FRENCH WOMEN NOVELISTS: DEFINING A FEMALE STYLE

Also by Adele King

CAMUS
PROUST
PAUL NIZAN: ÉCRIVAIN
THE WRITINGS OF CAMARA LAYE

Macmillan Modern Dramatists (*co-editor of series*)
Macmillan Women Writers (*co-editor of series*)

French Women Novelists: Defining a Female Style

ADELE KING

Associate Professor of French
Ball State University

MACMILLAN

First published 1989

Published by
THE MACMILLAN PRESS LTD
Houndmills, Basingstoke, Hampshire RG21 2XS
and London
Companies and representatives
throughout the world

Printed in Hong Kong

British Library Cataloguing in Publication Data
King, Adele
French women novelists: defining a
female style.
1. Fiction in French. Women writers, 1945–
Critical studies
I. Title
843'.009'9287
ISBN 0–333–41940–5

For Nicole
and
to the memory of Richard Coe

Contents

Preface

It is surely not a matter of interpreting the operation of discourse while remaining within the same type of utterance as the one that guarantees discursive coherence ... to speak *of* or *about* woman may always boil down to, or be understood as, a recuperation of the feminine within a logic that maintains it in repression, censorship, nonrecognition.   (Irigaray, 1985a, p. 78)

If a feminist criticism can be conceived, it must surely be on the side of excess, disturbance, simultaneity.

(Féral, 1980, p. 45)

Is it possible to *say anything* without using concepts?

(Kristeva, 1977a, p. 6)

If corporeal, libidinal *écriture féminine* moves against the grain of masculine, objectivity-claiming discourse, how is the critic to analyse such writing in abstract metalanguage? And how, if *parler femme* can never be codified, can a reader be confident that a critic has actually heard it?

(Jones, 1985, p. 101)

If we continue to deploy nature and culture in oppositional ways, we remain *inside* the modes of thought that got rigidified with Enlightenment rationalism and the emergence of modern science. But to reject nature and culture as thus understood is unsettling; it positions us as critics of modernity, and there is much in the modern world we do not want to jettison.   (Elshtain, 1987, p. 13)

Criticism based on the assumption that what makes a poem valuable and interesting is its author's awareness, enacted within it, of her own dilemma as a woman ... risks reducing everything to the personal.   (Montefiore, 1987, p. 5)

I refuse to enclose us in a ghetto, to say: women's writing is
characterised by points 1, 2 . . . so as to come back finally to
needlepoint.   (Pillet, 1977, p. 6)

Feminist discourse is the working out of our ambivalence
towards womanhood, our need to *overcome* and at the same
time to *affirm* experiences and values bound up in the
'feminine' and the 'female'.   (Schweickart, 1985, p. 161).

In attempting a coherent exposition of recent feminist thought
about women's difference, their use of language and their fictional
works, I can immediately be criticised by some of those I will be
discussing. Perhaps, however, this risk must be taken. If the
feminist movement, like much modernist and postmodernist
thought, is a questioning of subjective identity, of our normal,
socially constructed ways of perceiving ourselves and others, it
may none the less be useful to look at it within the perspective of
rational thought.

If in studying works of fiction written by women, we look at
possible differences from works written by men, are we continuing
to use a male norm as the basis of comparison, or at least to accept
some form of gender stereotype? Would it be possible to disregard
difference? Or to see women's writing by itself, without any
comparisons? Or is this type of radical separatism impossible in
literary studies?

Are we, in privileging gender, producing too limited and partial
a reading of literary texts? Even given the importance of some form
of desire as a motivation for creative activity, and given the
prominence of gender identification for the female subject in a
patriarchal society, is the writer *as* writer always aware of her sex?
Or are other factors of more importance? Questions perhaps to
pose rather than answer.

One of the organisational principles I have adopted has to do
with another kind of difference, that between Anglo-Saxon and
French criticism, theory and literary texts. I have compared de-
velopments in England, the United States and France, and tried to
combine theoretical approaches more prevalent in France with
practical textual analysis as practised by Anglo-Saxon feminist
critics.

Chapter 1 presents the basic questions of gender specificity
(what possible differences exist between men and women, are they

culturally or biologically conditioned, should women's capacities and qualities be given value in contrast to those of the dominant culture or should a bisexual or androgynous culture be the goal, is the whole question of difference valid or a way of introducing essentialism) and how these questions have been addressed by various critics. Chapter 2 discusses theories of difference in terms of language. It is to some extent artificial to divide theories of how women differ from theories of their use of language – especially given the contemporary concern with how identity may be constructed through language, a concern of Hélène Cixous, Luce Irigaray and Julia Kristeva, the most influential French women theorists. But positions on gender difference and language difference are not always parallel. Many feminists engaged in political struggles, including those who embrace gender differences as well as those who seek some kind of bisexual resolution, deny that differences exist in language. Chapter 3 is a consideration of other possible literary differences of form and theme.

The five novelists whose work is analysed in the following chapters are those whom I consider the most interesting women writers in France in the twentieth century. I am, of course, aware of feminist objections to any formulation of a canon (since most in the past have largely excluded women, members of the working classes and minority groups), and I present my choices as a personal preference. (While I discuss Simone de Beauvoir's ideas, I do not consider her novels as valuable as her other writing.) The novelists I have chosen are a mixed group from the standpoint of their attitudes towards feminist concerns, gender specificity and the possibility of a feminine style. If theories of what is feminine are not prescriptive, but descriptive of actual practices, however, it should be possible to apply them to women writers who might consciously deny their relevance.

I have been confronted with the problems of terminology that have bothered almost all Anglo-Saxon critics on women's issues as they are discussed in French. 'Feminine' has connotations of 'womanly', 'passive', 'soft' in English that it does not have in French. The term has been retained, however, since 'female' relates too specifically to biological gender. 'Feminine' then is used to mean 'related to the experiences of women and to qualities of character, language use and imagination that critics and theories have identified as more typical of women as a cultural group than men'. 'Feminine' also, however, may mean an approach differing from the socially dominant one (normally identified as 'masculine'), but not reserved to those of the female sex. 'Feminism' as a term has been attacked in France as part of liberal humanism, as a denial of the need for social revolution, or as relating to a celebration of a specifically 'feminine' essence. I have, however, used 'feminism' and 'feminist' in the looser, English sense, as relating to those who advocate improving the position of women, whether they are liberal, radical, separatist, lesbian, Marxist, etc.

Another term that presents difficulties of translation is *jouissance*. *Jouissance* means pleasure, enjoyment without worrying about the cost, and also orgasm. Feminists have given particular connotations to *jouissance*: 'Women's *jouissance* carries with it the notion of fluidity, diffusion, duration. It is a kind of potlatch in the world of orgasms, a giving, expending, dispensing of pleasure without concern about ends or closure' (Marks and Courtivron, 1980, p. 36). As there is no clear English equivalent, I have retained *jouissance* when necessary.

In parenthetical references to the works listed in the Bibliography, if two page numbers are given the first is to the published English translation, the second to the French. If no English translation is listed, the translation is mine.

My debts to many feminist scholars and critics will be evident in the following pages. I would like to acknowledge the help of the librarians in the Bibliothèque Marguerite Durand in Paris, for their excellent, well-organised collection of material. I thank Ball State University for a summer research grant in 1987, which enabled me to complete much of my work; and especially my two student assistants: Azita Naraghi for help with the Bibliography, and Lisa Mercer for very careful work in checking the translations and the manuscript.

ADELE KING

1

Ideas of Difference

'You're isolated, and undivided. Perhaps you are as obsessed with wholeness as we are with dualism.'
'We are dualists too. Duality is an essential, isn't it? So long as there is *myself* and *the other*.'
'I and Thou,' he said. 'Yes, it does, after all, go even wider than sex. . . .'   (Le Guin, 1969, p. 168)

If the distinction self/other is at the basis of any human thought, if dualism is thus unavoidable, it is the distinction man/woman that is the most fundamental of all dichotomies. The concept of race, Colette Guillaumin has suggested, did not exist in its modern meaning, before the reality of black slavery, but now is taken as belonging to the natural order. The 'difference' between races was only clearly seen to exist when it fulfilled a socioeconomic need (Wittig, 1981, pp. 48–9). While some feminists consider that the concept of sexual difference is similarly an imposition by the oppressor in order to dominate others, there is no identifiable era in human society in which this concept was not in existence, no human society in which divisions of roles, divisons of presumed capabilities between the sexes do not exist. Marcelle Marini quotes Georges Ballandier's *Anthropologiques*: 'The relationship man/woman is the deepest foundation of all unequal relationships', and points out that contesting this relationship is thus more menacing to society than contesting class and race relations (Marini, 1984, p. 248). 'Difference' is always defined, moreover, as 'difference from man', which is the 'norm'.

Current feminist thought in western societies has addressed this distinction and its effects in varying ways. The practical questions of equal rights have dominated most Anglo-Saxon movements: woman as oppressed by political, economic and social structures of the basically patriarchal order must be freed from this oppression. French feminist thought, however, while not denying the importance of these practical goals, has increasingly been concerned with

1

what might be considered as the basis of this oppression: woman as repressed by the very nature of the culture and the language of which she is a part.[1] The issues arising from this view of language and culture are of great magnitude and touch ultimately not only on the liberation of women but on the redefinition of human relationships, and a restructuring of thought and society.

The history of thought about women is often parallel between English and French societies. There are similar early strictures in religious and philosophical works on the 'humanity' of half the human race, or at least on women's claims to adult responsibility. There are similar moments when liberation of oppressed groups seemed possible; 'modern feminism and Romantic cultural theory emerged as separate but linked responses to the transforming events of the French Revolution' (C. Kaplan, 1985, p. 150). But in neither France nor England, and in neither practical effects nor changes in how woman figures in the male imagination, did the Revolution or Romanticism bring any transformations. Women who participated in revolution or political reform movements thought that they, as well as oppressed workers, racial or religious minorities, might be given rights, but these were moments of illusion, in which the largest group to gain nothing from political change was the female sex. There has also been, of course, in France and England, similar concrete progress. Although French women did not get the vote until 1945, long after English and American women (in 1918 and 1920, respectively), it is arguable that current practical benefits for women – child care, family support, equal pay – are more advanced in France at present. The exceptional woman – who moves beyond the prescribed roles and gains political power, or produces an artistic creation recognised and valued by her society – has, of course, existed in America, Britain and France for centuries, but such isolated incidents say little about the place of women.

In 1949 the publication of Simone de Beauvoir's *Le Deuxième Sexe* caused an uproar in Paris, but bore little immediate fruit there. The feminist movement was sufficiently dormant that Henri Peyre could declare in 1961: 'The fight is won today. The very many women writers of contemporary France have ceased to carry a feminine chip on their shoulders' (Peyre, 1961, p. 47). Rather, the fight was taken up by English and American women and led to the seminal feminist works of Betty Friedan, Kate Millet, Germaine Greer, Eva Figes and others. (*The Second Sex* has sold over one million copies in the United States.) It was only with the student uprisings in 1968, with the serious questioning of the authority of Charles de Gaulle – that great patriarchal figure – that French feminism began to catch up with Anglo-Saxon feminism, in terms of both political movements and theoretical discussion.

Le Deuxième Sexe is based on an existentialist ethic, in which the subject should, to assert her or his liberty, continually reach out towards the future, a mode of transcendence: 'There is no justification for present existence other than its expansion into an indefinitely open future. Every time transcendence falls back into immanence, stagnation, there is a degradation of existence into the brutish life of subjection to given conditions – and of liberty into constraint and contingence' (Beauvoir, 1953, p. xxix). In all societies, those who reach towards the future are men, not women: 'In no domain whatever did she create; she maintained the life of the tribe by giving it children and bread. .... She remained doomed to immanence, incarnating only the static aspect of society' (p. 73). Beauvoir praises even aggressive, warlike tendencies: 'The worst curse that was laid on woman was that she should be excluded from these warlike forays. For it is not in giving life but in risking life that man is raised above the animal; that is why superiority has been accorded in humanity not to the sex that brings forth but to that which kills' (p. 64). Beauvoir's view of motherhood is almost contemptuous: 'Ensnared by nature, the pregnant woman is plant and animal, a stockpile of colloids, an incubator, an egg ... she is a human being, a conscious and free individual, who has become life's passive instrument' (p. 495).[2] Woman, according to Beauvoir, accepts what is, holds ideas that are merely attitudes, takes no part in history, is more often conservative in her political opinions.

It is not surprising that Beauvoir's contemptuous attitude towards women as they exist, and her standard of greatness as being that of male culture, should have been attacked by a younger generation of feminists, even while they appreciated the great contribution she had made to the study of woman, and often agreed with many of her analyses. Beauvoir herself changed. Later she declared herself a 'feminist', having become more aware that the problems of women were not to be corrected through the socialist revolution:

In 1949, I believed that social progress, the triumph of the proletariat ... socialism would lead to the emancipation of women. But I saw that nothing came of it: first of all, that socialism was not achieved anywhere, and that in certain countries which called themselves socialist, the situation of women was no better than it was in so-called capitalist countries. Thus, I finally understood that the emancipation of women must be the work of women themselves, independent of the class struggle.   (Jardine, 1979, p. 235)

(Beauvoir's position in this respect might be compared to that of Aimé Césaire when he broke with the French Communist Party because he felt it did not address racial issues.) Beauvoir had become aware of the problems of combining the feminist and the socialist revolutions: 'feminism is one way of attacking society as it now exists. Therefore, it's a revolutionary movement . . . which is different from the class struggle movement . . . a certain alliance with revolutionary systems is necessary, even masculine ones . . . this is certainly a very tricky point: How to ally yourself to other leftist forces without losing your feminist specificity' (Jardine, 1979, p. 227).

While continuing to deny any female biological specificity, Beauvoir realised that as a result of their cultural situation, women have certain positive qualities as well as deficiences: 'they play fewer roles, are more authentic, closer to reality. They have more critical sense, more irony, more distance in relation to society's demands, more a sense of the concrete' (Francis, 1979, p. 570). She even seemed to deny her earlier praise of male aggressiveness: 'If women want to take power in the fashion of men, it's not worth the effort, that is exactly what we would like to change, all these notions and these values' (Francis, 1979, p. 589). 'Obviously, if you are truly on the left, if you reject ideas of power and hierarchy, what you want is equality' (Jardine, 1979, p. 226).

Politically, the French feminist movement since 1968 has been shaken by many disagreements. Many tendencies and limited interest groups developed (Albistur, 1977). Intellectually, the women's movement in France has been influenced by the dominant philosophical, linguistic and political theories that have emerged, particularly since the Second World War: existentialism, Marxism, structuralism, Lacanian psychoanalysis, deconstruction. Discussions may often seem, to the outside observer, like arguments with father figures. Breaking from male intellectual authorities has been harder for the French, undoubtedly because the educational tradition is less empiricist. If such discussion has increasingly become important to English and American critics, differences remain apparent. With few exceptions, French feminist critics discuss abstract theories, their own practice as writers, or texts by male authors seen as embodying less 'patriarchal' structures. The application of feminist literary criticism to texts by women, or even the task of pointing to the patriarchal attitudes in texts by men, has less often been undertaken in France than in British and American work. What has emerged is a series of often brilliant, if also often obscure and highly theoretical discussions of the role of language in the creation of the individual psyche of men and women. Such work has been criticised both for refusing to deal with practical realities and for setting up such difficult barriers for its readers that it appeals only to a very small élite. It has, however, produced some concepts useful for a more practical look at woman's psychology and her creative activity.

The principal question, addressed in varying ways by all contemporary feminists, is 'Difference'. Are women different from men? If so, how or for what reasons? And should differences be accepted, emphasised and revalued, or should they be eliminated in an ideal, androgynous society? (These questions concern, of course, psychological and mental distinctions, not the obvious physical differences between the sexes relating to reproductive functions.) Regardless of how difference is constructed, through Oedipal drama, language or social conditioning, what practical policies are required because of common perceptions of difference between the sexes? Cora Kaplan (C. Kaplan, 1985, p. 151) has distinguished three strategies adopted by feminist thinkers with regard to questions of difference: (1) women are basically the same as men, but have been conditioned to think and behave in different ways; (2) women are basically different from men, and can best advance their own (superior) capacities by radically separating from the dominant culture; (3) there is no point in focusing on differences.[3] All strategies have both practical and theoretical implications. Practically, politically, those who stress social conditioning advocate first of all 'consciousness raising', to undermine the effects of sex-role education; related efforts, to change images in textbooks, to fight advertising stereotypes, and so on, do not necessarily involve a radical questioning of the structure of modern western societies. (Materialist feminism can, however, include demands for such restructuring, on socialist or Marxist principles.)

The more radical feminists, those who would stress fundamental differences, often opt for a separate, woman-centred society, even if this can only be communes isolated from the main current of modern life and with limited political strength. Denial of differences, the third strategy, can produce an androgynous vision in which in practice women are expected to conform to the dominant culture, to become like men.

From a theoretical perspective, outlooks on difference produce variations in theories of the female psyche and female creativity, and all have their dangers. Emphasising social conditioning often makes women appear as primarily victims. Stressing innate differences can lead to a value reversal of the usual sets of opposites: woman is more emotional, more sensitive to others' needs, less rational; these become positive, rather than negative qualities. (The parallel to Negritude, reversals of the value of qualities attributed to whites and blacks, is evident.) Enthusiasm for a 'fantasy of untrammeled sexuality strives to undermine the closed masculine signifying conventions', but can pass into essentialism and biological determinism (McCallum, 1985, pp. 129–30). Those who would shift the emphasis from difference, and advocate androgyny, often wish to avoid any kind of essentialism, any definition of the eternal male and female. But such theories may be too far removed from political reality.

Perhaps a fourth strategy is possible, a realisation that the sexual impulses of every human being produce wide variations between individuals, that women are neither merely social victims, nor superior essences, nor androgynous, but are, as are men, particular creatures to be considered in their specificity. As Gayatri Chakravorty Spivak has said, 'woman's voice is not one voice to be added to the orchestra: *every* voice is inhabited by the sexual differential' (Spivak, 1987, p. 132). Such a strategy could lead to 'deconstructing' the categories 'man' and 'woman'. Marcelle Marini suggests that both those who want to make women like men (such as Beauvoir, who, Marini feels, proposes an equivalence between the 'liberated woman' and 'man') and those who want to transform 'woman' into a new, valorised universal (Marini's example is Hélène Cixous) finally refer to essentialist universal categories that must be overcome. For Marini, there can be only the concrete, no overriding theories (Marini, 1984, p. 250).

Julia Kristeva similarly distinguishes three phases of women's struggle. The first, which is where many Anglo-Saxon feminists have remained, she feels, is the struggle to gain a place in the world of rationality – equal pay, for example. The second phase is a distrust of politics, a movement to give language to the intrasubjective and corporeal experiences left mute by culture in the past, the phase, therefore, of radical feminism. Kristeva, however, wants a third phase, in which concern with differences between the sexes is replaced by concern with the singularity of each individual, the multiplicity of each person's possible identifications. She asks whether feminism will be able to break free from belief in Woman. Kristeva speaks of two necessary conditions for the 'solution' of the 'feminine problematic', both of which involve going beyond difference. First, women must be thrown 'into all of society's contradictions with no hypocrisy or fake protection' (Kristeva, 1980, p. 165). The second condition is not amenable to any social intervention, however. It involves going through 'an infinite, repeated, multipliable dissolution', so that the individual (male or female) has a voice to be heard in social matters, but a voice that is fragmented by breaks. The individual experiences a bisexual plurality, which Kristeva seems to see arising 'by virtue of communities that open up the family', 'by virtue of pop music' (pp. 165–6). (Thus Kristeva's 'third phase' may appear more radical than what I have termed a 'fourth strategy'.)

As Toril Moi has noted, Kristeva's second and third phases should not be read as mutually exclusive: 'For it still remains *politically* essential for feminists to defend women *as* women in order to counteract the patriarchal oppression that precisely despises women *as* women. But an "undeconstructed" form of "stage two" feminism, unaware of the metaphysical nature of gender identities, runs the risk of becoming an inverted form of sexism' (Moi, 1985, p. 13). Derridean deconstruction also suggests that when confronting the dilemma of whether to transcend the opposition between male and female or to celebrate the feminine, it is necessary to work on two fronts at once:

Analytical writings that attempt to neutralize the male/female opposition are extremely important, but, as Derrida says, 'the hierarchy of the binary opposition always reconstitutes itself,' and therefore a movement that asserts the primacy of the oppressed term is strategically indispensable.

(Culler, 1982, p. 173)

If categories are to be deconstructed, therefore, women must still be aware of social oppression. Otherness, as Pamela McCallum has observed, is a power relationship to be confronted in the real world. Michèle Barrett, while criticising the categories of 'man' and 'woman' and the philosophical basis of liberal humanism (which tends to see the 'universal' subject as white, bourgeois and male) recognises that humanism is an honorable tradition, and is needed for political action (Barrett, 1987, pp. 29–41). The problem is always contextual: 'Denial of difference can mean inauthenticity, while assertion of difference can mean retreat from supporting women's transcendent aspirations' (Gordon, 1986, p. 27).

Whether verifiable differences exist, therefore, and whether, if so, their causes are primarily social rather than biological, as a matter of practical politics those interested in the liberation of women must begin with the realisation that almost everyone (male and female) believes that there are differences and acts accordingly. If an ultimate goal might be a rejection of the dichotomy between the sexes, for the foreseeable future the goal must be to give women value as women. Thus there will be a tension between 'the celebration of the "female" and the advocation of "androgyny"' (Greene and Kahn, 1985, p. 24).

Scientific studies of possible differences between men and women have increasingly been undertaken, although the covert aims of some work need to be recognised. Schools of sociobiology often begin with comparisons of humans to primates, seeking a 'natural' explanation for male dominance. Even 'objective' studies, however, will always face the impossibility of separating genetic and cultural factors to account for any observable differences in behaviour between men and women. Nevertheless, some studies have laid solid foundations for what can be measured. Reviewing a number of psychological studies, Maccoby and Jacklin found a few quantifiable differences: girls have greater verbal ability, boys excel in visual-spatial ability and mathematics, boys are more aggressive. Findings on possible differences in tactile sensitivity, fear, dominance, nurturance were ambiguous. Unfounded were assertions that girls are more social, girls have lower self-esteem, girls are more auditory, boys more visual. (The observable traits, of course, vary from individual to individual, so that a particular woman might have greater visual-spatial ability than the majority of men.) Explanations, however, for certain psychological variations have been found in genetic inheritance. (Recessive genes, more readily inherited by males, for instance, cause a greater incidence of colour blindness in men, and similarly recessive genes *may* cause greater visual–spatial ability in men.) Other scientists, however, have considered that the small differences observed in mean group scores on verbal and visual–spatial abilities are insignificant, and that Maccoby and Jacklin ignore studies that find *no* sex-related difference in aggressivity (see Bleier, 1984, p. 97).

More important than what statistical differences exist is, of course, what does *not* exist. From the standpoint of female creativity, 'the underrepresentation of women in the ranks of the outstanding creative figures . . . would not appear to arise from any general deficiency in the "production of associative content that is abundant and unique"' (Maccoby, 1974, p. 114). In France, in a symposium on 'Le Fait féminin' under the direction of Evelyne Sullerot, studies were reported that found few quantifiable differences in biology between the sexes. Lateralisation of left and right brain functions appears to be less in women, with the possible results that women find it harder to do two things at once and to compartmentalise the emotional and the rational. Ruth Bleier, however, considers experiments on brain lateralisation to be inconclusive. It is not possible to formulate meaningful hypotheses about sex differences in brain processes, she says, as we do not know enough about these processes (Bleier, 1986, p. 58). (Thus Luce Irigaray's claim (Irigaray, 1985b, p. 10) that different lateralisation should destroy the pretension that the two sexes speak the same language, cannot be supported by scientific evidence, at least at present.) And, even if brain lateralisation were different, how important would this be in comparison with early childhood experiences and social conditioning?

Other possible biological variables were shown to be nonexistent or of limited interest. Even, as Sullerot noted, woman's reproductive role is no longer the essential, time-consuming occupation it once was. With birth control, lower child mortality, longer lives, women spend a much smaller proportion of their lives on childbearing and rearing. Sullerot concludes that 'it seems much easier to modify the facts of nature than the facts of culture' (Sullerot, 1978, p. 23), easier to change reproductive cycles than social attitudes. Discussions of hormonal differences should perhaps be seen in the light of Sullerot's comments about the relative ease of changing nature.[4] All existing human societies have moved far from the realm of 'nature' as seen in the animal world. So, if female rats who have given birth are more nurturing, because of their hormones, than male rats, the relevance to human behaviour is slight.

If, as seems likely, 'difference' is minimally explicable by factors that can be studied by experimental psychology, it lends itself, on the contrary, to a number of Freudian and other depth psychology interpretations. Perhaps the best known among American feminists is that of Nancy Chodorow, an objects-relations psychoanalytic theorist, who explains differences between the sexes largely by differences in the experience of being mothered: 'the fact that the child's earliest relationship is with a woman becomes exceedingly important for the object-relations of subsequent developmental periods.... Girls and boys expect and assume women's unique capacities for sacrifice, caring and mothering and associate women with their own fears of regression and powerlessness. They fantasize more about men, and associate them with idealized virtues and growth' (Chodorow, 1978, p. 83). Among the results of this experience of female mothering is what Chodorow terms 'more permeable ego boundaries' since girls experience themselves as less separate than do boys. As a consequence 'girls come to define themselves more in relation to others' (p. 93); a greater capacity for empathy is built into their primary definition of self. On the other hand, female social roles are more rigid and less varied than men's. As attractive in many ways as this analysis has been to feminists – among other strengths, it lends support to demands for more equal parenting by fathers – it is not subject to rigorous scientific testing, and, more significantly, has been interpreted by socially radical critics as neglecting how economic organisation leads to sexual inequality (Sayers, 1982). More radically still, Jacqueline Rose has commented that Chodorow accepts a notion of 'gender imprinting'; her account is based on the concept that the baby knows its gender, and thus sidesteps the problem of the 'acquisition of sexual identity' (Rose, 1982, p. 37). Chodorow remains, however, the major theorist whose work is based on psychoanalysis to be accepted by American feminists.

Dorothy Dinnerstein analyses the effects of female nurturing from another angle. The child, completely dependent on the woman who nurtures it, becomes resentful because it also inevitably experiences disappointments and pain. In compensation the child of either sex tends to identify with males; even the daughter wants to 'preserve her "I"ness by thinking of men, not women, as her real fellow creatures' (quoted in Culler, 1982, p. 53). Rather similarly, Nancy K. Miller has speculated on the social factors that may explain variations in male and female psyches: 'Because women have not had the same historical relation of identity to origin, institution, production, that men have had, women have not, I think, (collectively) felt burdened by too much Self, Ego, Cogito' (Miller, 1986, p. 106).

In general, among Ango-Saxon critics, distrust of Freud for his own patriarchal biases has outweighed acceptance of his insights into the structuring of the human psyche. A more useful approach is to consider Freud's work as a subversive science that can counter its own conservative aspects, to explore the potentially revolutionary powers of the unconscious.[5] Only recently, and particularly among critics responding to French theorists, has feminist work in English taken Freud seriously as the originator of more valid concepts than 'penis envy'.

Some feminist psychoanalytic theory argues against the Freudian valorisation of individuality and separateness as the goal of development, a concept which is seen as ultimately based on the structure of gender domination:

Since the child continues to need the mother, since man continues to need woman, the absolute assertion of independence requires possessing and controlling the needed object ... to make sure ... that her own subjectivity nowhere asserts itself in a way that could make his dependency upon her a conscious insult to his sense of freedom.   (Benjamin, 1986, p. 80)

Instead, feminist psychoanalysts argue that individuality is a balance of separation and connectedness; they offer an alternate model of gender evolution:

the girl sustains her primary identification with the mother and ... the boy must break that identity and switch to the father. It is this break in identification that brings about the attitude of repudiation and distance towards primary connectedness, nurturance and intimacy that characterizes the male model of independence ... maternal identification theory leans towards the revaluation of the mother.   (Benjamin, 1986, pp. 82-3)

Identifying with the mother, however, seems to mean identifying with a desexualised being. Mothers don't have sexual feelings; they are supposed to be selfless, always in control. A danger of identifying with the mother is that women may accept being 'righteous and de-eroticized, intimate, caring, and self-sacrificing' (p. 85). Jessica Benjamin suggests a possible reconciliation of gender oppositions, so that each individual child can express both male and female aspects of selfhood, so that both sides are seen as complementary rather than in opposition, so that both the mother and the father are subjects of desire. How this possibility can be realised is of central concern to those who would go beyond the emphasis on 'difference'.

In France, psychological theories of 'difference' have often been influenced by Freud and particularly by Freud as reread by Jacques Lacan, and then by Jacques Derrida's criticism of Lacan. For Lacan, difference is essential. The unconscious, like language in the Saussurean model, signifies through binary opposites. The structure of the unconscious and of language develops from the never completed break from the maternal body into the time of patriarchal language. Sexual difference is a function created by language; but this fiction is phallocentric (see Jardine, 1985, p. 107). Lacan makes the transcendental phallus the fundamental principle; man's and woman's relations to desire and to language are structured by the Oedipal drama of castration complex or penis envy. Using such theories as underpinning for feminist discourse has led to charges of a new 'essentialism' by those who feel that a psychological definition of female specificity plays into the hands of advocates of the theory that 'different from men means inferior'.

Feminist theories of 'difference' have also, however, been influenced by Jacques Derrida's radical interpretation of 'difference' as 'differance' (that is, both difference and deferral). Derrida, like many feminist critics, sees Lacan's work as subsuming the female to the male. Derrida's analysis undermines any simple binary opposition (such as male/female); any search for stable entities is metaphysical. A Derridean deconstruction of the way psychoanalysis establishes a hierarchical opposition between man and woman shows that it relies on premises that can reverse this hierarchy:

Since woman has, as Freud says, a masculine and a feminine phase, instead of treating woman as a variant of 'man', it would be more accurate, according to his theory, to treat man as a particular instance of woman. Or perhaps one should say, in keeping with the Derridean model, that man and woman are both variants of archi-woman.   (Culler, 1982, p. 171)

While many feminist theorists have embraced Derridean deconstruction as a way of moving beyond traditional, hierarchical distinctions, some have considered that even Derrida uses the feminine as a metaphor for the unnameable, thus still serving phallocentric mastery. Derrida, in a recent interview, has suggested that 'feminism' and 'phallologocentrism' may be the same thing (Russo, 1986, p. 225).

While American and French theorists differ in many ways, the ideas of Chodorow, Dinnerstein, Benjamin and others agree with those of the most prominent French writers – Hélène Cixous, Luce Irigaray and Julia Kristeva – in at least one central point: 'they intersect where female identity is concerned; for woman the delimited, the autonomous, separated, individuated self does not exist' (Hirsch, 1981, p. 211). Both Hélène Cixous and Luce Irigaray have reacted against Lacan and been influenced by Derrida. Both consider that the integrated, unitary self is basically a phallic self, which strives to keep itself immune to conflict and ambiguity (Moi, 1985, p. 8). Both seek instead a self that is not stable and unchanging. If many materialist criticis have seen such speculation as fostering a neglect of economic realities, these theories deserve serious consideration, both as attempts to explain the present condition of women and as interpretations of female creativity.[6]

Cixous seems to deny any biological gender determinism: 'sexual difference develops out of bisexuality which is the original condition of every individual and is subsequently displaced, transformed by culture' (Makward, 1976, p. 22). But in fact, often in Cixous's work 'masculine' seems to be the rejection of bisexuality, 'feminine' the acceptance of bisexuality. If there is initial bisexuality, Cixous claims that 'being a man' means eradicating the female elements. There does not seem to be a parallel choice 'to be a woman'; rather, it sometimes appears to be forced upon a woman by the dominant culture. At other times, 'being a woman' seems a more fundamental state of bisexuality. The female, as closer to the bisexual, has been made the norm, the male a deviation from it (see Moi, 1985, p. 110). Cixous says, however, that she does not like the opposition masculine/feminine. 'I speak of a decipherable libidinal femininity which can be read in a writing produced by a male or a female' (Conley, 1984, p. 129). Is this 'libidinal femininity' basically cultural? Sometimes, it seems so: 'No woman stockpiles as many defenses for countering the drives as does a man' (Cixous, 1976a, p. 881); 'More so than men who are coaxed towards social success, towards sublimation, women are body' (p. 886). At other times, the concept of a diffused sexuality seems clearly based on biology. So, a certain confusion remains. Is femininity based on the body – in which case it is hard to see how men can share it? Is it based on the experience of being suppressed as a woman in patriarchal culture? Again, how do men attain it? If we all begin bisexual, is it only men who lose the aspects of the opposite sex? In that case, are not women being elevated to an ideal role, as guardians of a bisexuality that existed in the individual's past? Enough questions, to which Cixous has no clear answer, and sometimes feels that none is needed, as she is not a 'philosopher'.

Underlying the conflict between asserting two essences and the denial of an opposition between the two sexes, and the confusion of bisexuality with women, is a conflict which could be defined as a conflict between Lacan (a desire for a Lacanian Imaginary before the intrusion of the symbolic) and Derrida (a denial of binary oppositions). As Diane Griffin Crowder has shown, Cixous is also ambivalent about the concept of motherhood as related to female creativity (Crowder, 1983, p. 136). Sometimes maternity is used to mean physically giving birth, elsewhere it seems rather a metaphor. Like Annie Leclerc, Cixous feels that motherhood has been repressed by the dominant culture. (For Monique Wittig, however, being a mother is the definition of being a woman in our culture, and must be attacked.)

Writing in itself will not change the world – Cixous believes in the necessity of transforming the socioeconomic structures – but writing is an essential part of the learning process necessary for women: 'the woman who does not know *herself*, who has not "thought *herself*," who has now reflected upon *herself*, who remains as she was – ignorant and blind about femininity, because she is alienated – will not be a good militant feminist, will not further her cause, and therefore can always be recuperated by all sorts of political movements' (Makward, 1976, pp. 25–6). Cixous's position, however, as well as affirming a radical, possibly biologically based difference, would seem to place women naturally outside a position of power, and therefore to call for a different world structure in which women would have a voice. She denies, however, that radical separatism is her aim: 'I, for one, am absolutely against marginalization . . . that would amount to going back to this sort of absurd dream: "a man's world/a woman's world." This is not so! This is a world of men *and* women where it is up to women to impose something which is their difference in equality' (Makward, 1976, p. 24).

Luce Irigaray's psychoanalytic approach to problems of 'difference' is based on a reinterpretation of Freudian theory, a radical criticism of both Freud and Lacan, and also on a Derridian 'deconstruction' of sexual opposition. While, like Cixious, she speaks of the interaction of social and sexual factors in the cultural construction of the concept 'woman', and speculates 'whether it is even possible to pursue a limited discussion of female sexuality so long as the status of woman in the general economy of the West has never been established' (Irigaray, 1985a, p. 67), it is the sexual and psychological that most interests her. In *Spéculum de l'autre femme*, Irigaray uses the words of various theorists – Freud, Hegel, Kant, Descartes, Plato – to criticise their representation of women, based on their fear of 'otherness'. She shows that in most western thought, woman is reduced to a mirror of the male, not allowed any immediate personal identity. Woman is always defined in relation to man, always the negative complement of man. She is barred from language, unable to express herself except through her body. For Irigaray, Marx's philosophy as well is inimcal to women; the class struggle is not to be equated with the struggle against the exploitation of women.

Irigaray is critical of those who advocate 'bisexuality', which she feels tends to lead towards sameness, and sameness becomes the masculine model. Advocates of bisexuality also ignore the problems of women's exploitation. Politically, she feels, it is not enough to become 'equal' to men: 'it is in order to bring their difference to light that women are demanding their rights' (Irigaray, 1985a, p. 166). This difference that must be brought to light is largely a matter of the body, the particularity of women's sexuality: 'Woman has sex organs more or less everywhere . . . the geography of her pleasure is far more diversified, more multiple in its differences, more complex, more subtle, than is commonly imagined' (p. 28). The 'mucous' – Irigaray's term for the intimate bodily perception of a woman – will disturb the concept of a transcendent, incorporal, immutable God. Often in fact, the female *body*, not a cultural concept, is the basis for defining difference: 'One of the differences between men and women is that these lips [Irigaray often speaks of the labia] do not come together according to the same system. If he needs the mother or her substitute, she is sufficient to be two, mother and woman' (Irigaray, 1984, p. 156). Irigaray finds in the 'possible' lesser lateralisation of the female brain a feminine value. Men's brains may be too exclusively laterialised: 'Women listen bilaterally, as they join their hands and their lips.' Thus, while sex cannot be reduced to simple biological differences, there is 'a bridge between body and culture' (Irigaray, 1987, p. 7). Irigaray's ideas of male and female sexuality – the distinction between seeing (male) and touching (female), different relations to time and space – are based finally on an irreducible duality. Difference is not to be denied, but rather to be rethought, so that maternal and paternal functions are no longer placed in a hierarchical order (Irigaray, 1984, p. 66).

Another prominent theme in Irigaray's work is the mother-daughter relationship, a relationship undervalued in patriarchal culture, which is based on discourse: 'Nourishing takes place before there are any images' (Irigaray, 1981, p. 63). The mother only exists, or more radically only keeps from disappearing, through the daughter: 'Was I not the bail to keep you from disappearing? The stand-in for your absence? The guardian of your nonexistence? She who reassured you that you could always find yourself again, hold yourself at any hour, in your arms . . . try to restore yourself to the world?' (pp. 64–5). Irigaray's plea is 'what I wanted from you, Mother, was this: that in giving me life, you still remain alive' (p. 67). The problem she addresses, the daughter's realisation of the mother's oppression by patriarchal culture, has practical relevance; but for Irigaray, it is also metaphysical: she speaks of the existence of a female 'divineness', between mother and daughter. She sees, however, a possible danger in love between women, 'confusion of identity between them, lack of respect or lack of perception of differences' (Irigaray, 1984, p. 66).

Jane Gallop has defended Irigaray against charges of falling into the Freudian folly of stating that 'anatomy is destiny'. While admitting that Irigaray's work is not simply a poetic, but based on an actual pluralistic, non-phallomorphic sexuality, that Irigaray is talking about bodies, not simply constructs, Gallop concludes: 'The new construction, the modernist, multiple body, will not be any more "real" in an essentialistic, numenal way, but might neverthe-less produce a rearrangement in sexual hierarchies, a salutary jolt out of the compulsive repetition of the same' (Gallop, 1983, p. 83). Irigaray defends herself against charges of a 'regressive recourse to anatomy or a concept of nature': 'It is rather a question of reopening the autological and tantological circle of systems of representation ... so that women can speak their sex' (Irigaray, 1985b, p. 272).

Is this, however, a satisfactory answer to the problems posed by a valorisation of the female body? As Ann Rosalind Jones has observed, sexual identity is always constructed from experiences in the family and reinforced by the ideologies of culture:

> most of us perceive our bodies through a jumpy, contradictory mesh of hoary sexual symbolization and political counter-response. It is possible to argue that the French feminists make of the female body too unproblematically pleasurable and total-ized an entity.   (Jones, 1981, p. 254)

Stephen Heath makes a similar point. He sees the danger in talk of female *jouissance* as dispersed, or in Lacan's insistence on woman as Other, because 'it matches perfectly with the historical positions of patriarchal society in which "woman" has been constantly identified as a locus of dis-order and women held to the forms of oppression constructed and justified in its terms' (Heath, 1978, p. 73). Heath feels, however, that Irigaray gets beyond this danger, that she does not equate woman with dis-order or the uncon-scious, but raises questions about 'the operation of an equation between the feminine and the unconscious ... within a history and economy of repression' and that this is 'a fully political task' (p. 74). Other critics have been less willing to accept the essentialist, ahistorical tendency in Irigaray. Toril Moi feels Irigaray has fallen for the temptation to produce positive theory. Christine Fauré, whose work is rooted in a post-1968 French radicalism, has criticised Irigaray's ideas, which she sees as a romanticisation of women's oppression and a glorification of female sexuality:

> This rigid devaluation of the temporal and historical dimension of women to the benefit of a single dimension – space, the female sex, that other place – takes on some of the characteristics of utopian thought: the idea that social change is initiated on the basis of new forms of behavior, thus protecting against the risks of unforeseeable chance and reducing individual responsibility for failure.   (Fauré, 1981, p. 85)

Again, there is the fundamental conflict between dealing with oppression or repression, between giving priority to the practical or the imagination.

Is the 'body', which seems to be the basis of Irigaray's theory of difference, 'natural' or a construct? Is there, in human understanding which proceeds from language, from distinctions (even if there are Derridean deferrals of meaning), anything 'natural'? Cixous and Irigaray say the body is socially constructed, but they often seem to be talking about biological distinctions between the sexes. In an analysis of psychoanalytic concepts, Stephen Heath states: 'Sexuality is not given in nature but produced; the individual subject is not constructed from sexuality, sexuality is constructed in the history of the subject, with difference a function of that construction not its cause, a function which is not necessarily single (on the contrary) and which, *a fortiori*, is not necessarily the holding of that difference to anatomical difference' (Heath, 1978, pp. 65–6). The problem for both Freud and Lacan, according to Heath, is that they keep appealing back to biology, keep making sexual reality the condition of the symbolic. Could the same thing be said of Cixous and Irigaray?

Julia Kristeva is careful not to suggest that any essential female nature exists. Her definition of woman as the marginal – what remains outside ideologies – is, as Toril Moi has shown, not a new 'essence' but a strategy. Kristeva has stated that believing that one 'is a woman' is almost as absurd as believing one 'is a man'. (Presumably the 'almost' is a recognition of woman's social oppression.) She wants to dissolve the notion of rigid sexual identity, to acknowledge each person's bisexuality, and to place women's struggle within a wider political context.

Kristeva's basic distinction between two modalities of experience and signification is not linked to a male/female dichotomy. One modality is the symbolic, a principle of law and Logos, what Lacan has called the Name-of-the-Father. The other is the semiotic, which speaks through nonsense or 'childish' language. The semiotic first occurs, according to Kristeva, in the phase of the infant's intense attachment to the mother's body. The semiotic is in close alliance with the unconscious and expresses itself through rhythm, intonation, gesture and melody. It is associated with the pre-Oedipal phase (when gender distinctions do not exist). Thus it is only associated with the feminine in so far as both the semiotic and woman are marginal to patriarchal culture and its use of language, to 'phallologocentrism'.

Kristeva believes that women must get beyond what she considers a 'mythification of the feminine' (Kristeva, 1977b, p. 106). She also rejects what she sees as 'existentialist' guilt forced on women. Does she, however, in her revaluation of woman's maternal role, perhaps reintroduce a kind of 'essence'? She believes that the feminist movement has made women feel guilty for having children: 'For me maternity as such has never seemed in opposition to a cultural activity' (p. 108). (Presumably Kristeva does not have child-care problems.) The experience of childbirth anchors women to the social, to the survival of the species. Woman participates in the crisis of identity of modern culture, but at the same time is divided: 'On one hand, she is part of the symbolic register since she speaks; on the other hand she is tied to biology, to the memory of cells, since the problem of reproduction comes up physically every month, and psychically is always present: this is the female counterpart of the male's obsession with death' (Kristeva, 1977a, p. 8). When she has a child who begins to speak, woman is then participating as mother in both nature and the symbolic culture. Thus the concept of the equality of men and women is another mystification. Woman is linked to the natural world, to life, as well as to the intellectual, and efforts to make her sexual and creative life equivalent to a man's have ignored this division.

Such an emphasis on the role of maternity seems to contradict to some extent Kristeva's earlier comments on bisexuality, on the symbolic and the semiotic as two modalities not directly related to biological genders. Or, again, has the feminine not become the new *norm*, since the woman as mother, nourishing and speaking to the child, combines the two modalities in a particularly significant fashion, and one that would seem denied to men? If Cixous's bisexual turns out to be female, Kristeva's merging of semiotic and symbolic is also female. Motherhood also seems to be an enriching moral experience, limited to women:

> The arrival of the child . . . leads the mother into the labyrinths of an experience that, without the child, she would only rarely encounter: love for an other. Not for herself, nor for an identical being, and still less for another person with whom 'I' fuse (love or sexual passion). But the slow, difficult, and delightful apprenticeship in attentiveness, gentleness, forgetting oneself. The ability to succeed in this path without masochism and without

annihilating one's affective, intellectual, and professional personality – such would seem to be the stakes to be won through
guiltless maternity. It then becomes a creation in the strong
sense of the term. For this moment, utopian? (Kristeva, 1981,
p. 31)[7]

Other French feminist writers (perhaps in her latest work
Kristeva cannot be considered feminist, however) although less
theoretically oriented, also address the central issues of biology
and culture, difference and bisexuality. Annie Leclerc's position
seems in many ways based on a biological essentialism. Woman
must express her body, a body that is largely defined in terms of
organs and physiological processes: 'To give birth is to live as
intensely as it is possible to live' (Leclerc, 1974, p. 39). Leclerc is
also aware, however, that woman's oppression is a result of
cultural conditioning; she analyses the difference between the
treatment of slaves, blacks and other subordinate groups and the
treatment of women. From women, men expect not only service
but also devotion. Submission is expected to be the 'fruit of respect
and love for the master' (p. 32). Her analysis is similar to Simone de
Beauvoir's in *The Second Sex*: 'The Negroes submit with a feeling of
revolt, no privileges compensating for their hard lot, whereas
woman is offered inducements to complicity; . . . the delights of
passivity are made to seem desirable to the young girl' (Beauvoir,
1953, p. 298). Because of this social role, Leclerc says women have
come to devalue themselves. If men desire women but not love
them, women hate themselves. In revaluing themselves, however,
women should not attack men: 'We must not make war against
man. That is his way to win. . . . We must simply debunk his values
through ridicule' (p. 15).

Much feminist discussion has addressed the question of how
women differ from oppressed minority groups and from the
oppressed lower classes. 'Women present a special case to the
historian: neither class nor caste nor minority, they are more
closely allied to the men in their lives than they are to women of
other classes and races, and so are more closely integrated with the
dominant culture than is any other subordinate group. They have
in some sense consented to their subordination, internalizing the
ideology of the oppressor' (Greene and Kahn, 1985, p. 14). Edwin
Ardener's concept of a muted culture has been influential in
English and American feminist thought. According to Ardener, the

experience of any individual depends on many elements – social class, nationality, race, age and sex. Even among individuals otherwise of the same cultural group – for instance a white, middle-class English couple – the experience of the woman will not totally coincide with the man's. There will remain a 'no man's land' reserved to women, and a 'no woman's land' reserved to men (Showalter, 1982, pp. 27–32). (If Leclerc is right, the 'no man's land' will include an acceptance of submission, of inferiority, of self-hatred.)

Leclerc sees the liberation of women from this submission and domination as part of a more general economic liberation, but does not seriously consider any restructuring of society. She would like to have the traditional roles of women as nurturers given more value by society, but does not see the division of labour as economic exploitation. Christine Delphy, in discussing *Parole de femme*, makes criticisms pertinent as well to other primarily psychological approaches: they are often, in fact, 'reverse sexism', essentialist and based on biology. They pay too much attention to the ideological superstructure, to how the subject constructs him or herself psychologically, through language, and not enough to the ways ideology is determined by social organisation (Delphy, 1975). Pamela McCallum sees the theories of Irigaray and Cixous as 'very near to what Habermas has referred to as an archaic neo-conservatism in French post-structuralist writing' (McCallum, 1985, p. 132).

Similar points have been made by Catherine Clément, who has stated that the notion of feminine specificity is an ideological trap, and that overemphasis on language leads to a neglect of the political struggle.[8] In *La Jeune née* Clément considers the woman who refuses to accept the patriarchal order – the witch or the hysteric – as bisexual. This is not what has usually been considered bisexuality, which 'is always dominated by masculinity', such as the phoenix myth in which the male engenders himself; rather, the hysteric denounces sexual roles, goes beyond the spectacle, 'the circus where too many women are crushed dead', towards a noncontradictory status, a true synthesis (Cixous and Clément, 1975a, pp. 109–11).

The concluding section of *La Jeune née*, a discussion between Cixous and Clément following their individual essays, clarifies the fundamental oppositions between two approaches to the question of the liberation of women. Clément's position is clear: 'I accept that the cultural system is phallocentric; but to try to make another one through anticipation is based on nothing; . . . to want it already in place is utopian' (p. 252). For Cixous, using the coherent language of male discourse leads inevitably to a kind of repression. But Clément replies that, in the present, women must use the objective discourse of mastery of a subject to communicate: 'I don't see how to conceive of a cultural system where knowledge is not transmitted through coherent statements' (p. 259). Revolution cannot be made at the level of language. Cixous agrees to this, but adds that there is no revolution without raising consciousness, which she elaborates as 'people who begin to get up and howl'; 'I think that what cannot be crushed, even in the class struggle, is the libido, desire; it's by starting with desire that you can bring forth the need for real change' (p. 291). Clément replies that these words have only a poetic meaning; 'desire' and 'the class struggle' are on different levels of language.

If Cixous can be accused of one kind of Utopianism with regard to the liberation of women, another, often diametrically opposed kind of Utopianism might be found in the work of Monique Wittig. Like Cixous and Irigaray, Wittig wants to displace the traditional binary opposition man/woman. She does this by making the norm the lesbian. The lesbian, because she occupies a position outside the male/female pair, is beyond difference, and not a 'woman' in the sense in which the term has been used culturally. Wittig rejects the idea of 'woman', which she sees as necessarily contingent on a relationship to 'man'. She agrees, therefore, with Beauvoir's famous dictum, 'One is not born a woman, but becomes a woman': 'what makes a woman is a specific social relation to a man, a relation that we have previously called servitude, a relation which implies personal and physical obligation as well as economic obligation' (Wittig, 1981, p. 53). She wants to 'dissociate "women" (the class within which we fight) and "woman", the myth. For "woman" does not exist for us: it is only an imaginary formation, while "women" is the product of a social relationship' (p. 51).

If Wittig's celebration of lesbianism is first of all an attack on the cultural construct 'woman' as a norm in any society, it is also a celebration of lesbian desire. Desire, she believes, has 'nothing to do with the preliminary marking by sexes' (Wittig, 1979, p. 114). She wants to go beyond categorisation, to value the individual as individual, and to desire not limited by social norms: 'Heterosexuality is a cultural construct designed to justify the whole system of social domination based on the obligatory reproductive function of women and the appropriation of that reproduction' (p. 115). 'Lesbianism opens onto another dimension of the human (insofar as its definition is not based on the "difference" of the sexes)' (p. 117). Just as Cixous and Kristeva find male representatives of 'feminine' modality or style, Wittig calls Baudelaire a 'lesbian poet', who speaks of 'pleasure for pleasure's sake' (p. 117). Lesbian sexuality, going beyond the reproductive function, involves 'the search for pleasure and the creation of a unique being, irreplaceable, self-sufficient' (p. 119). Politically, Wittig considers lesbianism as related to feminism: 'Feminism reminds lesbianism that it must reckon with its inclusion in the class of women. Lesbianism warns feminism against its tendency to treat as immutable and determining essences what are simple physical categories' (p. 118). The feminism she has in mind is the movement of those who fight 'for women as a class and for the disappearance of this class', not those who want to enforce a myth of specificity (Wittig, 1981, p. 50).[9]

Beyond fighting for the liberation of women as an oppressed class, Wittig wants to fight for individuals as *subjects* not merely as *objects of oppression*. One of the dangers she sees in Marxist theory is its reduction of individuals to members of a class, whereas 'for everyone to exist as an individual, as well as a member of a class, is perhaps the first condition for the accomplishment of a revolution' (p. 53). Wittig's attitude towards 'woman' is similar to that of Simone de Beauvoir, whose analysis showed how 'woman' has always been considered the 'Other' against which man has defined himself. Beauvoir, however, has often been reproached for taking the male standard as the norm. Wittig's denial of difference is more radical.

2
Theories of Language

The very form of the sentence does not fit her. It is a sentence made by men; it is too loose, too heavy, too pompous for a woman's use . . . this a woman must make for herself, altering and adapting the current sentence until she writes one that takes the natural shape of her thought without crushing or distorting it.   (Woolf, 1967, p. 145)

Most feminist critics agree on several general points: that language has been representative of the dominant culture and therefore reflects masculine values only; that most women when attempting to express themselves verbally are alienated from culturally-accepted symbols and forms, and that other written and spoken modes exist that would express the *un*alienated language of women.

(Gelfand, 1977, p. 245)

Theories of how women use language and how women write creatively begin with language as a reflection of the dominant culture. But they have led to sometimes contradictory views: is women's language inferior and to be changed, or is it expressive of values that have been neglected? Is difference in language a reflection of cultural submission, or a way of subverting the dominant culture? If women feel uncomfortable expressing their experience within the language of male culture, they may use language less forcefully than men; language use may reflect a position of social inferiority. On the other hand, rejecting the dominant language may also mean rejecting the conventional point of view and may result in increased creativity among women motivated to find their own means of expression.

The 'Précieuses' movement in France in the seventeenth century is perhaps best known now because in *Les Précieuses ridicules* Molière mocks their pedantry, affectation and use of euphemism. But it was an attempt to appropriate speech for women, to

24

establish a place in patriarchal society by asserting difference (Yaguello, 1978, p. 39). In the nineteenth century, Clémence Royer, who taught philosophy at Lausanne, took the opposite approach. In her *Introduction à la philosophie des femmes* (1859) she wrote: 'The two halves of humanity, because of a too radical difference in education, speak two different dialects' (Albistur and Armagathe, 1977, p. 404). What she wanted was access to the dominant language, not a vindication of difference.

Distinctions between speech and writing, and between ability to communicate effectively in social situations or in learned discussion and creative ability, must be borne in mind in considering the questions of women and language. In addition, there are differences in approach from country to country. French feminist literary theorists have largely filled a prescriptive role, talking about woman's writing (*l'écriture féminine*) as it should be, rather than as it is. Anglo-Saxon critics have been more likely to examine the actual work of women writers, to look for structural patterns, imagery, themes that reflect the author's gender. To some extent this is, of course, a difference between a rationalist and an empirical approach. Perhaps, as well, it is a reflection of the greater pre-eminence of women writers in English. The canon of major English writers, as defined by male criticis, will almost always include Jane Austen, George Eliot, Virginia Woolf. The canon of major French writers may well not include a single woman.[1]

A number of impressionistic essays have been written about how women use language in ordinary life. Some differences between men's and women's speech, at least until recently, have seemed obvious. Within 'polite' society, certain lexical items are considered male or female, certain words not to be used 'in front of the ladies', for instance. One of the first books in English was Robin Lakoff's. She considers that women use more flowery but empty adjectives ('divine'), more intensifiers, more tentative statements ('I guess'). Such language, she argues, shows woman's marginal role in the power structure, her fear of being aggressive, her concern with smoothing the relationships between individuals, avoiding conflict. Lakoff also suggests that women tend to use hypercorrect grammar. Language correctness, like neat physical appearance and following fashion, is a way of gaining status when real power is missing.[2]

If Lakoff's book was important in stimulating discussion on possible differences in language usage, its approach has been

questioned by both linguists and feminists. A major criticism is
that women's language has no positive value for Lakoff, and that
woman is reduced to the role of a victim. Many of her observations
have not been substantiated by scientific study. Studies by linguists, rather like studies by experimental psychologists, have
found a range of language uses, and few points at which a
differentiation according to the sex of the speaker was clear.
Several linguists comment that beliefs about sex-related language
differences may be as important as actual differences; the extent of
specificity is less than general opinion would expect.[3] It is common
to consider that women's language is more emotional, less precise,
and thus to accept traditional stereotypes: men are rational,
women intuitive. Janet Radcliffe Richards suggests that the acceptance of a woman's way of going about everything is a bad legacy of
patriarchy; reasoned argument is neither male nor female
(Richards, 1981, p. 15). According to Sally McConnell-Ginet,
assuming that sexual difference is more important than the differences among women continues the view that all women are alike
(McConnell-Ginet, 1980).

Dale Spender, in challenging Lakoff's implicit acceptance of
male language as the norm, sees women as the muted group,
having therefore access to a broader range of meanings, being less
dogmatic and more concerned with human ends: 'Marginality can
be productive' (Spender, 1980, p. 93). Unfortunately, such a position seems to imply that women should remain passive, give up
attempts to gain power, in order to use language more effectively.
The problem is how to value what may be specifically feminine
without indirectly denigrating it by a comparison with what is
masculine.

In *Les mots et les femmes*, Marina Yaguello discusses how women
use language in the practical, down-to-earth manner more often
associated with Anglo-Saxon feminism. She comments on the
difference in words referring to male and female genitalia; words
for male organs are more specific and also more often words of
praise; for female organs they are less specific and normally
insults. Woman is often treated in popular vocabulary as a product
to be consumed. Yaguello says that many of the feminist attempts
to change vocabulary can have little effect until fundamental
attitudes are changed. She sees many American strategies as at
best Utopian, at worst ridiculous, and notes that trying to change
pronoun usage is particularly difficult (*illes*, for example, to com-

bine *ils* and *elles*). She concludes that useful action is mainly changing sexist dictionaries, school books, administrative titles, television programmes, rather than inventing words such as 'herstory'.

Yaguello considers that any linguistic variants are preferential rather than exclusive, and that it is important to speak not of *natural* differences in women's use of language but rather of *cultural* differences. These differences, however, are not treated as 'negative' values, as they often seem to be for Lakoff. It is not a matter of women learning to 'speak male', but of giving women's speech a positive value. At the same time that language difference is revalued, however, equality of political rights must be demanded. 'Difference', in other words, must not extend to social and political matters in which it could be used to oppress women:

> Women feel differently, so they talk differently, have a different relationship to words and to the ideas of which these are the vehicle. Asserting difference at the same time as demanding equal rights is obviously the position to take.... We must impose female cultural models which have a universal value in a world where 'universal' equals 'masculine'. In other words cultivate marginality until the margin takes up half the page. We have a long way to go.   (Yaguello, 1978, pp. 67–8)

Christiane Rochefort does not distinguish between masculine and feminine styles of writing, feeling, rather more pragmatically, that 'one must be doubled-sexed to be a creator' (Rochefort, 1979, p. 108), but she does distinguish between the style of the oppressed and that of the oppressor. The oppressed have more flexibility, more subtlety. 'One must almost write as if twice removed, frame everything in irony and derision, or find other forms, another syntax, break down the whole thing' (p. 109). In *Les mots pour le dire* (1975), an account of her psychoanalysis, Marie Cardinal speaks of discovering how she found it difficult to say certain words: 'I understood that words could be my allies or my enemies, but that in any case they were strangers to me' (Cardinal, 1975, p. 283). She begins to think about what being a woman, having female genitalia, entails: 'Not even a word to protect them. In our vocabulary the words for this part of a woman's body are ugly, vulgar, dirty, grotesque or technical' (p. 305). Cardinal also speaks of the different connotations words have when used by men and women. If a

woman speaks of 'freedom', for example, she must be sure this is
not interpreted to mean 'license', whereas a man speaking of
freedom is under no such constraint (Cardinal, 1977, p. 89).

Even Simone de Beauvoir, who opposed theories of the specificity of women's writing, spoke of the practical problems of women's
use of language: 'I know that language in general use is full of
traps. While pretending to be universal, it shows traces that men
have elaborated it. It reflects their values, their pretensions, their
prejudices' (cited in Yaguello, 1978, p. 65). Women *write* differently, however, according to Beauvoir, only because of their present
cultural situation. When this situation changes, women will be as
creative as men, but not in a different fashion. They will 'not bring
new values. To believe they will is to believe in a female nature,
which I have always denied' (Francis, 1979, p. 248). In the interim,
can language be used as a weapon? Here Beauvoir said she
changed her ideas. She used to think that problems of masculine
dominance in grammar, for instance, should simply be ignored.
Later she realised, 'Certainly this is not the ground on which to
begin the battle. But to ignore it is to risk closing our eyes to many
things' (Francis, 1979, p. 258). This does not mean, however, even
temporarily, a 'woman's language'; Beauvoir felt that some present-day writers only reach a small circle of initiates, and that their
writing is élitist:

> You can't address yourself to women by speaking a language
> which no average woman will understand. . . . There is some-
> thing false in this search for a purely feminine writing style. . . . I
> consider it almost antifeminist to say that there is a feminine
> nature which expresses itself differently, that a woman speaks
> her body more than a man, because after all, men also speak
> their bodies when they write. Everything is implicated in the
> work of a writer.   (Jardine, 1979, pp. 229–30)

Before considering feminist positions on women's writing, it
may be useful to look at a few male perspectives on writing. Serge
Leclaire sees male and female discourse as resulting from different
positions in relation to castration, to the phallus:

> Because man has in his body a relation with his *penis as the
> representative of the phallus*, schematically, his natural inclination
> leads him to forget the fact that the phallus ('God') is invisible,

unseizable, unnamable. But woman does not have this representative in her body; therefore, her relation to the phallus is less veiled. She is less tempted to forget the fact that the phallus is always absent. . . . In the whole evolution and history of woman, nothing has ever come as a screen between the invisible 'God', phallus, and the way she speaks. . . . The important thing is that two types of relation to the phallus determine two types of discourse which are, of course, always blending. (Leclaire, 1979, p. 46)

Both sexes then write the body, but differently, because of an essential psychological difference. From a less theoretical standpoint, some comments by Alain Robbe-Grillet indicate a distinctly masculine perspective on writing: 'I had found a sentence in Kafka's *Diaries* where Kafka says that the act of description is an erotic act, in the way the sentence espouses the form of the object' (Robbe-Grillet, 1979, p. 88). This formulation – 'espouses the form', particularly – makes writing appear a male act – and also a position of power. Robbe-Grillet believes that fantasies, and therefore their artistic expression, vary according to biological type. As he describes how he works the 'masculine' elements of 'construction' dominate. Since feminist writing has been compared with modernism and postmodernism, it is necessary to remember that Robbe-Grillet too is a postmodernist, and that his method of working and even the vocabulary with which he describes this method are clearly antithetical to descriptions of *l'écriture féminine*:

All my books are organized around a kind of panoply of stereotypes that are *carved out* of the language society provides me. I live in society. . . . The system . . . consists of detaching fragments from society's discourse and using them as raw materials to *construct* something else. In society's discourse, these are concepts, but I detach them from their context, take them as *building blocks, I push them back* to the status of signifiers in order to build another language, which is my own. (Robbe-Grillet, 1979, p. 93, my italics)

The starting point for feminist theorists is often what is wrong with the dominant discourse as represented by Robbe-Grillet: its objective, impersonal stance is a way of asserting 'mastery' over its subject matter. Its 'grammatical and syntactical completeness' corresponds to 'the uni-directional drive of masculine need to resolve itself' (Gelfand, 1977, p. 245). Thus, women's language will be less 'objective', less 'uni-directional', presumably.

In 1974 several events of importance for the history of *l'écriture féminine* occurred. A double-page spread on women's writing, 'Existe-t-il une écriture de femme?', was planned for *Le Monde des livres*, but rejected by the editor, Jacqueline Piatier, who felt that the texts were 'absurd' and 'incomprehensible'. They were instead published in *Tel quel*. Xavière Gauthier, who introduced the selection and interviewed several writers, attacked both 'feminine' literature as it has traditionally been conceived, and also the idea of women writing 'like' men, which, she felt, would lead only to alienation. It will be necessary, she said, to *'make audible* that which agitates within us, suffers silently in the *holes of discourse*, in the unsaid, or in the non-sense' (Gauthier, 1980, p. 163).[4] Marguerite Duras speaks with Gauthier about the empty space, the rejection of syntax, the madness in her own writing. Julia Kristeva, in her interview with Gauthier, also speaks of ruptures and holes, though identifying their use not with women writers, but with a largely masculine avant-garde. For Kristeva, 'feminine' and 'masculine' are attributes or attitudes of writers of either sex who multiply meanings.

Also in 1974 Annie Leclerc's seminal *Parole de femme* appeared. Her work is emphatically not obscure or theoretical. For her the question of women's writing is largely one of reception; women's writing is not metaphysically different, but its themes have not been considered of value by the dominant culture. She is 'writing the body' in terms of themes rather than style. It is not so much preconscious or 'bisexual' issues that come to the fore, but the forthright discussion of the female body which has often been censured in literature. Birth in *Anna Karenina*, for instance, is described in terms of Levin's emotions, not in terms of the physical process Kitty was going through. Annie Leclerc therefore wants to invent a female language starting with the body: 'it is really in my gut that it began, by little signs, hardly audible, when I was pregnant' (Leclerc, 1974, p. 11). She speaks of the need to talk about menstruation, childbirth, breastfeeding. Woman, being closer to nature, can give new emphasis to the physical. Woman is also, according to Leclerc and other theorists, less obsessed with death. Men, she feels, need to dominate and need to have a good death, as can be seen in writing by such men as Malraux and St

Exupéry, and in the film genre of westerns.

For Annie Leclerc, 'masculine' and 'feminine' refer to men and women, not differing facets of a fundamental bisexuality. A woman's body apprehends time in a circular fashion; a man's in a linear fashion. Men read into ejaculation a dialectic of life and death: the penis rises and falls; women have a menstrual cycle. Does such a relationship to time affect a relationship to language? Leclerc's description of childbirth might suggest some parallel between the creation of a child and the creation of a work of art: 'I lost bit by bit everything that previously made me say "I", limits, separation, a feeling of time passing. I reached a dazzling awareness of raw life, a single life in all its fragile forms ... mad, disrespectful of any permanence, basic, drunk' (p. 79). The description might be compared to Chodorow's idea of women having more permeable ego boundaries, not in this case because of being raised by mothers but because of being mothers. It differs, however, from Kristeva's more theoretical consideration of motherhood as a relationship of semiotic and symbolic between mother and child. For Leclerc, it is a purely personal experience of joy, having nothing to do with the child. Leclerc also considers, rather as Irigaray does, the equation of sight with male domination of the world. The senses she praises as 'feminine' are hearing and smelling, which she equates with *jouissance* rather than *desire*.

In 1976 two special issues of *Les Cahiers du GRIF*, the Belgian feminist periodical, were devoted to the question of women and language.[5] The *Magazine littéraire* (no. 180, January 1982) asked a number of male writers and editors if there was a specifically woman's writing. Replies ranged through 'it doesn't mean anything', 'there is a different sensibility, but that doesn't mean a different way of writing', 'writers are necessarily individualist; women's writing is a political label', 'in writing the principal archetype to be expressed is the Androgyne', to 'when a woman writes, her relationship to her body and to the world is different. ... Women have overthrown certain notions of eroticism.' Only the last opinion seriously admits a specific woman's writing. Several of the editors, however, in spite of denying female specificity, were willing to judge characteristics as masculine or feminine. Women's writing is 'elliptical ... dissonant, anxious to prove its originality'; women's writing shows 'a simplicity in the love relationship'; 'an attention to concrete details, such as clothing'; it is a 'seductive writing'. If a woman's sentences are 'hammered', 'brutal', one might think they were written by a man. In other words, critics want to deny any metaphysical difference in writing, but show by their own vocabulary that they have internalised many social stereotypes. Women's opinions on writing as a woman range from Yaguello's practical assertion that she finds it difficult enough to write without thinking of whether she is writing as a woman, through Beauvoir's denial of specificity except in terms of the writer's situation, Kristeva's careful distinctions of semiotic and symbolic language (distinctions that still are most often expressed within a language that is itself 'objective', 'rational'), to texts in which the libidinal economy is given full power and the 'explanation' of female creative language is itself creative and not readily paraphrasable.

For many French feminist writers, women's language will assert the presence of the imaginary, the libido, the unconscious. Such language is not *merely* a means of artistic expression, it is a tool for gaining power. Why should female libidinal energy be expressed in a multiform way, whereas the male drive is seen as 'unidirectional', 'phallocentric'? Some theorists tend to talk about the female body as the source of the energy of 'female writing'. There is often an unfortunate tendency to reduce the opposition (the dominant male culture) to a single position/phallus. This is particularly hard to justify when much of the writing praised for its feminine nature was written by men, who, if in tune with their unconscious, nevertheless possessed a male body and a male organ.[6] The expression of a multiform, liberated unconscious has to be seen as cultural rather than biological. It is not a physical difference between male and female bodies that matters, but the cultural interpretation of them. Once this is granted, some of the work about 'writing the body' makes more sense. Considering 'feminine' as meaning '"bi-sexual" in the sense of non-repression of sexual differences in the self' (Gelfand, 1977, p. 245) is one way of approaching the problem. 'Feminine' writing, then, is seen as what allows greater diversity, less domination, less 'mastery', less of the 'phallologocentric' approach to the world.

'Writing the body' is a development from Leclerc, but especially from the work of Hélène Cixous, whose conception of *l'écriture féminine* aims at undoing the Lacanian notion that woman enters language through a lack or negativity. For Lacan, human subjectivity is organised in relation to language. As a result of the castration complex, the child no longer exists in the order of the Imaginary, where it perceives no incompleteness and is in close relation to the mother. Rather, the child enters into the Symbolic, which is dominated by the phallus, the law of patriarchy. Language depends upon awareness of the phallus (Cameron, 1985, pp. 119ff). Through language, Lacan has said, the individual internalises the values of the patriarchal societies in which we live. These powers he calls the 'Name-of-the-Father', that is, social identity given through the patronym, the process of naming under patriarchy. The Name-of-the-Father confirms in the child its attempts to situate itself in reality. The child learns its place in a system of names (*le nom*) and in a system of negatives (*le non*). In Lacan's view, we all take into our psyches this Name-of-the-Father as we acquire language within the network of familial and social relations. The female, however, because she lacks the castration complex, is what does *not* exist within the system of language. For Lacan, the 'I', the subject, is the position of men, possessors of the positive symbol of gender: 'because masculine desire dominates speech and posits woman as an idealized fantasy-fulfillment for the incurable emotional lack caused by the separation from the mother, Lacan can say "Woman does not exist"' (Jones, 1985, p. 83). For Cixous, this negativity is a cultural 'repression of the feminine'; a female text, a text which inscribes female pleasure (*jouissance*), will dislocate this repression:

> That women are particularly close to everything that is interior and related to bodily gestures is not surprising, since that is the realm to which they have been relegated. Woman ... does not need the social recognition so important for man. She is indifferent to selfish motives. Closer to her unconscious, more anguished, but also more courageous, she wants to take erotic pleasure in writing [*jouer de l'écriture de façon érotique*]. (Cixous, 1976b, p. 20)

(This citation seems to prove that Cixous is taking an idealistic position, not describing real women, who are not all 'indifferent to selfish motives'.) Plurality is valued over fixed meaning. In teaching literature, Cixous says, she first wants the student to feel the surface, to isolate figures and metaphors that give a text continuity. Only then can the student consider 'meaning' (Makward, 1976, p. 29). Structure is fluid, not linear.

Some of Cixous's descriptions of *l'écriture féminine* are essentially descriptions of her own writing practice: 'It is perhaps a *continuum* that is the most visible sign of a feminine libido. In my texts, there are no chapters, no ordered framework' (Cixous, 1981a). Writing is a descent into the unconscious, which Cixous has described as for her a descent into hell; but it is also an act of love, and an act of giving: 'Writing is also milk. I nourish' (Cixous and Clément, 1975, p. 54). At other times she is either analysing texts produced by others, or, more frequently, prescribing for the future: 'A feminine textual body is recognised by the fact that it is always endless, without ending'; 'what takes place is an endless circulation of desire from one body to another'. Feminine texts are 'close to the voice', have 'tactility' (Cixous, 1981b, pp. 53–4). Writing thus liberates what is suppressed by male desire to dominate, to order the world. Cixous considers that a 'feminine libidinal economy has a more supple relation to property'; therefore 'you will have literary texts [note the prescription, in the future tense] that tolerate all kinds of freedom ... which are not texts that delimit themselves, are not texts of territory with neat borders, with chapters, with beginnings, endings' (Conley, 1984, p. 137). Writing should be as close as possible to the unconscious, working on the level of myth and dreams.[7] Cixous's own writing is the opposite of order, domination. It attempts to break down all binary oppositions. It is filled with metaphors and word-play.[8] It subverts the either/or logic of rational (masculine) discourse. Hysteria is reclaimed as a valid mode of being and of using language.

Luce Irigaray's comments on women's use of language are largely prescriptive and based on the need to contradict the dominant, masculine discourse. Like Cixous, Irigaray defines this discourse as linear, systematic, logical, based on binary oppositions. Irigaray herself in *Spéculum de l'autre femme* disturbs this discourse by imitating it in such a way as to show its contradictions, its false assumptions. Mimicry, a way of subverting the masculine and articulating the feminine, is defined as 'an interim strategy for dealing with the realm of discourse (where the speaking subject is posited as masculine), in which the woman deliberately assumes the feminine style and posture assigned to her ... in order to uncover the mechanisms by which it exploits her' (Irigaray, 1985a, p. 220). Women's writing 'resists and explodes every firmly established form, figure, idea or concept' (p. 79). It is 'tactile' rather than 'visual'. (The visual implies an appropriation of the world as object, the tactile, a fluidity among things.) It resists linear meaning.

In *Spéculum de l'autre femme* Irigaray describes what woman's language should be (a language which woman has only been able to use publicly in the western world, Irigaray feels, in the language of mysticism); she speaks of insisting on the blank spaces, using ellipsis to deconstruct the logical grids of the masculine discourse, overthrowing normal syntax. A female syntax would have no subject or object, no distinction of identities. (Here we may again remember Chodorow's theory that women have more permeable ego boundaries.) This is not, however, a 'natural' use of language, a spontaneous outpouring, for it requires patience and rigorous application. There is, perhaps, an unresolved contradiction here, however, for later, in *Ce sexe qui n'en est pas un*, Irigaray speaks of women's language as setting off in all directions:

> She steps ever so slightly aside from herself with a murmur, an exclamation, a whisper, a sentence left unfinished.... One would have to listen with another ear, as if hearing *an 'other meaning' always in the process of weaving itself, of embracing itself with words, but also of getting rid of words in order not to become fixed, congealed in them.* For if 'she' says something, it is not, it is already no longer, identical with what she means. (Irigaray, 1985a, p. 29)

Perhaps there is a distinction between a spontaneous use of woman's spoken language and woman's written expression, but this is not clarified.

Irigaray's views on language, like her views on sexuality, posit an essential difference, partly based on metaphysical or psychoanalytic theories, but also on her empirical analysis of the language of schizophrenics, where she found:

> The typical sentence produced by a man is:
> *I wonder if I am loved*, or *I tell myself that I am perhaps loved [Je me demande si je suis aimé ou: Je me dis que je suis peut-être aimé].*
> The typical sentence produced by a woman is:
> *Do you love me? [Tu m'aimes?]* (Irigaray, 1984, p. 128)

Essentially, in both cases, the *subject* of the typical phrases is male. The difficulty of changing the use of language is, Irigaray feels, immense: 'All the speaking body of the subject [*le corps parlant du sujet*] is in some way structured archaeologically by a language that is already spoken. To tell the subject that this language can or should be modified is to demand a modification of the body, something that can't be done in a day' (p. 165).

Irigaray's discussion here of speaking subjects and their relation to language is rather similar to Julia Kristeva's emphasis on language as a process between speaking subjects, an emphasis which tends for Kristeva, but not for Irigaray, to lead away from any binary opposition between male and female use of language. Artistic creation, for Kristeva, is a dialectic, a harmony between the libido (the semiotic) and the symbolic: 'Innovating is never either the repetition of paternal discourse nor a regression to an "archaic mother". ... we can say that all creativity comes not from difference but from sexual *differentiation* between these two borders' (Boucquey, 1975, p. 25). While she rejects 'writing the body' as incapable of communication, Kristeva does consider the woman writer, like others who are 'marginal' to the dominant society, as involved in a different process of creation. Some of her descriptions of this process are not that far from the theories of Cixous and Irigaray. Women should reject what is definite and structured, should disrupt 'phallic' discourse. The creation of 'gaps' in meaning, a modernist, avant-garde technique is, however, open to both sexes, and its most famous practitioners have been men: Mallarmé, Lautréamont, Joyce, Artaud.

If Kristeva obviously does not consider a writing based solely on the body as a valid approach, she does see women as well situated to bridge the gap between the conceptual and the subjective: conceptual because of the necessity to communicate, of which women are particularly aware; subjective because 'intellectual, paternal, symbolic values are always only secondary in relation to female experience' (Kristeva, 1977a, p. 7). Women, however, find it more difficult to create since 'the process of sublimation' is particularly arduous for a woman 'because of her difficult paternal identification' (p. 8). Indeed, Kristeva castigates much of what has been recently written by women, terming it 'a reiteration of a more or less euphoric or repressed romanticism and always an explosion of an ego lacking narcissistic gratification':

> Thanks to the feminist label, does one not sell numerous works whose naive whining or market-place romanticism would otherwise have been rejected as anachronistic? And does one not find

the pen of many a female writer being devoted to phantasmic attacks against Language and Sign as the ultimate supports of phallocratic power, in the name of a semi-aphonic corporality whose truth can only be found in that which is 'gestural' or 'tonal'? (Kristeva, 1981, p. 25, p. 32)[9]

Is an insistence on the primacy of language another way of ignoring power, of retaining, therefore, a theoretical approach that will leave women in a marginal position? According to Deborah Cameron it may well be. Lacan's 'theory of language and sexual identity offers no explanation *why* the symbolic order is patriarchal. It can deal with matters of sexual differentiation, but it cannot deal directly with sexual power ... the feminists who have taken it up (Cixous, for example) have been grievously misled as to what its significance is, and they have overestimated its political useful-ness' (Cameron, 1985, p. 124). 'Radical feminists must be intensely suspicious of theories that invalidate experience and make the subordinate status of women a consequence of something other than their mere womanhood' (p. 132). Irigaray rejects not only Lacan's theory of women's negative relation to language, but more radically linguistic determinism, any one-to-one correspondence between the signifier and the signified. This, too, according to Cameron, is dangerous, as with no linguistic determinism there is 'no control of meaning by men, no privilege of the phallus as signifier and thus no alienation'. In other words, there is no longer a ground from which to fight. Cameron also sees dangers in Kristeva's position, finding the distinction of semiotic and symbo-lic an artificial separation existing in writing but not speech. Thus Kristeva's theories 'do not apply to the vast majority of language users and language events' (p. 166).

I want, however, to relate these theories – which may well be dangerous for liberating women from oppression, and incapable of explaining the relations between language and social reality – to the more limited realm of creative writing, where perhaps they will yield interesting insights. The creative writer's relation to the language he or she is using is not that of the propagandist – all literature is not committed – nor that of the individual involved in daily life. Rather, it is a construction from the materials of the psyche – materials which will reflect both the pressure of the symbolic (society and the cultural order) and the pressure of the semiotic (desire, the realm of the imaginary). Writing is 'an activity of transgression, breaking with the fixed positions of language, opening out a moving tissue of meanings' (Heath, 1978, p. 78) and in this may not the 'transgressions' differ according to the specific pressures the individual feels? These pressures will necessarily be individual: 'The unconscious is not anatomical, from a given division of the sexes, but symbolic, from a division of the individual as subject in language, meaning, difference' (p. 109). Female creativity then will not be an essential innate quality of women, but rather creativity typical of what being a woman has meant at the particular time and place in which a writer is situated, and also typical of personal factors, as for any writer. Stephen Heath's position in some respects is similar to Simone de Beauvoir's: 'each person has his or her own very particular history . . . and after all, the unconscious is the most secret part of ourselves. In any case, if the unconscious must express itself it will do so through the work that you do consciously' (Jardine, 1979, pp. 230–1). Kristeva at times seems to favour such a position. We must not

> sexualise cultural production. The problem is rather, I feel, the need to give women the economic and libidinal conditions for analysing both social oppression and sexual repression, so that each one can realise what is personal to her. . . . Why should a woman write like all women?   (Boucquey, 1975, p. 27)

Monique Wittig wants to develop a language not based on sexual difference, a concept that, she believes, is largely a cultural construct. She wants to strip language of masculine attitudes, of words the dominant culture has used to describe, for instance, the female body. She is particularly suspicious of metaphor, too often a way of denying women's political reality. But this does not mean abandoning rational language and especially does not mean developing a language for 'woman'. Wittig considers *l'écriture féminine* to be, like *la littérature engagée*, a 'myth'. Literature has to do with *forms*, not individuals, social groups, or social themes: 'To write a work of literature, one must especially be modest and realise that everything isn't determined by the fact of being "gay" or any other comparable sociological category' (Wittig, 1985a, p. 41). For Wittig, language is a means of innovating, remaking literary tradition. Far from advocating a language of the unconscious, she appropriates male language and genres and turns them into weapons.

A few English-language writers or critics have described their writing in ways similar to those defined by Cixous and Irigaray. Adrienne Rich has spoken of the need to listen for the 'silences, the absences, the unspoken, the encoded – for there we will find the true knowledge of women' (quoted in Greene and Kahn, 1985, p. 26). Wendy Mulford writes of the importance of altering syntax, 'the logical tendency of our linear-directed language that makes it impossible to think across structures of main and subordinate intention, categories of negative/positive and binary logic' (Mulford, 1983, p. 34). Michèle Roberts describes her own difficulty in writing straightforward linear narratives, a difficulty she associates with the place of the woman in culture (Roberts, 1983, pp. 66–7). In general, however, English-language writers are less likely to construct philosophical or poetic theories around their own practice.

Among academic critics there is a range of attitudes. Adrienne Munich suggests that 'rather than invent female language, we can appropriate what is at least half ours anyway' (Munich, 1985, p. 252). Mary Jacobus has said 'Utopian attempts to define the specificity of women's writing – desired or hypothetical, but rarely empirically observed – either founder on the rock of essentialism (the text as body), gesture toward an avant-garde practice which turns out not to be specific to women, or, like Hélène Cixous in "The Laugh of the Medusa", do both' (Jacobus, 1982, p. 37). Josephine Donovan, however, attempts to identify such traits: 'A female prose style is or should be one which enables the writer to deal with the psychic, personal, emotional "inner" details of life in a way that is neither analytical nor authoritarian' (Donovan, 1973, pp. 345–6). She analyses sentences by Jane Austen, George Eliot, Virginia Woolf and Kate Chopin in which there is a 'décollage' between the surface and the 'under-conversation'. Annette Kolodny feels that Donovan is too consciously looking for recurring traits in women writers, and that a definition of a female style would necessitate a definition of a male style as well. (Myra Jehlen makes a similar point in a plea for more comparative studies [Jehlen, 1981].) Kolodny herself, however, identifies such recurring patterns in women's writing as 'reflexive perceptions', when a character (in a work by Margaret Atwood or Sylvia Plath, for example) is shown 'discovering herself or finding some part of herself in activities she has not planned or in situations she cannot fully comprehend' (Kolodny, 1978, p. 41). Kolodny also finds 'inversion', in which traditional stereotypes of women are turned around, and the frequent use of clothing as iconography.

Texts written by a woman may show particular characteristics of language influenced by her gender, whether or not she is conscious of these characteristics. It is of interest, however, to see what the authors I will discuss have said on this subject. To my knowledge, Colette never directly addressed the question of whether she was conscious of writing as a woman, although she was always obviously conscious of using an 'I' which was a female voice. Nathalie Sarraute said: 'at the level where tropisms are found, everyone feels in the same way' (Besser, 1976, p. 284). Marguerite Yourcenar seemed to believe that certain qualities – kindness, gentleness, delicacy – are feminine; and also that in great male authors there is a tendency towards total impersonality, which is much rarer in women (Yourcenar, 1980, pp. 267–72). Nevertheless, she was against theories of sexual specificity in literature. She accepted a rather conventional distinction between masculine and feminine, but then denied its validity, at least for her own work.

Marguerite Duras says that in order to write she must not think in an analytic manner, speaks of the silences in her work, and seems to accept some gender specificity, such as women being closer to madness. She sees her work as differing from what a man would write. In reply to a question of Xavière Gauthier: 'Would a man show like that blank space?', she replied: 'I don't think so, he would intervene. *I* don't intervene' (Duras, 1974, p. 19). She rejects, however, any programme: 'It is false for me and for all women and for all homosexuals and for all writers who claim to an original alienation. . . . All writing which claims to adhere to a class is "transitive" writing. But writing is "intransitive", without direction, without any goal but its own, essentially without utility. Or else it is pornographic.'[10] Monique Wittig is consciously stripping her language of masculine attitudes, but has denied that a 'woman's writing' exists. Of the five women novelists whose work I shall discuss, only Marguerite Duras has to any extent described her writing in such a way as to suggest some of the premises of the theories of women's writing. These opinions do not necessarily invalidate theories, but they do suggest that we must approach theories of 'women's language' with a critical eye. Theories about form, structure, themes, being less abstract, are perhaps less tendentious.

3
Forms and Themes

It may well be, however, that the story has to be told differently. Take Oedipus, for instance. Suppose: Oedipus does not solve the riddle. The Sphinx devours him for his arrogance.   (Lauretis, 1984, p. 156)

Then all stories would be told differently, the future could not be calculated, the forces of history would change, will change, hands and bodies, another way of thinking, not yet thinkable, will transform how all societies function.
(Cixous and Clément, 1975a, p. 119)

Virginia Woolf's speculations about a 'woman's sentence' or Hélène Cixous's descriptions of *l'écriture féminine* constitute only one area of enquiry into the possible specificity of women's novels. The use of distinctly feminine themes is another obvious possibility. The mixing of traditional types of novel as they have been defined by a predominantly male literary theory is still another. Could comments about female/male perception of time (linear or cyclical), or about a vision/touch dichotomy be relevant to the structure, the imagery, the narrative point of view, the characterisations of the woman's novel, if such a thing exists? If the theoretical writing of most French feminist critics has tended to explore style, English-language critics have more often studied questions of theme and form.[1]

It is useful to remember at the start that we need to avoid ahistoricism, to study the writing of women in relation to its social and cultural contexts. If women are not strictly a class, neither are they outside the movement of history; thus it is important not to judge writers before the 1960s (Colette, for example) as lacking 'an ideal of self-development and sexual awareness that belongs to the late twentieth century' (S. Kaplan, 1985, p. 51). As Annette Kolodny has observed:

what women have so far expressed in literature is what they
have been *able to express*, as a result of the complex interplay
between innate biological determinants, personal and individual
talents and opportunities, and the larger effects of socialization,
which, in some cases, may govern the limits of expression or
even of perception and experience itself.   (Kolodny, 1978, p. 39)

Any woman writer is also aware of the power structure of
publishers, editors, critics, a power structure that has often been
hostile to women. If she is not silenced, the woman writer may
silence or disguise some of her thoughts in order to reach her
audience.[2] And, psychologically as well as practically, a woman's
relationship to literary institutions is likely to be more problematic
than a man's, as women have often been educated to feel guilty
about self-affirmation: 'To find in oneself her own justification is
difficult for those who have learned to define themselves in
relation to an Other' (Collin, 1984, p. 9). Virginia Woolf doubted
that any woman had solved the problem of telling the truth about
her own experience: 'She still has many ghosts to fight, many
prejudices to overcome' (Woolf, 1967, p. 288).

It is also necessary to avoid the autobiographical fallacy of seeing
creations by women as only personal confessions. Such a reading
has been used as a way of denigrating the importance of women's
work. (Mary Jacobus, for instance, has criticised what she sees as
the complicity of Gilbert and Gubar with the idea that the female
text *is* the author [Moi, 1985, p. 61].) Women may often use texts as
ways of defining themselves. The resulting text, however, must be
read as a product of value in itself, and as not merely a psychological document.

In considering themes, critics frequently observe that women's
fiction is more often concerned with the personal than the political.
For Simone de Beauvoir the culturally constructed condition of
women keeps them from the greatest themes of literature: 'to
question the world, one must feel deeply responsible for this
world. But women can't to the extent that it is a man's world'
(Francis, 1979, p. 471). Virginia Woolf, however, as early as 1929,
thought that the situation was already changing, that women had
intellectual and political as well as emotional relations, and that as
their lives became more impersonal they would deal with 'the
wider questions which the poet tries to solve – of our destiny and
the meaning of life' (Woolf, 1967, p. 147). Perhaps Woolf was more

optimistic, or simply less aware of the pervasiveness of patriarchal control of culture.

Eliane Boucquey's analysis suggests that neither Simone de Beauvoir nor Virginia Woolf may have been aware of the extent to which women are constrained by their culture, and were perhaps naïve in expecting them to create authentically merely by gaining access to realms beyond the domestic. Boucquey suggests that all women who wish to create confront an impossible choice: try to be part of the dominant culture, which entails self-mutilation and will negate the possibility of real creation; or remain 'authentic' and only have at one's disposition a cultural ghetto, always regulated by the orders of the superior culture. 'All really feminine works show the signs of this laying aside, this sacrifice, this acceptance of being taken and devoured, this masochism' (Boucquey, 1975, p. 20). For Boucquey, this masochism, which often prevents women's genius, is a result of culture, of course, not biological essence.

One major theme of women's writing is the problem of personal identity as experienced by women. At least two factors are at work here. Culturally, women have been the 'Other', defined by men. 'To be a woman' has been, at least until very recently, to fit into what men want. A woman's 'self-portrait originates in the distorting patriarchal mirror' (Weigel, 1985, p. 61). She thus seeks an emancipated self: 'the striking coherence we noticed in literature by women could be explained by a common, female impulse to struggle free from social and literary confinement through strategic redefinitions of self, art and society' (Gilbert and Gubar, 1979, p. xii).

Psychoanalytic theories such as Chodorow's theory that women have more permeable ego boundaries provide another explanation of the problem of defining oneself, a problem that may figure in characterisations and narrative point of view in fiction by women, as well as thematically. Might it be possible to find in novels by women less clearly separate characters, or characters who take their identity primarily from the reactions of others, or feel less individual than in fiction by men? (The problems of self-definition and ego boundaries might explain the confusion of pronouns often found, for instance, in Duras's work. Or the impossibility of separating Colette the author, Colette the character and Claudine. Or, again, Nathalie Sarraute's refusal to create well-defined characters.)

Cora Kaplan suggests that women's place in culture as subordinate makes them less in tune with romantic individualism (C. Kaplan, 1983, pp. 58–9). Nancy K. Miller says that Barthes's 'Death of the Author' is not relevant to women, who, rather than valorising dispersal, need to overcome it (Miller, 1986, pp. 106–9). You have to have an identity before you can desire death! Woman, for Kristeva (though of course this is woman as a marginal member of society, not as a biological essence) is 'aware . . . of the inanity of Being' (Kristeva, 1980, p. 146), thus not primarily concerned with defining a self. Rachel Blau du Plessis suggests that 'making the narrative center be the multiple individual is a strategy expressing the psychic oscillation between boundaries and boundlessness, characteristic of the mother-child dyad' (Blau du Plessis, 1985b, p. 155).

Is the subject 'decentred' because of a tension between what Kristeva terms the semiotic and the symbolic? And might this decentring be particularly evident in writing by women? Kristeva points out that 'the male writer, at battle with the maternal space, but separated from it, can turn elsewhere for his narcissistic gratification – to his "muse", his mistress, his mother. But the woman writer who has been both excluded from and forced to conform to the symbolic system, drawn towards and yet forced to exclude (ignore/repress) her attachment to the mother, is in exile' (Jardine, 1981, p. 230). As Margaret Homans comments: 'Where the major literary tradition normatively identifies the figure of the poet as masculine, and voice as a masculine property, women writers cannot see their minds as androgynous, or as sexless, but must take part in a self-definition by contraries' (Homans, 1980, p. 3). Women poets must face the problem that the muse is normally feminine and that nature is usually a mother.[3]

Annette Kolodny finds in women's fiction a 'fear of being fixed in false images or trapped in inauthentic roles' (Kolodny, 1978, p. 45), a theme that again relates to a tension between the semiotic and the symbolic, as this tension is reflected in cultural constructs. This contradiction, particular to women, who are caught within a masculine world that they accept and reject at the same time, often produces the theme of the other, the double, someone else to embody part of the tension.

Another theme in women's writing related to self-identity is madness, or the fear of going mad. 'Narratives in which a hero can only rebel with the ironic but futile "acting out" of the unfeminine behaviour that society finds "insane" are staples of women's fiction' (Pratt, 1981, p. 52). As Catherine Clément shows in *La Jeune née*, the hysteric is the woman who has 'taken on in her symptoms all the history inscribed in feminine mythologies'. Like the witch, the hysteric refuses to fit into rational society, incorporates a 'lost childhood that survives in suffering', a childhood of desires that cannot be assuaged (Cixous and Clément, 1975a, pp. 12–13). If she tries to revolt against society, she is incarcerated. She is the victim and the symbol of the tensions of the patriarchal family structure. Women's writing often presents a reality that seems neurotic within the perspective of the average (presumed male) reader. Often, as well, men's fear of madness has been projected on to women as the 'Other', the embodiment of nature rather than culture, of the unconscious rather than rational control; and women have accepted and incorporated within themselves this projection of madness.

Annette Kolodny's device of 'inversion', which works on the level of style, also works with themes: 'Love is revealed as violence and romance as fraud; suicide and death are imaged as comforting and attractive, while loneliness and isolation become, for their heroines, means to self-knowledge and contentment' (Kolodny, 1978, p. 43). Inversion can affect the structure as well, producing, for example, the unhappy ending of Kate Chopin's *The Awakening*. Women's fiction often rejects the dominant cultural pattern of always defining a woman in relation to a man. Among the patterns Annis Pratt finds is a clash between an ideal of liberty and 'norms of monogamous, wifely chastity' (Pratt, 1981, p. 9). Adolescent female heroes resist these norms by a retreat into nature, a green world, which is later seen as a lost state of innocence. (To some extent this theme is present in Colette, although with her persistent sensuality she depicts the natural world as always filled with sexual symbols: 'The rasping sound of a very real existence, a very real exigency, the thrust of the bud, the twitching erection of a bloodless stem just given its liquid nourishment, the greediness of water-logged stems . . . the big scarlet poppy which forces open its green, slightly hairy sepals with a little *cloc*, then hastens to stretch out its red silk beneath its sprouting seed capsule' (Colette, 1986, pp. 116–17). Most often, however, there is no easy escape: 'authors conceive of growing up female as a choice between auxiliary or secondary personhood, sacrificial victimization, madness and death' (Pratt, 1981, p. 36).

Another pattern Pratt identifies is the novel of social protest, although most often when women authors find an alternative social system it too is undermined by the sexual politics of patriarchy. Novels of love between men and women often show eroticism becoming criminal, with the female hero experiencing self-doubt and blame. Often 'self-censorship, both conscious and unconscious, drowns the revolutionary power of Eros in these novels' (p. 89). Novels of love and friendship between women do not escape this discrepancy between desire and fear of punishment by society. Strong bonds between female characters were, Pratt feels, more acceptable before 1920, when there was less acknowledgement of lesbian sexuality. Later novelists, however, often treated passions between women 'as passing phenomena on the road to marriage' (p. 97) or as objects of satire. Even with openly lesbian novels, there is often a sense of desperation. Catharine Stimpson has commented that lesbian novels have developed two patterns: 'the dying fall, a narrative of damnation ... and the enabling escape', the first of which has been dominant (Stimpson, 1982, p. 244). Colette more often fits the first pattern; Monique Wittig is a salutory exception to the sense of desperation. Novels about older women often depict characters who go beyond female roles and duties to pursue a 'mode of mysticism' (Pratt, 1981, p. 131), characters thus similar to the adolescent girl. (Again Colette's later work provides an example.) Pratt's patterns, therefore, are all variants of the struggle to overcome the barriers to self-realisation imposed upon women by their social roles and often by their own acceptance of these roles.

A theme related to the search for identity, one that may be almost specific to women's writing, is how women relate to one another. As Virginia Woolf commented, women are rarely portrayed in relation to each other in fiction written by men.[4] The relationship to one's mother is a major theme, a particularly charged case of relationships among women. While to some extent perspectives on the mother are similar for children of both sexes, as Dinnerstein has shown, and while, according to Kristeva, the woman who wants to create has to confront a difficult relationship with her father, women writers often express particular ambivalences towards their mothers, or, alternately, particularly deep, less-problematic attachments to them. Irigaray describes trying to reach her mother, who has, like most women, accepted her role in society and therefore cannot comprehend her daughter's revolt from social standards. The mother, once she ceases to be the

all-powerful nurturer of infancy, often is seen as no longer dominating, but dominated, and does not provide an adequate model
for the daughter. Or, on the contrary, by idealising the mother, the
daughter feels guiltily that she cannot reach standards too far
above her. The conflict between identifying with the mother as
admirable and rejecting her as victim can lead to the creation of a
character that Judith Kegan Gardiner terms the 'mother-villain'
who 'is so frightening because she is what the daughter fears to
become and what her infantile identifications predispose her to
become. One way in which the author may dispose of this fear is
by rendering the mother so repulsive or ridiculous that the reader
must reject her as her fictional daughter does. Another tactic is for
the author to kill the mother in the course of the narrative'
(Gardiner, 1982, p. 186).

The search for definition, and the uncertainty about the very
existence of the self, might explain the frequent mixture of autobiography and fiction found in women's works (Colette's and
Duras's for example). As woman has often been seen as an art
object, the 'sense that she is herself the text means that there is
little distance between her life and her art' (Gubar, 1982, p. 81).
Although the breakdown of the integrated character of nineteenth-
century fiction is seen in much twentieth-century literature, men,
according to Judith Kegan Gardiner, often split 'characters into
disjunct fragments, while female characters in novels by women
tend to dissolve and merge into each other' (Gardiner, 1982,
p. 185). (This is, of course, the type of subjective observation
difficult to verify empirically.) Mixtures of fiction and autobiography may also be explicable as a refusal to conform to traditional
genres as defined by the dominant literary culture, or as a
subversion of these genres to 'deconstruct' their normal significance. Wilson Harris has argued that new forms of fiction are
necessary to undo the roles of victim and victimiser in the culture
of former colonies. A similar strategy may be found in some recent
women's fiction. Angela Carter, for example, has spoken of
women's writing as part of a process of decolonisation of language
and thought, and says she feels allied to Third World writers
(Carter, 1983, p. 75).

To what extent are the possible characteristics of style and form
either found in women's writing or prescribed for women's writing
similar to those of modernist and postmodernist writing in general? If the feminist movement has been a questioning of stable

identities and accepted cultural values, does it primarily parallel
the openness of avant-garde literature by men as well? In discussing how women's work fits into the larger categories of modernism and postmodernism, no clear distinctions need to be drawn.
Both modernist and postmodernist ideologies can be interpreted as
undoing previous certainties of narrative, character and point of
view.

A useful summary of distinctions has been made by Rob Nixon.
Modernism includes the cult of the estranged artist, open-ended
forms, the use of myth or symbol for formal coherence, a reduced
reference to the material world, a hostility towards technology.
Postmodernism, on the other hand, includes the death of the
author, severely fragmented forms, no overarching formal structures, self-reference and extreme narcissism, and a submission to
technology (Nixon, 1984, p. 29). Nixon points out that significant
strains of recent literature are excluded from a narrow definition of
postmodernism, and cites among his examples Third World authors such as Gabriel García Márquez and Salman Rushdie. As
women, too, are writing from a 'marginal' position within 'high
culture', their work may also not fit neatly into a category. Thus,
for example, Duras may share the 'extreme narcissism' and lack of
'overarching formal structures' of postmodernism, but not the
'submission to technology'. Wittig uses myth or symbol 'for formal
coherence' but not the 'hostility towards technology' of modernism.

The postmodernists have been said to try to 'expose that system
of power that authorizes certain representations while blocking,
prohibiting or invalidating others' (Owens, 1983, p. 59). The representations that are normally authorised require a male hero:

> Opposite pairs ... appear to be merely derivatives of the
> fundamental opposition between boundary and passage; ... all
> these terms are predicated on the *single* figure of the hero who
> crosses the boundary and penetrates the other space. In so doing
> the hero, the mythical subject, is constructed as human being
> and as male; he is the active principle of culture, the establisher
> of distinction, the creator of differences. Female is what is not
> susceptible to transformation.   (Lauretis, 1984, p. 119)

As Craig Owens has observed, 'the representational systems of the
West admit only one vision – that of the constitutive male subject'

(Owens, 1983, p. 58). Thus it would seem that women writers might naturally tend towards the postmodern, at least as so defined.[5]

In *Writing Beyond the Ending* (the normal ending which leads either to marriage or death for the heroine), Rachel Blau du Plessis suggests that

> To change story signals a dissent from social norms as well as narrative forms. . . . If a novelist's maleness is expressed 'manfully' in receiving the commands of the dominant form without flinching, a novelist's femaleness might, at very least, consist in 'leaving a blank or outraging our sense of probability', at most, it might lead to a rejection of dominant narrative. (Blau du Plessis, 1985b, pp. 20–1)

She feels that any woman writer whose practice makes 'the meaning production process' a site of struggle may be considered feminist, even if the writer doesn't consider herself as a feminist. Thus to the extent that struggle with the master narrative can be found, feminist writing is present.

If this desire to disturb the 'master narratives' is the conscious attitude of many contemporary women writers, might it also be found, less prominently, in earlier writers? Or would the desire to be accepted (and published) have carried more weight? Critics have often felt that women writers have usually shown respect for form, as women in general are considered to show more respect for correct grammar. Culturally such respect may be the result of needing to be accepted within the dominant culture, of fearing to be excessive and to be judged 'mad', although there is possibly a persistent irony beneath the surface.

Recent feminist writers are consciously iconoclastic in various ways. Some, such as Cixous, who consciously mix styles,[6] are not afraid to be judged 'mad', since they want to liberate the unconscious. Those, such as Monique Wittig, who subvert traditional genres are often deliberately using this means to appropriate dominant forms for new purposes. Cixous chooses excess, effusion, Wittig irony and satire. Wittig wants to use the 'master narrative' for her own purposes; Cixous strives to unravel this narrative. The difference is comparable to that between J. F. Lyotard, for whom the 'master narrative' of any ideology has lost all credibility, and Fredric Jameson, the Marxist critic who wants to retain a 'master narrative' and who sees postmodernism as schizophrenic (Owens, 1983, pp. 64–5). Thus from more formal considerations, we return to a distinction between emphasis on the social (Wittig) or the psychological (Cixous). Teresa de Lauretis opts for a position closer to Wittig's:

> The most exciting work in cinema and in feminism today is not anti-narrative or anti-Oedipal; quite the opposite. It is narrative and Oedipal with a vengeance, for it seeks to stress the duplicity of that scenario and the specific contradiction of the female subject in it, the contradiction by which historical women must work with and against Oedipus.   (Lauretis, 1984, p. 157)

Or, more radically, de Lauretis suggests that political and personal are ultimately one:

> Since one 'becomes a woman' through the experience of sexuality, issues such as lesbianism, contraception, abortion, incest . . . are not merely social (a problem for society as a whole) or merely sexual (a private affair between 'consenting adults' or within the privacy of the family); for women, they are political and epistemological.   (p. 184)

Another way of approaching the problem of structure is the concept of the 'palimpsest': 'The orthodox plot recedes, and another plot, hitherto submerged in the anonymity of the background, stands out in bold relief' (Showalter, 1982, p. 34). The idea of the 'palimpsest' has been criticised as too much a reliance on finding a 'hidden message'; the reader, like Oedipus, tries to discover 'meaning', rather than considering a subtle interplay of tone, ambiguity and imagery, or the tension among various meanings (Moi, 1985, pp. 62–3). The 'palimpsest' theory may also blur the distinction between life and literature. Nancy K. Miller suggests that the plots of women's novels are not about 'life', but about the plots of literature, about the difficulty of portraying a female life in fiction (Miller, 1985, p. 356), an approach fundamentally contrary to that of the palimpsest.

Many critics have found tendencies in women's fiction to imagine a better society, utopian visions of a world in which the tensions of trying to fit into a role will be eliminated. Pratt identifies such visions in novels about mystical escape to a 'green world' of

nature, both by adolescents and by older women, in some science
fiction (such as Ursula Le Guin's *The Left Hand of Darkness*), and in
descriptions of all-female societies. The theme of the better world is
as well implicit in much of women's theory, from the hopes for a
socialist revolution in *The Second Sex*, through Yaguello's sugges-
tions that one must fight until women 'occupy half the page' to the
visions of *la jeune née* (the newly born woman) of Cixous and
Clément who, in spite of their divergences, both postulate a
possible world of bisexuality. A comment by Milène Polis in *Les
Cahiers du Grif* is typical:

> I hope, however, that when an authentically feminine culture
> will exist – free and strong – we will have a Baroque civilisation
> . . . no longer a dominant, masculine civilisation in the form of a
> circle, with a centre . . . but a civilisation in the form of an ellipse,
> that is with two focuses, two centres, both necessary.   (Polis,
> 1975, p. 16)

If realising such a vision in practice is obviously difficult, even in
fiction it is more often destroyed than successful.[7] Kristeva,
however, sees feminist Utopias as copies of masculine power. For
her an alternative is 'a permanent questioning of everything
established; humour, laughter, self-criticism, even of feminism'
(Boucquey, 1975, p. 23).

Related to questions of genre and formal structure are those of
narrative points of view. Are some more used, or more suited, to
writing by women? A female aesthetic might incorporate an
expression of mutuality, in, for instance, antiphonal, many-voiced
works in which there is not one single authoritative voice. Such a
refusal of authority, linked to patriarchal structures, is not, of
course, limited to works by women, although women, like other
marginal groups, may be more conscious of the need to resist
authoritative pressures. Besides the use of varied points of view,
the use of a single voice, if this voice is tentative, uncertain, is
another technique perhaps typical of women's writing.

Marthe Robert's work on the origin and structure of the novel
has implications for women's writing. In *Origins of the Novel*, she
distinguishes two ways of writing a novel: 'the way of the realistic
Bastard who backs the world while fighting it head on; and the
way of the Foundling who, lacking both the experience and the
means to fight, avoids confrontation by flight or rejection'. The

Foundling, who imagines himself (or herself) as having been adopted, who rejects his or her parents, is, Robert says, 'imprisoned in the pre-Oedipal universe', and 'flies in the face of reality, ignoring or jostling history and geography' (Robert, 1980, pp. 37–9). Among her examples: Cervantes, Melville, the Flaubert of *Les Tentations de Saint Antoine*. The Bastard, who rejects only the father, claims to be true to life, naturalistic. Such novelists are Balzac, Proust, Dickens, the Flaubert of *Madame Bovary*. The distinction has nothing to do with literary merit. Although the Foundling, existing in a pre-Oedipal world, is psychologically prior to the Bastard, 'the Bastard can never betray the Foundling who survives within him without running the risk of a *literary* impoverishment – a loss of depth, ambiguity and poetry – and of losing at least some of the social advantages due to him' (p. 112). The contemporary novelist, according to Robert, is dominated by a dialectic between the two childhood tendencies, between acceptance and negation of reality. Might Robert's distinction have anything to do with the gender of the author? The Oedipal drama, the rejection of the father, would seem to be primarily a masculine form, as is evident in Robert's description of one tendency of the nineteenth-century novel as enacting possible conquests – of women, authority, wealth. Although women have written the Bastard novel of psychological realism, Robert gives few examples. The pre-Oedipal Foundling story, that of a bisexual vision, might be more congenial to women.[8] At least, Robert's category of the Foundling novel fits well with both Kristeva's semiotic and Cixous's *écriture féminine*.

A salutory practical perspective can be found in Béatrice Didier's *L'Écriture femme*. While rejecting any theory that would see all women's writing as a single entity, she identifies some tendencies:

(1) A lyricism resulting from social prohibitions on women talking about themselves, which makes them write about themselves instead.
(2) Interest in rather artificial detective stories and in tales of the marvellous; that is, those outside the rational organisation of society. (Didier points out that in Agatha Christie's novels death is quite unreal.)
(3) Frequent use of images of childhood and the relations between mother and daughter.
(4) Fewer events, more breaks in narrative.
(5) The body presented as women feel it, not as men thought they did.

Didier concludes, however, that many of these tendencies can be found in Proust as well, and are thus not limited to women authors.[9]

Among French feminist critics, Claudine Herrmann has also made a significant contribution towards a practical definition of how typically feminine experiences have influenced literary techniques. Herrmann begins from the concept that a woman is always conscious of not being dominant, is always aware of her relations to others. A realisation that the world is not made in her image influences the woman's relation to space and time, and thus the form in which she writes:

> Woman, who is always obliged to take others into account, and also to consider a material reality from which she escapes less easily than man, can only conceptualize a cosmos of which she is not the center.   (Herrmann, 1980, p. 88)

> Physical or mental, man's space is a space of domination, hierarchy and conquest, a sprawling, showy space, a *full* space. Woman, on the other hand, has long since learned to respect not only the physical and mental space of others, but space for its own sake, *empty* space. ... to escape man's habitual urge to colonize, she must conserve some space for herself, a sort of *no man's land*.   (p. 169)

Angela Carter makes a similar point about the lesser dominance in writing by women:

> Everything is determined by different circumstances, and the circumstances of women are different from those of men. Somehow women writers really do keep on making this point, and sometimes they don't even know that they do it.... It's a point which men don't make when they write – unless they-'re loopy like Dostoevsky, or gay – because they really do believe that the world is made in their image.   (Carter, 1984, p. 38)

Similarly, time is seen differently. Men are more likely to deny themselves in the present for some future goal, women to insist on the primacy of the present moment:

> As soon as a woman speaks up, it is usually to reclaim the right to the present moment, to affirm the refusal of a life alienated in

social time, which is so hostile to interior time. (Herrmann, 1980, p. 172)[10]

Man has, says Herrmann, made woman responsible for the continuity of daily life and of the species, while he is engaged in discovery and change. Therefore woman must refuse their continuity, by fragmenting space and time into 'moments and places that are not linked together, in such a way that each is a sort of innovation' (p. 172).

Herrmann's theories invite various comparisons. There is an echo of Beauvoir's immanence/transcendence dichotomy. There are some similarities to Kristeva's distinction of the symbolic and the semiotic. Annie Leclerc also has spoken of how men see time differently; she explains this perspective by bodily distinctions, however, whereas Herrmann's concepts are based on cultural constructs. Béatrice Didier speaks of cyclical time, always beginning again, in women's writing, as a possible explanation for the relative lack of events in their fiction (Didier, 1981, p. 33). Often, she finds a denial of the myth of technical progress, and reminds us that Frankenstein was created by a woman. Annis Pratt says that 'Since women are alienated from time and space, their plots take on cyclical, rather than linear, form and their houses and landscapes surreal properties' (Pratt, 1981, p. 11). Is Herrmann's suggestion that women should fragment space and time contrary to Cixous's advocacy of fluidity? or merely another way of reordering feminine experience so as to counter the rational structure of masculine discourse? While these various critics start from different theoretical perspectives, their ideas converge on the ways in which women's position in society has affected how women writers use narrative.

Another, radically different approach to the question of 'difference' in literature is from the perspective of the female reader: 'from a feminist viewpoint the question is not whether a literary work has been written by a woman and reflects her experience of life, or how it compares to other works by women, but rather how it lends itself to be read from a feminist position' (Furman, 1985, p. 69). The question of the reader is linked to the politics of culture; it was feminism, as Laura Mulvey remarks, that gave a new urgency to consideration of the politics of culture (Mulvey, 1979, p. 178). Emphasis on the reader excludes the '*disembodied* voice of some neutral, impartial and absent speaker' (Furman, 1980, p. 52), a speaker who as neutral will, in fact, be read as male. Such emphasis is similar to Jonathan Culler's 'reading as a woman', which is largely a deconstructionist reading.[11]

Interesting work in film criticism has been based on the theory that as the camera eye is usually male, just as the reader is usually presumed to be male, only the male spectator can fully be engaged with its perspective:

> the feminist critique of representation ... has conclusively demonstrated how any image in our culture – let alone any image of woman – is placed within, and read from, the encompassing context of patriarchal ideologies, whose values and effects are social and subjective, aesthetic and affective, and obviously permeate the entire social fabric and hence all social subjects, women as well as men. (Lauretis, 1984, pp. 38–9)

How might women's films differ? Gertrud Koch has speculated on how different childhood experiences may affect the structure and images of films:

> If it is correct that in a socialisation differentiated along gender lines, male infants receive more support in their motor efforts than female infants, then one might also understand the tendency in many films made by women to rivet the desiring gaze onto objects that are both beyond physical grasp yet fixed within the scope of vision. (Koch, 1985, p. 149)

Teresa de Lauretis finds in women's cinema techniques that resemble those in women's fiction: disjunction of image and voice, strategies that alter the forms of traditional representation, reworking of narrative space (Lauretis, 1985, p. 175).

Discussions of female specificity in language and aesthetics end, as do discussions of more general possible differences between the sexes, in a quandary. Should differences be identified and given value, or should we aim at a genuine bisexuality or androgyny? Annette Kolodny feels that while a separate feminist criticism is needed, and will be needed for some time, the goal ultimately is 'to so enlarge the boundaries of all literary criticism that we finally achieved a fully "humane" literary criticism' (Kolodny, 1978, p. 55). There are dangers in an emphasis on difference in literature, as in politics: 'if women forfeit the culture men have dubbed "male" when it is, in fact, human, they will have deprived themselves of too much' (Heilbrun, 1982, p. 294). The question, of course, is whether this culture is genuinely human or whether, as many would argue, it is really 'male'. To answer such a question would be to determine the place of women within any culture (both part of it and to the side, and always dominated, seems to be the most accepted view) and to determine which essential features of the culture are within that sector of which women are fully a part, which features are implicitly based on gender domination.

Silvia Bovenshen warns against defining differentiation in feminine aesthetics as merely inversion of masculine aesthetics, and concludes that while there are feminine modes of sensory perception and feminine aesthetic awareness, there is no feminine specificity in artistic production or theory of art (Bovenshen, 1985, p. 136). Teresa de Lauretis suggests that the specificity of a feminist theory resides not in a new essentialism or in a private female tradition but in 'that political, theoretical, self-analysing practice by which the relations of the subject in social reality can be rearticulated from the historical experience of women' (Lauretis, 1984, p. 186).

Turning from theory to the practice of women writers, shall we find that this 'self-analysing practice' is more important than any of the specific techniques, patterns or structures that many feminist critics have tried to identify?

4

Colette

> She presents women as they are (for her), no longer as they were supposed to be (for men) or as they would like to be (for feminists).   (Biolley-Godino, 1972, p. 63)

Colette's work fits certain theories of women's writing in its refusal to be categorised easily into genres. Robert Phelps has identified at least four categories among her short stories – *chroniques*, autobiographical sketches, non-narrative lyrical meditations and short stories proper – categories that 'tend to metamorphose into one another' (Colette, 1986, p. xv). Often she appears as a character in her novels; the line between autobiography and fiction is thus blurred. Joan Hinde Stewart has defined Colette's favourite genre as 'autography': 'the writing of an author who records events *in her own name and as if they were true*, but without giving anything like a self-history' (Stewart, 1983, p. 93). Christiane Makward gives some interesting examples of how Colette recreates her experiences. When Colette wrote *Break of Day* 'which deals basically with the same quest for feminine autonomy and the same refusal to let a young man enter her life [as *La Retraite sentimentale*], she was already deeply involved with Maurice Goudeket, sixteen years her junior and her future husband'; and 'the famed "pink cactus" of Sido's letter at the opening of *La Naissance du jour* – if it existed at all – did *not* prevent Sido from accepting de Jouvenel's invitation to visit the couple' (Makward, 1981, p. 188). If Colette is a feminine author, it is not in an artless, autobiographical directness.

Colette is a test case for any theories of female writing that discuss work prior to that created by contemporary feminist awareness. To many, including Marguerite Duras, Colette is the epitome of 'feminine' writing that plays up to male expectations of what women should be interested in (Horer and Socquet, 1973, p. 176). This type of writing is often considered particularly evident in the early Claudine stories, which were written to Willy's specifications. For Simone de Beauvoir, Colette is, like Virginia

Woolf, feminine in the best sense of the word, more sensitive to
nature, more contemplative (Jardine, 1979, p. 233). (It is obvious, I
think, that Beauvoir doesn't quite know what to say about Colette,
however.) Cixous cites Colette as an example of women's writing
in 'The Laugh of the Medusa', but a year later, in 'Rethinking
Differences', she is not so sure. While granting that Colette
'communicates the body as few texts do', she is not 'excessive'
enough for Cixous, and is too much concerned with 'a certain
social milieu'.[1] The comments are perhaps more valuable for the
light they shed on Cixous than on Colette! Male critics have
stressed qualities similar to those Beauvoir praises, but have often
sought to reduce their value. For Pierre de Boisdeffre, for example,
Colette is 'limited, and remains too indifferent to what makes the
nobility of man' (quoted by Richardson, 1984, p. 239). To others,
Colette is a precursor of recent feminist concerns:

> the presence of the body, a diffuse sensuality, an unrepressed
> female desire, the celebration of marginality ... those narrative
> techniques which depart from patriarchal convention, leading
> toward the generation of the female text: the reversal of sexual
> stereotypes, the transcendence of genre, the alteration of image
> structure, and the discovery of new lexical codes.... The
> androcentric optic is displaced; a new subject appears: the
> woman who desires. (Eisinger and McCarty, 1981a, pp. 1–2)

Not the nobility of man, but the sensuality of woman.

Feminist critics have seen in Colette's work the beginning of a
gynocentric optic in French literature – a vision of the world of the
female in which she exists as a subject, rather than merely an object
of desire, and in which her basic identity is centred on her
relationships with other women. If it is undoubtedly unfair to
many earlier French women writers to say that Colette inaugurates
this vision, it is also an exaggeration to deny the importance of the
relationships between the sexes in her work, to focus her vision
exclusively on relationships between women. The claim is, however, an understandable revision of the earlier reading of Colette as
a writer portraying women as men wanted to see them.

A more interesting approach is to see Colette's work in terms of
the marginality of her characters. Mari McCarty speculates that
'women can only overcome their Otherness by becoming consciously marginal'; she sees Colette's world as a fringe world, 'a

refuge from phallic constructs' (McCarty, 1981, p. 367). Colette's marginal people, living in the 'refuge from phallic constructs', are not, however, all women. Often her male characters are also marginal, and lacking in 'phallic' aggressiveness. This is indeed one of the striking parallels between Colette's work and that of Marguerite Duras. The life of the marginal takes place not in a 'no man's land', but in a land without a 'masculine' drive towards worldly success or power. It is still, however, a world of sexual desire, desire often directed towards men. And it remains a world in tense contact with the socially-approved world of ambition and success, although Colette does not often portray the 'real' world directly. In the short story 'Belle Vista', the hotel caters for marginal people; if others arrive they are quickly shunted away. One could read *Chéri* without being aware that there was a society in France at the time profoundly out of sympathy with Léa's world. The marginal world of *Gigi* has its own standards, parallel to but separate from those of respectable society. The reader is always aware of experiencing a 'fringe' society, whose enclosure is partly self-chosen, partly, that is, a deliberate rejection of respectability, but also partly forced upon individuals who cannot attain the larger society's approval. Women do not necessarily choose marginality to be safe from masculine domination; marginality is often forced upon them, and they then find the advantages possible within it. Colette is, I feel, much less advocating a conscious choice than showing what can be gained from necessity.

A related problem with feminist readings of Colette's themes is the tendency to divide her female characters into positive and negative categories, according to how well they exemplify values not contemporary with Colette's world. This is evident in Sylvie Romanowski's 'typology', where Vinca, in *The Ripening Seed*, is considered positive partly because she does not wear 'self-consciously applied makeup' (Romanowski, 1981, pp. 67–8). I doubt whether Colette, who continued to wear heavy eyeliner in her old age, would have considered this a 'positive' quality in itself! Similarly, Romanowski places Léa among the negative exemplars of the mature woman because she has had so many lovers, chooses a lover much younger than herself, and is aware of getting old and less physically attractive; none of these would be faults for Colette herself. It is not possible to recuperate Colette for a narrow 'burn-the-bras' school of feminism, any more than for a 'women should only be interested in themselves as beautiful objects' approach. Colette had her own morality – seldom directly expressed – of sympathy for and refusal to dominate others, openness to the natural world, ability to nurture. Colette's 'gynocentric optic' is not a refusal of physical beauty; rather, beauty should be enhanced by any available artifice (the character 'Colette' in 'Le Képi' is proud of her ability to refashion Marco with skilfully applied makeup). Nor is there a refusal of any contact with men. Rather Colette recognises the right of women to have their own sexual desires, their own passions, and to withdraw, if they want, from the roles men would impose upon them.

Colette's 'gynocentric optic' is also not a radical lesbian position. She treats lesbian, homosexual and heterosexual love as basically the same experience, making moral distinctions only on the basis of the refusal to dominate another human being and on the authenticity of the emotions. She does not give a preference to lesbianism, and she continues to think in terms of masculine and feminine. Colette is no Monique Wittig, asking women to withdraw from any contact with the patriarchs or to give up distinctive features of female identity. Nevertheless, relationships among women are at least as important in her work as relationships between men and women, because the former include dimensions beyond the erotic: mutual nourishing, friendship, and especially maternal ties:

> Women who love women come together in Colette's world because they are fleeing from a painful experience with a man and are looking for a *retraite sentimentale*, 'Sido's' warmth with its attendant garden and animals. Lesbianism is a *pis aller*. It is a copy of either mother–daughter or male–female love or both. (Marks, 1979, p. 369)

Colette's work may seem particularly feminine in its reliance rather on linear love stories than complex plots. Her plots, often similar, frequently involve one man and two women, one older and maternal, the other younger and a rival. Her texts might also be particularly feminine in the importance given to sensual experience. Colette said that heroism is banal; her characters are not heroic, but are passionately in tune with the pleasures of erotic desire, the natural world, food, jewellery, visual beauty. But especially, of course, the writing is feminine because the desiring subject, the voice of the text is feminine: 'We never see Chéri except as Léa sees him or as he has internalized Léa's perception of him' (Relyea, 1981, p. 159). Colette's exploration of her own identity is built upon feminine experiences, experiences essentially of being in love or being out of love.

Can Colette then be 'recuperated' by modern feminist critics? A first problem for the feminist critic is those texts that speak of a woman's need for a dominant male. As Claudine says in *Claudine à Paris*: 'what I had been searching for for months – for far longer – I knew, with absolute clarity, was a master. Free women are not women at all' (Colette, 1976a, p. 353). This could, of course, be considered writing to Willy's specification. Or an early view, later revised, since there are numerous texts that seem to suggest the true fulfilment for a woman means reaching a state beyond any need for the presence of men. But the recognition of dependence as part of many women's emotional and sexual desires persists well beyond the Claudine stories (see Biolley-Godino, 1972, pp. 127ff.). Many of Colette's most aggressively self-assured female protagonists share the dual nature of Claudine: the need to be independent and the need to submit. Colette's characters are not going to play simple exemplary roles as modern heroes in charge of their own destinies; they are not immune to the erotic attractions of the male or unaware of their own frequent need for emotional and financial support. Her interest lies in describing what exists. More fundamentally, she is not going to treat woman's dependence as only an unfortunate result of social conditioning: 'If it is often difficult in her novels to be a woman, the origin of the difficulty is never attributed to society, but rather to love, and Colette does not treat love as a socially determined phenomenon' (Marks, 1960, p. 65).

Dependence is a feminine trait not limited, however, to women. There are many portraits of strong women, who rise above the burden of being female in a predominantly male world without losing their feminine qualities. And among her notable characterisations, men perhaps more than women may be submissive, dependent on passions – Chéri being the greatest example.[2] Colette 'often stated her preference for men who develop a weakness that opens them up to nurturing and being nurtured, and for women who develop a strength and resilience in the social and personal spheres' (Stockinger, 1981, p. 87). There is considerable sexual ambiguity in her work. Characters may be androgynous, or capable of acting as a member of the opposite sex, as in

'Belle-Vista'. Often her females are the aggressors, and tend to treat males as sexual objects. (They can only do so, of course, because they have gained economic power, through careers as rich courtesans or through marriage.)

Looking at someone seems to be the primary activity of Colette's characters. Dialogue is less important than observation, and the observer is usually curious and detached. The male character is 'demythified', not reflected (as Virginia Woolf remarked he often was in both life and literature) through a magnifying glass of female adulation or love. Female characters are also seen clearly, whether Léa or Marco, for whom the reader is invited to have some sympathy, or Rose in 'Le Rendez-vous', for whom we have very little. This technique reflects Colette's underlying vision of life. It is not only important to look closely at nature, at the external world, but also to look clearly at other human beings, and at oneself. The most admirable characters are those (such as Léa) who can recognise their own weaknesses. (Marco is an object of pity because she cannot.)

As a result of her insistence on honesty, Colette is particularly unromantic. Colette's world, in spite of the luxurious milieu in which some of her characters exist, is a hard world, a world in which the survivor is the person who can manage to keep her or his eyes clear, even in the midst of love. The novels and stories seldom are seen through the eyes of a character in love. Rather, it is an observer detached from emotion who presents the story and who draws the reader's attention to the difficulties that love can entail. This detached observer is increasingly the character 'Colette', whose commentary on the progression of the action deflates heroism and romanticism.

Such a perspective is, I would think, the opposite of what is often considered a 'feminine sensibility'; it is indeed curious that readers of Colette have so often seen her as reflecting a 'womanly' vision. Her interest, for example, in clothes, make-up, household furnishings, is often based on the use of such objects as weapons in the battle for survival. The woman's perspective lies in the recognition that most life is experienced at the level of the small detail, that we are not often called upon to make large, heroic choices. For Colette 'the personal is the political' in the sense that all life is a struggle to endure in which the essential decisions are made as tactics rather than as grand strategies.

Colette is also, because of her insistence on love as first of all physical, strikingly modern. She treats sexual passion with a directness and honesty rare in any era, and with no touch of prudishness. What interests Colette particularly in men is their physical qualities, the erotic desires they arouse in women. Often, indeed, they seem to be 'sexual objects', whose only function is to make love. Their business interests, if they have any, are never discussed. If 'love' is what motivates many of her characters, this 'love' is closer to the pure sensuality of Claudine than to romantic adulation, or to an aggressive assertion of a dominating ego. Colette's insistence on the importance of the body as the source of pain and pleasure is connected to her respect for and love of animals. Colette's animals are seldom sentimentalised, but are creatures also trying to survive and find pleasure in a cruel world. If they – like human beings – must sometimes act the clown, it is ultimately with a practical goal in mind. Indeed, Colette's fiction, in which human beings are often described with metaphors from the animal world and are often valued for their physical qualities, in which the sexual act is reduced to its most elementary level, does not make a great distinction between human and animal.

It is hard to imagine a character of Colette's caught in the desire to 'fuse' with another being. If the woman often wants to submit, as often she wants to flee, and Colette seems critical of any desire to lose one's liberty. Nor can the man as object be possessed, incorporated into the self. Rather he is an object to be looked at and admired. Léa's relationship to Chéri is far different from Marcel's relationship to Albertine. Colette's perspective is that of woman in the sense defined by Claudine Herrmann. She is well aware that she does not dominate the world, or even a small corner of it, and especially that she cannot dominate another human being.

Because of their greater power in the 'real' world, men cannot, however, be reduced to their physical qualities. Marcelle Biolley-Godino speculates that Colette is often hard on her male characters – in her satiric descriptions, in her plots where the possibly dominating males are conveniently killed off – as a kind of revenge (Biolley-Godino, 1972, pp. 150–1). Colette wants to be strong, independent, free of emotional entanglements, and portrays some of her heroines in this fashion. But she realises that such independence – given the society in which her heroines live – can only be gained through a 'retreat' or 'flight' from the powerful male. In the hard world of survival, the female's weapons are still limited.

Colette's relationship to the fact she was a woman is rather ambiguous. She seems to have accepted that women should be giving, should not be aggressive, although she also saw women as strong, sympathetic, naturally courageous. She incorporated within herself, at least in her early years as a writer, this difficult tension between the socially ordained role of women and the role played, for example, by her own mother. In becoming more successful and independent, in needing to live as a divorcée who had failed, in society's eyes, to be a proper woman, she felt that she would have liked to be more 'womanly', but was at some point 'masculine'.[3] Colette was, in other words, of her era; she is not a partisan of the kind of equality sought by, for instance, Simone de Beauvoir. She saw womanly qualities as different from manly ones. Sharing in both natures, she also has many of her characters share in this cultural androgyny, an androgyny intensified by bisexuality. She does not, however, envisage eliminating 'difference'.

If we accept that 'sexual mobility would seem to be a distinguishing feature of femininity in its cultural construction' and that 'it is understandable that women would want to be men', Colette's tensions may reflect that of many creative women. She was upset to be told she was 'masculine' in behaviour; yet on the other hand, she valued her independence. Another way of approaching her work, therefore, is through the concept of the 'masquerade', the assumption of an excess of femininity, in order to hide possession of masculine powers.[4] This might be related to Irigaray's concept of 'mimicry'. This is not to deny the validity for Colette of a psychological desire to submit, but to suggest that she may have exaggerated certain 'feminine' qualities – especially the desire to be dominated – in an effort both to conceal her feeling of being superior to most men and to adopt almost a 'caricature' of the docile, domestic female, as a protective role.

Fundamental to Colette's work is the dichotomy between the lost paradise of childhood – of which animals are an important element, and which is always connected to her love of her mother, who had a great passion for nature – and the world of adult sexual passion, deceit and perversion. Such a dichotomy might remind us of the divide between Combray and the world of Sodom and Gomorrah in Proust; for Colette, however, there seems to be no snake in the grass of paradise, no implicit criticism of the mother for rejecting the child's demands. Indeed, Colette is unusual in her abiding, largely uncritical view of her mother, whose only notable weakness would seem to be a tendency to believe the best of human nature.[5] The paradise is lost, in spite of the mother, when the girl moves to Paris.

The world of Paris, in which most of Colette's fiction is set, is often a world removed from harsh economic necessity, a world removed as well from middle-class sexual mores. Many of her characters seem to live in a milieu of chic restaurants and are singularly lacking in any interests beyond *foie gras*, pearls and other accoutrements of living well. There is, however, another group of characters, the victims of society: the actresses, seamstresses, stringers of pearls whose labour is exploited, as Colette's was exploited by Willy, but who, like Colette herself, are often survivors through their resilience.

Claudine à l'école (Claudine at School, 1900), Colette's first novel, was perhaps made deliberately salacious at Willy's insistence, but cannot be simply dismissed as a comissioned work, for it shows many of her later themes in embryonic form. Claudine is a first example of Colette's 'autography', for she shares many qualities with her creator. The form of the novel – a deliberately naïve diary, full of mockery, a parody of traditional autobiographies (Stewart, 1981b, p. 263) – is thus also for Colette an intentionally disguised version of her own early life. The greatest discrepancy between Claudine and her creator is that Claudine is without a mother, thus without a counter balance of affection and sensitivity, to the eroticism and cynicism of life in her school. The novel is not a story of an earthly paradise. We could speculate on the absence of Sido in this work, in terms of Colette's own unhappy separation from her mother by her marriage to Willy and especially by the life she was expected to lead in Paris. Sido does not belong in Willy's world or even in a version of Colette's childhood written to conform to Willy's intentions. Perhaps, as well, Sido does not belong in the world of newly awakened sexual passions that Colette herself was experiencing at the time. It is not necessary, however, to dwell on the 'gaps' in the text of the novel to find Colette's first attempt at self-definition. Claudine is in search of her own identity, including a sexual identity that she finds some difficulty in accepting. Critics have often speculated about the paucity of *Bildungsroman* by women writers. The Claudine novels are exemplary exceptions.

Claudine à l'école begins not with the school and society, but with the natural world. The village of Montigny-en-Fresnois is of value to the child because of its woods, its animals, the possibilities of escape and solitude that it offers. Claudine begins by establishing herself as an individual apart from the world of 'femininity' – the girls who shudder at the approach of insects, who are afraid to get dirty. Yet the description of this world of the 'tomboy' (which we might compare to that of the children in Monique Wittig's *Opoponax*) is immediately followed by 'Two months ago, when I turned fifteen and let down my skirts'. The juxtaposition of the 'natural' Claudine in the woods and the 'young lady' Claudine is the beginning of a tension in the search for identity that will inform much of Colette's work. Colette is not, however, merely bemoaning the passing of the 'tomboy in the natural world' phase; she also welcomes the onset of more active sexuality, in spite of the problems it will raise.

The young Claudine at school has from the beginning a need to set herself apart. She feels superior to her schoolmates, whom she takes pleasure in describing satirically. She sings well, without effort gets the best marks in composition, is the first to attract the adult men who enter the school. Her superiority is also manifest in her quick tongue and her ease in dominating others, a tendency that leads towards what might be considered an incipient sadism; Claudine loves to hit people. And Luce Lanthenay seems to love being hit. At the same time, however, Claudine wants someone 'stronger and more intelligent' than herself. 'I don't love people I can dominate' (Colette, 1976a, p. 111). Both her independence and her desire for love (the two sides of her nature and perhaps of the nature of Colette herself) are thus established at the start of the cycle.

Claudine's adolescent sexuality finds it first expression in her attraction for Aimée, who is also the first of Colette's portraits of the unfortunates, the victims of society. Sexuality, however, is always androgynous, or polymorphous perverse. The ridicule to which the young assistant masters at the school are subjected by Claudine does not prevent them from being objects of sexual desire as well as objects of curiosity. *Claudine à l'école* captures with accuracy the adolescent's interest in sex for itself, and need to assert one's own desires and to test one's own attraction for others. What seems most striking, when we consider the date of its publication, is less the lesbian episodes in themselves than the frankness with which female sexual desire and curiosity – for members of both sexes – are described.

The wider community is no better than the school. The local

officials give parties with nude women; a poor farm girl feeds her newborn child to the pigs. Colette's adolescent heroine is well aware of the hidden aspects of desire. She is still, however, basically untouched by any of the nastiness around her. She uses various simple ruses to see many sexual or emotional exchanges that are not intended to be seen by a third person. This appears, however, to be simple adolescent curiosity, not real voyeurism, and often, in fact, is a rather awkward literary device.

Colette also shows in this first novel a sympathy for the victims of society. Claudine may mock the stupidity of her classmates and the job of school teacher but when the *brevet* examinations take place she realises the importance of the education these girls have received:

> They were bravely preparing to spend three years at a Training College, getting up at five a.m. and going to bed at eight-thirty p.m. and having two hours recreation out of the twenty-four and ruining their digestions. . . . But at least they would wear hats and would not make clothes for other people or look after animals or draw buckets from the well. (Colette, 1976a, p. 124)

Underneath the humour, there is a serious criticism of the discrepancy between the subjects the girls are made to study and real knowledge (they are like caricatures of *Les Femmes savantes*, a text cited in their examinations) and also between the questions they are asked (a man earns 22,850 francs on the stock market) and their lives (75 francs a month as a teacher). When Claudine defends Michelet at her oral exam, is not Colette taking a stand for a less sexist interpretation of history?

In *Claudine à Paris* (*Claudine in Paris*, 1901), where Renaud becomes the father 'that I missed and needed' (Colette, 1976a, p. 285), adolescent reactions to parents and a supposed love story are so intermingled that emotions are muddled and much less rings true than in *Claudine à l'école*. The reader cannot help but feel that Colette was inventing a story to justify her own largely unhappy marriage to Willy, just as Claudine invents stories of her own lesbianism to satisfy Marcel. When, however, she reacts so strongly to Luce's degradation, and says that in her 'heart of hearts' Luce is a 'decent girl' (p. 307), or when she decides that Luce can be understood as only an animal (willing to forget her family, as Fanchette will forget the two kittens that are drowned), Claudine's common sense approach to life shines through the fog of that part of the novel dealing with Renaud. We must, however, accept Claudine's assertion that 'free women are not women at all' (p. 353) as expressing an important side of her creator's own feelings, even though 'the delicious langour of someone who has been beaten or caressed almost to death' (p. 351) may well be overstated for salacious effect.

Claudine en ménage (*Claudine Married*, 1902) continues the story of a marriage that seems unreal, a projection of what Colette imagines life with an older husband could be, an attempt to work out in literature her personal ambivalences. The insecurity in the treatment of the theme is reflected in the episodic formal structure and lack of plot. A visit to the school in Montigny seems mainly an excuse to show Renaud's and Claudine's interest in young girls. Episodes alternate with diary entries mainly bemoaning Claudine's feeling of being uprooted. If Claudine was often characterised as a tomboy or masculine in the earlier novels, her feminine side is most prominent here: her desire to be dominated, to submit, but also her desire to adapt. Claudine submits, but she is never passive. She refuses, for example, to let Renaud undress her on her wedding night, although she cannot explain why. Yannick Resch, in examining later heroines of Colette's fiction, finds that they treat nudity as natural, that they do not try to be coquettes (Resch, 1973, pp. 31ff.). Such an attitude is instinctive to Claudine; her body is her own, not merely an object of desire for her husband. Claudine is also herself in remaining close in spirit to the garden of Montigny, in refusing to enter completely into her husband's world: 'Have I no real dwelling then? No! I live here with a man, admittedly a man I love, but I am living with a man!' (p. 407).

Renaud is Claudine's initiator into sexual 'delight'; nothing else about him – and particularly his frivolous interest in society – is very admirable, but 'I don't despise him for all that frivolity. And, besides, it wouldn't matter if I did, because I love him' (p. 425). Especially difficult for Claudine is his easy acceptance of lesbianism and the way in which he pushes her towards an affair with Rézi. For Renaud, lesbianism is 'charming', 'of no consequence', 'a consolation for *us*, a restful change' (p. 439). Claudine is initially shocked. Gradually she develops her own sense of morality. To have a lover because of love or simple desire is natural and honest; vice is 'doing wrong without enjoying it' (p. 453). Even after she is aroused by Rézi, however, and makes love to her with Renaud's approval, she finds that his attitude is scandalous. Her affair with Rézi is not a mere diversion, can be considered 'moral' by her own definition (although it is not love), but Renaud's connivance shows a libertine attitude she cannot readily accept. When she discovers Renaud and Rézi together, she must assert her own identity: 'I was Claudine' (p. 491), and return to Montigny, her beloved country and to the grass 'that would heal me' (p. 502). Then she writes to tell Renaud to come and to 'dominate' her.

We might overlook the lesbian episodes as written to fulfil Willy's expectations. Beyond them, however, lie deeper tensions, not explored or resolved. The impossibility of reconciling her need to be her own Claudine with her need of a strong husband makes the tone seem false. Only the final chapters, describing Claudine's joy in seeing the countryside again, are at the level of Colette's better writing. *Claudine en ménage* is thus an example of a woman's writing not yet capable of confronting fully the problems of female identity.

Claudine s'en va (*Claudine and Annie*, 1903) again circles around the tension of independence and submission. The narrative voice is no longer Claudine's but Annie's and Annie is initially the subdued, dominated little wife Claudine could never be, happy to have a husband 'intelligent and strong-minded enough for the two of them' (Colette, 1976a, p. 535), more completely an object than any other of Colette's characters, an object created by her husband: 'it is my own work I am admiring; a lovable child, fashioned little by little and without great difficulty into an irreproachable young woman and an accomplished housewife' (p. 547). This portrait of Annie is sufficiently exaggerated to forewarn the reader that Annie must change. A comparison between Annie and the docile wife that Claudine has often said she would like to be makes it clear that Claudine could never fit this mould. When Annie does become herself, no longer a creation of her husband, and realises she does not love him, Claudine's advice is eminently moral: 'One can't live with a man one doesn't love, its filthy indecency' (p. 616). Annie, incidentally, never had a mother as a model; she must make her own way, inspired only by a Claudine whose marriage is seen too idealistically to be a pattern to be copied. Annie reaches self-knowledge, however, and learns to adapt to life. If there is a certain romanticism in her desire for 'the hoped-for miracle that may lie round the next bend of the road' (p. 632), there is also the realism of admitting that, as a wealthy woman travelling alone, she may be found raped and murdered.

The curious choice of a different narrative voice is a means of avoiding an analysis of the 'happily married' Claudine from the inside, therefore of portraying the existing tensions. And Renaud hardly needs to exist; for Annie he is 'silent and detached as if he had transferred all his life to the woman he called his "darling child"' (p. 579). The Renaud–Claudine marriage can seem an idyll. They 'follow each other ... without being like each other' (p. 592), though Claudine adds that when one loved, one followed the man 'whether he kissed you or beat you' (p. 593). The Claudine novels thus seem an example supporting Gilbert and Gubar's theory of the 'palimpsest', the text written on top of another underlying text, which is not given overt expression. Rather than writing a direct self-portrait, Colette gives facets of herself to various characters, including Léon, the novelist shut in and ordered to produce so many lines a day. What would seem pathetic, if not tragic, as a description of a wife, turns comic as a description of a dominated husband. But while putting parts of herself into various characters, Colette avoids anything approaching a picture of the whole.

In the last of the Claudine novels, La Retraite sentimentale (The Retreat from Love, 1907), Renaud's death is reported, and Claudine retreats into an asexual existence in a country house. It is a novel where nothing happens; Renaud's death is situated in a blank space.[6] What happens is rather a series of memories, recreated as spoken language, leading at the end to silence and solitude. Claudine's retreat can be seen as a more peaceful version of the asexuality that Léa achieves in La Fin de Chéri, a retreat in which Claudine's relationship to the world of nature functions to replace other emotions, especially the love of men. Colette herself thought of La Retraite sentimentale as 'the sequel and the end of "Claudine"', the end of her domination by Willy and thus the end of her need to 'spice up' a text to order.[7]

In the Claudine novels, Colette worked through, if very indirectly, her marriage to Willy. With La Vagabonde (Renée, the Vagabond, 1911) and L'Entrave (The Shackle, 1913), she was able to confront her themes more squarely, drawing upon her own experience, by creating a character whose story is self-contained, and sufficiently distanced from autobiography that it can be told without the sometimes uncomfortable 'holes' of the Claudine novels.[8] In La Vagabonde the separation from the unfaithful husband is in the past. Renée has chosen to live her own life, to earn her own money, not to rely on men. A divorced woman, like Annie, she accepts the danger inherent in her social position – greater danger as, unlike Annie, she does not have financial security. The novel thus examines woman's place in society from a wider perspective. In the first part of *La Vagabonde*, devoted to Renée's tactics for survival, there are no desires, no hopes for a miracle.

In the second part, Renée has a male admirer, Maxime Duffe-rein-Chautel. He cannot imagine the small compromises required of her because of her poverty. Yet his infatuation, she says, 'casts the light of self-revelation upon me', revealing 'some unguarded trait in face or figure' (Colette, 1931, pp. 104–5). The observation is of interest; Renée, in many ways an 'emancipated woman', is none the less capable of feeling a 'secret sense of shame' (p. 104) at the inadequacy of a life that does not meet a man's expectations. The reader is aware that Renée protests too much, is too eager to proclaim her desire to be alone, to forgo love. There is always a tension between love and her fear of 'the enemy', 'the man destined to possess me' (p. 258). Possession means a loss of her independence, a submissiveness. She is frightened by Max's claim always to get what he wants from his mother, thus to dominate a woman. She is aware as well that he is her inferior in wit, energy, vitality. There can, therefore, be no real communication between them. Renée's distrust of men is conveyed much more sharply than her love for Max, which always seems a bit nebulous (although still more realistic than Claudine's love for Renaud). She is also frightened, however, because she is thirty-four and unsure how long she can hold him with her beauty. A realistic appraisal of her value in her society.

Later, when she is working and travelling, Renée finally chooses the freedom to be herself, to accept the natural world as an alternative source of sensual pleasure to that offered by the enemy, man, and to devote herself to her art. It is finally a solipsistic choice, a *retraite sentimentale* similar to that of Claudine, but without Claudine's 'excuse' of widowhood. *La Vagabonde* can be read as Renée's search for her own identity, an identity which is finally an acceptance of being 'free' but also 'alone'. Renée's choice can be read as one of 'androgyny', of a world without sexual roles. She thinks with joy of her wild and free childhood (pp. 127–8), a time when communion was with nature, not with a being of another sex. Her work in the music-hall is also essentially devoid of erotic overtones. With Brague, her partner, the relationship is of two equals in work; when she dances, it is for herself alone, not for display as a sexual object to an audience.

The novel, which for late twentieth-century feminist critics is a 'rejection of the traditional female sphere of house and family for the androgynous world of freedom and creativity' (Eisenger, 1981c, p. 95), leaves its tensions unresolved. That Colette returned to her character, and changed the choice to be made, in a subsequent work, is one indication of this lack of resolution. Even within the frame of *La Vagabonde*, however, the identity Renée chooses is described as inherently fragmented. 'But time will dissolve it, like all others – all its sister shadows – and you shall know no more of me, till the day comes when my steps must halt and one last, small shadow shall rise from me and wing its flight – who shall say whither?' (p. 314).

In *L'Entrave*, Renée's retreat has narrowed. Having come into a small private income, she is no longer a dancer and a mime. Her life seems centred on observing other indolent, pleasure-seeking creatures, withdrawing from them emotionally, but without a will to assert herself in a more positive way. There is no suggestion that she may begin writing or dancing again. Her life in the hotel at Nice, watching the quarrelsome affair of May and Jean, holds much less of value than her life as a music-hall artist. Thus Colette prepares the reader, from the beginning, for Renée's eventual submission to a subordinate role. Perhaps, as Anne Duhamel Ketchum has suggested, *L'Entrave* reflects the 'feeling of apprehension and helplessness' of Europe on the brink of the First World War, as well as changes in Colette's own life with her second marriage and the birth of her child (Ketchum, 1981, pp. 25–6).

Renée is initially shaken by having seen Max with a wife and child, thus by having been reminded of what she gave up. In spite of the wife's 'slightly cowlike placidity' (1976b, p. 9), (a quick judgement on Renée's part, as she has hardly looked at the other woman) and in spite of feeling that lying in Max's arms 'was like lying in a tomb made to my measurements' (p. 34), Renée is aware of her 'frailty', of the 'delirium' bordering on 'hysteria' of her thoughts. Such a reaction is, she says, typically feminine: 'It is as if I were establishing the fact that I may still be good for something – from the sexual point of view' (p. 6). Renée is, in other words, a woman who cannot completely reject the gender role against which she feels she has rebelled. It is not only a role of being subservient to a man, and expecting in return to obtain sexual pleasure; it is also a role in a sadomasochistic game. May is amorous and triumphant after 'she knuckles under and humiliates herself in private' (p. 62). Renée escapes momentarily to 'chaste Switzerland' (p. 64), a retreat from even watching others in love, a retreat into literature and into the peace of the natural world, where describing seagulls becomes a sublimation of 'pent-up desire' (p. 69). In Geneva, however, when she goes to see her old stage partner, Brague, she feels as out of place beside him and his new partner as with May and Jean in Nice. Suddenly freedom seems to her rather 'escape'.

Renée is always aware of being a woman, and of how women may be different from men. She is prone to generalise about her sex: 'for a woman . . . the sight of another woman's suffering is often poignant' (p. 42); 'I think all women make the same gestures at certain moments. . . . To adorn themselves – in other words, offering themselves. And to touch, which is the same as taking' (p. 99). (The emphasis on touch may be compared to various comments of Irigaray.) Jean calls her on this tendency: 'I don't find it attractive, this way you have of treating women with contemptuous pity, as poor little creatures' (p. 100). (Perhaps self-reproach on the part of Colette for some of her early writing?) Jean suggests that in spite of her desire to identify with her sex, Renée really thinks she's not like other women. He has indeed caught an ambiguity in her attitude. When she wants support, shelter, love, from which she has been fleeing, she wants to see this need as natural to women, in order to reach some justification for her emotions; at the same time, she always judges herself to be more than a pitiable creature, to be a worthy adversary of a man. When she begins to feel Jean's attractiveness, she sees it as the effect of a stronger will forcing itself upon her, not as a merely 'feminine' reaction. When she makes love to Jean, their love-making is a battle of wills, which seems to Renée to be a battle between equals on one level, 'a harmonious wrestling-bout' (p. 132), while on another, it may be a surrender. What she finds initially with Jean is an 'intelligent pleasure of the flesh that instantly recognises its master' (p. 132). But it turns to love, which means a recognition of the impenetrable barriers between two people: 'Love is that painful, ever-renewed shock of coming hard up against a wall which one cannot break' (p. 179).

L'Entrave is a striking example of how Colette makes a story out of very few incidents, but rather a series of encounters between people, and a series of introspective self-appraisals, in which the setting – the play of light in a fireplace, the sight of flowers, the trickle of water – is more charged than any dialogue or event. It is in this reliance on the small detail, on how things look and feel, that Colette's writing often seems particularly feminine, attuned to a vision of the world in which there are no heroes, no great actions to be undertaken, but rather bodies to be admired, and one's own body to be listened to, a world with, as Renée says, 'the narrow range and the eye for small, sometimes subtle details, of a woman' (p. 189). Yet, of course, we must be wary of any tendency to let this world seem trivial, for the themes underlying the subtle details are as rich as any in literature: the misunderstanding inevitable between human beings, the difficult search for identity, the tension between individual achievement and the need for love.

Does Renée, in yielding to Jean in *L'Entrave*, become the anti-feminist recent critics have sometimes castigated? Was she really, in *La Vagabonde*, as independent and free as she sometimes claimed to be? Mari McCarty gives a rather doctrinaire reading of the novel: 'The Shackle shows that all attempts to reach the new space are not fortuitious, and that, once having arrived, one must be constantly on guard against an unwitting return to male confines' (McCarty, 1981, p. 369). The heroine fails to continue in the woman-centred space she reached in *The Vagabond*. McCarty quotes Colette as saying she was unhappy with the ending of *The Shackle*, but was 'unable to change it'. The question remains, however, why Colette did not change the ending. She did not give the novel the more positive value McCarty would like, I think, because she was not trying to create an exemplary heroine but was being true to the difficulties and tensions of the life of her character. The tension between liberty and a love allied to submission runs deep in Colette's work. If she was much later uneasy about the ending of *The Shackle* (written in 1913, the comment is in *L'Étoile vesper*, 1946), such evidence cannot be used to deny the depth of the two conflicting impulses. Renée sees herself as 'in flight', admits her fears of a barren, old-maidish existence, realises that at her age 'tears are a disaster' (p. 174). She accepts the place of a woman, not as an adversary, but as someone for whom the man is 'the limit of my universe' (p. 220), and she accepts Masseau's definition of a woman's love as one that does not engage her lover in any way.

But this acceptance is to some extent a deliberate decision, in which the intellect is still involved, a submission of emotions, but not a denial of her own personality.

Undoubtedly, there was an ambivalent stance on Colette's part in this novel. But such a position should not be merely condemned. As Sigrid Weigel has said, in commenting on a number of nineteenth-century women writers:

> Within the fictional space of the plot, escape is imagined, resistance is tested, indignation formulated. Without denying herself the pleasure of fantasising, the author can, because she is responsible for the thoughts and actions of her heroine, remain conformist either by punishing her heroine or by letting her (understandingly) renounce. And so, perhaps, the message will still get through to women readers, but in a subversive way. (Weigel, 1985, p. 71)

Chéri (1920) and *La Fin de Chéri* (*The Last of Cheri*, 1926) present a story of love, a love that begins as eroticism, desire for pleasure, need to mother or to be mothered, but that moves beyond its origin and beyond the rather humorous situation of a spoiled young man being admired as a sensual object by an ageing courtisan. (Critics at the time saw the novels as rather slight and Chéri as a character who was not really worthy of two novels.) It is only gradually, however, that we become aware of the depth of the love that Léa and Chéri feel for each other. It is a love between two individuals in which, finally, neither their ages nor their biological sex is of primary importance.

Léa sees Chéri initially as a beautiful physical creature. Love, which she does not expect, comes gradually and is rooted in daily, physical reality, not in any blind passion. Léa exemplifies lucidity, in the midst of love and in the midst of grief. She is surprised to find herself grieving for Chéri after his marriage, because it is a new experience for her, and she poses to hide her grief. Chéri, on the other hand, cannot attain to her lucidity. He cannot analyse his emotions, but rather retreats into a pathos of passion that cannot be fulfilled. The contrast between Léa and Chéri can be considered as a contrast between energy and inertia, or a contrast between self-knowledge and dreams of a proud, ideal identity. Léa emerges as stronger because she is able to survive, to adapt to life, not to live at a level of absolutes. Léa is able to equate love with nurturing – building Chéri up physically through food and exercise, sacrificing herself with nobility when he marries. Chéri, on the other hand, can only see a choice between allowing Léa to dominate him, and dominating Edmée. When neither absolute is possible – Léa no longer wants to dominate him, Edmée has become her own person – Chéri has no choice but death.

Léa is, however, still a woman in love and in *Chéri* she only just manages to survive. Her flight from Paris after Chéri's marriage might be compared to the flights of Claudine from Renaud, Claudine's 'sentimental retreat' or Renée's flight from Max. The differences are that Léa takes lovers on her trip out of Paris, does not escape into a gyneceum, and on her return is able to take up normal life again. Chéri tries a similar tactic of flight, but it is a flight into opium dens and cabarets, a flight into forgetfulness, not an attempt to establish roots in another way of life. In *La Fin de Chéri*, Léa reaches a state of peace where she can exist without a man. This is not a state of recaptured childhood, however, or reunion with the natural world, but an acceptance of another mode of existence within her society. In *Le Pur et l'impur*, Colette speaks of herself as among the survivors, who dare not show their need of each other. Léa is such a survivor. If Léa survives, however, Colette can only show this survival indirectly. In *La Fin de Chéri*, she does not present Léa's thoughts or emotions.

Initially, in *Chéri*, the action is narrated largely from the point of view of Léa. After Chéri's marriage and Léa's departure, however, Chéri becomes the character through whom the action is focalised. The contrast is striking between Lea's self-awareness and Chéri's self-deception, in, for example, his drunken conversation with Desmond, where he tries to treat Léa 'with severity' (Colette, 1951, p. 69). In the final scene of *Chéri*, events are sometimes seen through Chéri's eyes; he 'asked himself vaguely. Why does she look so happy?' (p. 112). Primarily, however, Léa is again the point of focalisation. Léa loses momentarily her ability to see clearly, and thinks Chéri has returned to her. She is no longer able 'to play her scene without a fault' (p. 101): 'It was like bad theater' (p. 113). She then manages to dominate herself and let him go back to his wife. By combining the two points of view, Colette is able in this scene to underline the lack of communication between the lovers. At best, Chéri can tell her that he can only be a child in her presence. They are separate creatures, unable in spite of mutual love to be completely honest with each other. The novel ends in the solitude of both the lovers.

In *La Fin de Chéri*, almost all the action is focalised on Chéri, a Chéri six years older, but still unable to see himself clearly. Between the two novels is the era of the First World War. Chéri is disillusioned not only with the ageing Léa, but with an ageing world. Irrevocably changed by the war, he can neither find pre-war certainties, nor the heightened sensations of his time at the war front. If he chose Edmée over Léa because she was younger, easily dominated, he finds her, after the war, an independent woman, immersed in hospital work in which he has no place. The boudoir has become her study: 'Before she's done she'll have to have a prescription to make love to me'. Even Desmond, who had been a 'perfect parasite' (p. 68) before the war, 'managed a night club and sold antiques to Americans' (p. 135). In this world Chéri has no place.

After Edmée stops loving him, he begins to think of Léa. When he goes to see her, however, at first he does not recognise her. She has a 'sexless dignity' (p. 172), seems 'like an old man' (p. 173). In the scene between them, Chéri imagines his double kneeling before her, and Léa herself as hiding within the heavy body of an ageing woman. The surface, banal conversation hides these ghostly beings of a past that he cannot reconcile with the present. This single meeting with Léa, the destruction of his last illusion, leads to his end. His flight to La Copine, a parallel to his flight to Desmond in the earlier novel, brings memories and false memories of Léa, but no hold on present reality. So he kills himself. Colette, however, does not suggest that their love is foolish; an interpretation of *La Fin de Chéri* that suggests that Léa now 'lives in a new space free from men' (McCarty, 1981, p. 369) ignores the depth of Léa's passion and seems a simplistic feminist reading.

Chéri is, of all Colette's creations, the most fully delineated male character, and also the male most closely allied to a feminine sensibility. Indeed, one can read his story as an inversion of the more usual sexual dilemma of the young woman who attaches herself to an older man for protection and affection, whose main concerns are her own beauty and living well, luxuriously, and who falls when protection is withdrawn. If we imagine a female Chérie, however, the story might well become sentimental or melodramatic. By giving the role of beautiful sexual object to a man – and a man without need of financial support – Colette changes the tone. The story can be both more humorous and in its conclusion more purely a story of lost love, as there is no element of easy pathos, no simple identification of victim and victimiser.

Chéri is first of all a sexual object, one that Colette obviously enjoyed creating:

> I gave Chéri good measure from the start: twenty-five years old, dark hair, white skin, glossy as a six-month-old tomcat. Sometimes I stepped back to observe him. I never tired of adding to his beauty. Eyelashes and hair like the wings of a thrush.
>
> (Colette, 1966, p. 246)

As Colette assumes the role of all-powerful creator, is there not an implicit criticism of the arrogance of a man who, in life or in fiction, invents the role which women are given to play? *Chéri* and *La Fin de Chéri*, however, are not pure inversions, because Léa cannot play the role of the rich male with a young mistress. Léa grows old, and, as Colette is well aware, age for a woman has more devastating consequences than it does for a man. Léa knows from the beginning that Chéri will be her last love affair. She can be honest with herself in realising how her neck has aged, while cleverly not wearing her pearls in bed, so that Chéri will not notice the neck. Colette seems to accept the problem of female age without anguish. Love is related to the body and the body changes; this is a fact of life. If, therefore, *Chéri* and *La Fin de Chéri* reinstate the woman in a role of power, there is no suggestion of any possible revolution that would give the ageing Léa a means to retain that power.[9]

Like many of Colette's works, *La Chatte* (*The Cat*, 1933) involves a 'trio' of individuals, the striking difference being that one of the three is a cat. Alain rejects his young wife, Camille, in favour of his cat, Saha. The novel presents another inversion of normal gender roles. Alain seems out of touch with everyday reality, dreamy, soft, a creature of sentiments. Camille is harder, more aggressive, more willing to act. The novel explores the tensions between two individuals, tensions arising more from temperament than from biological differences.

La Chatte seems to invite two radically opposed possible readings: Alain is right to reject his aggressive, rather uncultured wife for the natural nobility of Saha; Alain is 'mad', incapable of functioning in normal society, whereas Camille is merely fighting for her right to consideration. The structure and point of view of the text, as Mieke Bal has demonstrated, seem to invite the reader's sympathy with Alain; his thoughts are privileged, whereas we only know what Camille says. As a result, the feelings of Saha as well are presented more directly than those of Camille, as Saha is more comprehensible to Alain. Even in the aborted murder scene, when Alain is not present, Saha's feelings are presented much more fully than are Camille's. Saha 'would have died rather than have uttered a second cry'. In contrast, Colette writes, Camille 'showed no temptation' (p. 535). Camille is shown from the viewpoint of an outside observer, Saha from the inside.[10] Colette's own attitude towards animals often seems to resemble Alain's. Animals are purer creatures, whose love is more direct, who give as much to their humans as they receive. Much of the tone of the text – especially in the descriptions of Saha – seems to require us to agree with Alain. The novel might therefore seem comparable to the short story 'Le Rendez-vous', in which the female protagonist is firmly criticised for her lack of sympathy for a suffering creature, in which the reader's response is directed towards accepting the man's decision to leave her. Yet, if we step back from the text we may indeed wonder how Alain can justify his preference for a cat to a human being.

La Chatte is partly about the 'inevitable hostility between Man and Woman' (Colette, 1951, p. 516), a hostility that does not exist between Man and Animal. Alain and Camille have differing expectations from life, and cannot satisfy each other. Saha, on the other hand, because she is a simpler creature, makes no demands upon Alain's view of himself, nor upon his desires. She can accept him as a fellow being divorced from a society from which she is naturally separated. Alain can see Saha as a perfect creature, unchanging in her needs, needs he can readily understand and satisfy. Saha has almost human emotions: she 'knew very well how to divert him, to win him back' (p. 487) when she has annoyed him; 'Cat dignity shown again in the pure gold eyes' (p. 499). Camille changes; he would love a 'Camille fixed, brought to perfection' (p. 478), a Camille who would resemble, therefore, a cat. For Alain, a major fault of Camille is her lack of dignity. (He is even shocked at seeing his wife naked, a shock that, of course, Saha could not produce.) Camille is also incapable of submerging herself in Alain's world, will not learn Saha's feminine wiles. She finds it difficult to accept a matrimonial 'we'. At the same time, she is jealous of Saha and 'to kill what troubles her ... is a woman's first thought, especially if she's a jealous woman' (p. 562).

There is sympathy for Alain when he thinks of the inevitably short time he will have with Saha, and promises her that if he takes another woman he will never take another cat. But Colette is surely mocking Alain's fear, in his dream, of his own nudity, as she is criticising his refusal to accept Camille as an independent creature. Colette is also, we feel, sympathetic to Camille's jealousy, a passion she describes in *Le Pur et l'impur* as having often felt herself, a passion that 'thrives on homocidal desires' (Colette, 1968, p. 165). Perhaps the ambiguity of the story is the inevitable result of Colette's realisation that the pure love of Alain and Saha is a dream, like the dream of the retreat into the natural world, that a different, more difficult passion for human beings is inevitable, even if it often leads to failure. At the end of the novel, Saha seems more 'human' than Alain, who retreats into a childish state. Saha is living fully within her world; Alain is not. He is fundamentally unwilling to accept an adult relationship with another person; he seems adolescent in his conversations with his mother, almost childish in his attitudes towards business. He is also a snob. Camille's family are *nouveaux riches*, Saha is an aristocratic, pure-bred cat. This attitude, as well, is seen as childish. Alain's mother, though aware of the social differences, accepts the marriage. She sees Saha as Alain's 'delusion' (Colette, 1951, p. 557).

Le Pur et l'impur (*The Pure and the Impure*, first published as *Ces plaisirs* in 1932 and re-edited in 1941) is Colette's examination of all kinds of physical love. The book is hard to classify: not a novel, but a series of discontinuous sketches, juxtaposed with commentary. One thread uniting the episodes is the exploration of all the gradations of human sexuality, which cannot be comprehended by a simple male/female division. Heterosexual, homosexual and lesbian love are in some ways the same – coming from 'that barrier reef, mysterious and incomprehensible, the human body' (Colette, 1968, p. 31). Often Colette sees physical pleasure as a mere habit: 'I fear there is not much difference between the habit of obtaining sexual satisfaction and, for instance, the cigarette habit' (p. 102). This pleasure cannot be defined merely in terms of the sex of the body, though Colette sometimes suggests that women are more demanding of physical satisfaction than men.

Bodies are similar in their needs, but Colette is aware of great differences between the hearts of men and women. Women such as Charlotte often have a maternal affection for their lovers, as well as an ability to sacrifice themselves, including, in Charlotte's case, the willingness to fake orgasm for the sake of her young lover's ego. Love between women is, for Colette, a matter of many kinds of sensual pleasure, combined with a mutual attraction that is more a feeling of kinship than of sexual need. Women lovers have 'a mutual trust such as that other love can never plumb or comprehend' (p. 117). If lesbianism is praised as a shelter or refuge, Colette never openly espouses it as superior sensually, but only as a more nurturing relationship. Men, even the homosexuals Colette knew as Willy's young bride, have a virility arising from their social role: 'A human being with a man's face is virile by the very fact that he contracts a dangerous way of life and the certainty of an exceptional death' (p. 139). She scorns men for their talk of victories, for their boredom with their own sex and for their frequent misogyny.

Those who give nurture to their lover – whether Charlotte or the elderly homosexual poet-scholar – meet with approval. Those who seem only interested in physical satisfaction – whether Damien the Don Juan or the lesbian poet Renée Vivien – are judged as going too far. How are we to read Colette's account of the 'Ladies of Llangollen'? Some critics have seen it as the most successful story of fulfilled lesbianism in the book; others have felt that Colette disapproved of them for their loss of individuality. When she wonders what Sarah Ponsonby thought, when she objects to Sarah being subsumed within an all-encompassing 'we' by Lady Eleanor, Colette is presumably talking of the dominance that should be avoided in any relationship. It is good to nurture, but less good to be the lover who is nurtured. The tension between Colette's desire for independence and her need for submission to love is clear in this ambiguous story. For Colette equality between the two lovers, which seems to be what is lacking in the relationship between Sarah and Eleanor, is nevertheless, finally, 'madness' (p. 170).

Colette does not favour an androgyny that would deny sexual difference. Her homosexual friend Pepé is disgusted by a man dressed as a woman. She criticises masculine women, who seem by their behaviour to want to be men, who childishly would like to 'do *pipi* against a wall' (p. 108). Lesbian relations should not be an apeing of masculinity but a way of discovering the realities of womanhood, both physical and cultural. All men are part of the male power structure; homosexual women are subject to the social subservience expected of all women. Colette's homosexual friends feel at ease in her presence; her lesbian friends can only speak freely in the absence of men. Theirs is a veiled world, a darkness that is a refuge from society. The condition of women in general is finally a greater concern for Colette than is lesbianism. She can praise Proust for his portrayal of Sodom, criticise his misunderstanding of Gomorrah, but cannot, as a woman, be as open in her portrayal of her own sexual tendencies as would be a male writer of the period, Gide for instance. Colette knows that it is 'hard for a woman to refuse herself' (p. 39) to a man. As Sherry Dranch has shown, moments when Colette feels herself drawn sensually towards another woman, as in the taxi with Madame Charlotte, can be read only by filling in the holes, the ellipses of the text (Dranch, 1983, p. 180).

In the final chapter of *Le Pur et l'impur* Colette comments on her relationships with young people and with animals, relationships built on nurturing and mutual needs, relationships thus purer than those she has described between human beings in love. She also speaks of the jealousy that often results in strange, indefinable relationships between two women attached to one man – relationships that seem particularly impure on the surface, often leading to homocidal desires, but that are also often resolved into a kind of mutual dependence, as the two women come together in spite of the man, as they too reach a state of 'purity' transcending normal social morality. If, as she states 'The word "pure" has never revealed an intelligible meaning to me' (p. 172), it is because she is always conscious of all the ambiguities and difficulties of human beings, with their needs for nurture as well as their passions.

Colette is closer to Flaubert than to most women authors of the nineteenth and early twentieth centuries in her insistence on seeing clearly, her refusal of any romantic attitudes, and in her use of concrete details, rather than psychological notations, to describe her characters. The result is not, however, a complete, realistic portrayal of event or character, but rather a 'series of snapshots', 'a dispersed world' (Biolley-Godino, 1972, pp. 31ff.). Again, I am reminded of Herrmann's theory that woman's space is not as full as that of a man.

To what extent, then, can Colette's work be considered 'feminine' or 'feminist'? Perhaps above all in its refusal to place the woman simply in the role of the Other? And in its advocacy of woman's right to her own specific nature, rather than to any 'equality' with men? Her work departs from the expected 'women's literature' of her time in her definition of how the sexes differ. Her females are often stronger, more geared to survival, her males more often sentimental and romantic, than we might expect. This is a reflection of how she saw her own parents; Sido was the tower of strength, Captain Colette was a dreamer, whose love of his wife kept him from achieving his ambitions. Colette herself, while glorifying and mythologising Sido, frequently portrays with sympathy characters that derive more from her father. Finally, she refuses to make any simple moral judgements.

Colette recognises, however, the ambivalence of emotion towards the desired Other, particularly, the frequent female desire to submit. Women may be tougher, less romantic and survive more successfully the loss of love, but when in love they often seem to enjoy being deceived, mistreated, considered as an object. This attitude, often masochistic, is presented as a given fact, even as an instinct of the female; it is not directly criticised. The tension between wanting to submit to a man and wanting to be independent pervades Colette's work and is never completely resolved. Marcelle Biolley-Godino has suggested that in her more autobiographical works Colette's heroines (Claudine, Renée) can only escape by flight, whereas in her more fictional works she creates strong heroines, such as Camille and Léa (Biolley-Godino, 1972, p. 150). Thus there is a 'literary compensation' for Colette, through the creation of women who do not submit to masochistic conditioning.

If Colette's work privileges the female experience – though undoubtedly it is less of an initiator in this realm than some recent critics would claim – does it assert 'not only woman's right to sexual pleasure, but the positive superiority of the female libidinal economy' (Eisinger, 1981b, p. 256)? Could it be accurate to claim Colette as a partisan of separatism for women, or a believer in the primacy of one sex over the other? The total impression gained from her work would argue otherwise. Colette's moral values are those of sensitivity to all living creatures, of honesty in the expression of emotion; they are values informing characters of both sexes, or singularly lacking in characters of both sexes. Sexual passion has its pleasures and its dangers, also shared rather equally among characters of both sexes.

Is Colette's world of the physical sensation, of the struggle to survive and to find sensual pleasure in any sense particularly feminine? It is obviously a denial of great projects, of schemes to change the order of things, of revolutions and kingdoms. It might therefore merely reflect what was possible as a sphere of interest and influence for women, as Simone de Beauvoir has speculated. Or is it a more deliberate insistence that only the physical is of value? Colette's characters might agree with Camus's Meursault, who thought that clean washroom towels and the smell of the sea on Marie's hair were more valuable than abstractions. But, finally, Meursault launches a revolt against God and society, a revolt that one cannot imagine in Colette's world.

In presenting the varieties of the sexual and emotional responses of women, Colette reaches an uncommon kind of honesty in the description of the self, ultimately either the male or the female self. While her fiction is primarily told from the standpoint of one of the sexes, implicit in her descriptions is a recognition that for both men and women hostility goes with desire. Because of her own emotional ambivalence towards love and towards the opposite sex, and because of her recognition of the subordinate place of women in society, Colette can be particularly direct in her portrayal of all sexual life, seen from the perspectives of both sexes. In other words, being a woman makes it easier to break down hypocrisy and self-deception, to admit less than noble impulses.

5

Nathalie Sarraute

When I write, I am neither man nor woman, cat nor dog. I am not me. . . . I don't exist. (Rykiel, 1984, p. 40)

I have never understood how some writers can display their life as they do. . . . What counts is the books. (Saporta, 1984, p. 23)

Nathalie Sarraute's strong 'political' feminism does not, she has said, have a direct relationship to her creative work. She does not think as a woman, she says, and one must not consider men and women as separate, for this leads to a 'destructive segregation'. Any definition of *l'écriture féminine* would include elements found in works by male authors, Proust, for example (Rykiel, 1984, p. 40). Women in her work are not militant feminists or even career oriented: 'These images of women that I have shown are images of feminine behaviour as you continue to see it everywhere. Many women accept playing the role that society imposes upon them' (Besser, 1976, p. 286). She also considers that her own life has no relevance to her work: 'You will find nothing there; or else you will be making arbitrary interpretations' (Saporta, 1984, p. 8). Sarraute's experiences as a Jew in occupied France, for example, have no overt relevance to her work. We are far from the autobiographical work of Colette or Marguerite Duras. Yet while granting the possible divorce between beliefs held and books written (easier to do, perhaps, than granting the divorce between personal experience and written work, as Sarraute also requests us to do), we may find underlying her work a vision of the world that reflects her position as a woman, a use of writing that shows a conscious or perhaps unconscious assumption of gender.

When Sarraute says that at the level of human behaviour and use of language with which she works there is no distinction of gender, she implies a fundamental human nature underlying any divisions. She denies not only gender, but also racial, national and

85

class differences. Yet, in spite of her theory, Sarraute's characters have a certain number of external traits, among them sex. They are *il* or *elle*, not *on* (Brulotte, 1984, p. 45). Sarraute says that the use of *ils* or *elles* for a group is 'sometimes determined simply by a concern for the sound [*un souci de phonétique*] or by a desire to diversify' (Sarraute, 1972, p. 35). When she describes movements of consciousness before they exist in words, a level of 'pre-language', however, are not these movements to some extent based on perceptions that will vary according to what has been felt before? Will not the sensations she describes in some way reflect previous relations with other people and thus how one's gender is perceived by others? Sarraute is aware of how men and women are perceived differently, as can be seen in her reply to a critic who says she has an emotional relationship (*rapports affectifs*) to language: 'you would not look for emotion in Flaubert because he is not a woman' (p. 57). How could such awareness not be reflected in 'tropisms'?

Sarraute's works do not usually have female protagonists. She is seeking what is common to all human beings and is aware that women cannot, at least now, represent this communality. She refused, for example, to let an all-female cast perform one of her plays because 'Women can never, alas, represent the neuter'.[1] She seldom treats directly of what are considered typically feminine themes, such as maternal relations, sexual love, the female body. The lack of communication between individuals in her work, the impossibility of fully comprehending another individual, of which she speaks in *L'Ère du soupçon* (*The Age of Suspicion*), is not a result of a battle of the sexes, as in Colette. Where, then, should we look for possible indications of 'writing as a woman'?

Tropisms, as Sarraute herself defined them, are 'purely instinctive and are caused in us by other people or by the outer world and resemble the movements called tropisms by which living organisms expand or contract under certain influences, such as light, heat, and so on. These movements glide quickly round the border of our consciousness, they compose the small, rapid, and sometimes very complex dramas concealed beneath our actions, our gestures, the words we speak' (Sarraute, 1961, p. 428). These movements of approach and withdrawal, of contact and distance between individuals can be considered, according to Ellen W. Munley, as explorations of identity, as a process of alternative merger with or separation from other persons, a process particularly feminine, if we accept Nancy Chodorow's theory that 'women's sense of self is continuous with others', that women have 'more permeable ego boundaries'. In other words, the psychic reality underlying conscious thought – a reality which for Sarraute is shared by everyone – is nevertheless a reality of which women, because of their cultural conditioning, beginning with their experience of being mothered by women, may be especially aware (Munley, 1983).

In speaking of the *Nouveau Roman* as a possible literary movement, Sarraute makes an important distinction. What interests her is not objects themselves, which are merely 'catalysts', but rather 'the inner movements they release'. For Robbe-Grillet, on the contrary, what is important, she feels, is the 'play of surfaces'. A text is 'living' when its source is in 'a sensation', but it dies when it moves away from sensation to mere games, 'the "beauty" of language' (Saporta, 1984, pp. 21–3). As Valerie Minorgue has commented, Sarraute's work combines 'psychological realism with intense linguistic and literary reflexivity'; it is not concerned merely with the play of language, however, but aims at articulating 'human truths' (Minorgue, 1981, p. 18). Christiane Makward has observed that while 'l'écriture féminine', like the 'nouveau roman', does not distinguish between form and content, it nevertheless postulates 'a direct relation with non-linguistic, non-literary reality'. Sarraute's work is always concerned with this non-literary event.[2]

Sartre's definition of Sarraute's style in *Portrait d'un inconnu* (*Portrait of a Man Unknown*, 1948) may suggest a feminine approach, in the sense that the style is tentative, not aggressive; 'a style that approaches the object with reverent precautions, withdraws from it suddenly out of a sort of modesty, or through timidity before its complexity, then, when all is said and done, suddenly presents us with the drooling monster, almost without having touched it, through the magic of an image' (Sarraute, 1956, p. xiv, p. 14). Sarraute herself has described the importance she gives to the unfinished quality of her sentences, to the use of points of suspension: 'They give my sentences a certain rhythm, through which they breathe. And also they give my sentences this hesitating, groping aspect, as if they were trying to seize something that each minute escapes, slips away, comes back' (cited Brulotte, 1984, p. 51).

Sarraute's analysis of her style recalls some descriptions of

l'écriture féminine: 'My sentences are unfinished, suspended, cut
in pieces. Sometimes in defiance of strict grammar' (Besser, 1976,
p. 285). Although this may appear opposed to the fluidity of which
Cixous speaks, it is another means of depicting how sensations are
not fixed, and is similar to Cixous's advocacy of a language in
which rationality (here 'strict grammar') is sacrificed to the need to
capture emotions unanalysable in terms of logic. Sarraute's use of
separation and suspension might also be compared to the use of
'blank spaces' in the work of Marguerite Duras, for example. The
lack of conclusion (the 'unfinished sentences') is allied to a lack of
exciting intrigues, a refusal similar to Colette's to write of great
themes, of the destiny of man. What is important is psychological
states, an individual's response to events and other persons. More
radically, Sarraute has suggested that she is not interested in
events at all: 'In reality all my books are written on two levels.
There is the level of the most banal external appearances . . . and
then there is the invisible level, which interests me: the level of
tropisms' (Rambures, 1972, p. 16). To read at the level of banal
appearances is to read falsely. Sarraute defines her form as similar
to that of other recent novelists, essentially a refusal of previous
conventions of the novel: the character is only a *trompe-l'oeil* and is
often part of a group, the plot is almost nonexistent, there is no
chronological order, the dialogue is transformed (Sarraute, 1972,
p. 26). She refuses any description of her characters; if one could
say that a character was 'timid' or 'miserly', she feels, he would no
longer be of interest, as he would be defined in conventional terms.
If, after the appearance of tropisms, the reader is still interested in
the character of Martereau, Sarraute is, she says, distressed (p. 53).
Related to this refusal simply to tell a story with well-defined
characters is the lack of a clear genre, another connection between
Sarraute's work and various definitions of women's writing. Her
books are hardly novels, but rather 'prose texts which are in a
vaguely defined area between interior monologue, intimist theatre
and Proustian introspection' (Arnette, 1976).

Sarraute's quest for tropisms has been described as a quest for
spontaneity, for lucidity, a fight against conformism and the
language of 'correct society':

> She comes to the defence of the madness and the passion that
> people want to lock up. She takes the side of rebels against
> conventional values . . . against 'One must not', 'That's not

done', 'That's the way it is'.... For real contact. Against classifications, labels, definitions. (Brulotte, 1984, p. 40)

This, as well, is a link to *l'écriture féminine* in its refusal to accept the categories of thought and language prescribed by conventional (patriarchal) society. There are no absolute truths. In her defence of 'passion', of 'madness', Sarraute's work might be allied to that of Duras. It is not, of course, working with the same overt themes, is not concerned with the extreme traumas of love and passion that haunt Duras; but it is a similar rejection of the socially acceptable. Might not the narrator of *Portrait* in his voyeuristic obsession with the elderly father and his daughter be compared to Jacques Hold in *Le Ravissement de Lol V. Stein*? The self for Sarraute has been characterised as *'a space*, unstable and open to attack', a space without a language. The self without language occurs as well in Duras's work, but for Duras the self retreats into silence or madness. The self in Sarraute's novels often retreats rather into empty mechanisms and clichés. It is only the artist who seeks a language of truth, and the artist is sometimes equated with the 'mad prophet who denounces the established order' (Britton, 1982, p. 581).

Sarraute is always consciously concerned with the act of creation, how words influence our perceptions and emotions, how each human being organises his or her own world around clichés as well as individual experience. Narrators are thus, intrinsically, unreliable. Narration may be a search for truth, but it is also 'an act of presumptuousness and even of aggression' (Minorgue, 1981, p. 23). The absence of the omniscient narrator is also the absence of an authority figure: 'We know that usually the narrator is presented as a projection of the old paternal role in the family. The father–narrator is installed as head of the story.' Sometimes Sarraute uses narrators who are limited, sometimes she multiplies the points of view. Often she invites a dialogue with the reader. The world of her novels is 'polymorphous and changing' (Brulotte, 1984, pp. 48–9).

Portrait d'un inconnu, Sarraute's first 'novel' which Sartre in his influential preface termed an 'anti-novel', is the story of a man watching an elderly father and his daughter. The narrator is very tentative in his approach, wary of what others may say to him, uncertain, incapable of reaching firm conclusions. He may, therefore, strike the reader as a 'marginal' individual, full of vague fears, lacking in aggression, or even in any self-confidence. He seems to want to be proved wrong. He cannot always control himself: 'I must keep my distance – but I couldn't stop myself. I felt already the attraction they still have for me, like a rush of air that draws everything along, a sort of dizziness, a plunge into the void' (Sarraute, 1956, p. 32, p. 31). He sees himself not as the seeker, but as the sought, the victim: 'Underneath his every action, even the apparently trivial and innocuous ones, there is a sort of wrong side, another facet, a hidden one, known only to us, and which is turned in my direction. It is through this, no doubt, that he attracts me and continues to have such a strong hold over me' (p. 91, pp. 92–3). His description of the old man recalls Claudine Herrmann's theory of the male who dominates his world: 'It is not only because of the look he has of waiting for his prey when he sits there withdrawn into himself, but also because of his position: in the center – he is in the center, he sits there in state, dominating everything – and the entire universe is like a web of his own weaving, which he drapes at will about himself' (p. 113, p. 116). The narrator has no such assurance. More radically, he knows that the old man has no such assurance. The feeling of domination that Herrmann ascribes to the male is an illusion in Sarraute's world. There are no essences: 'Above all, one must be aware of an impression of easy victory which he can give at times, when he accepts a little too willingly, for instance, a frontal attack, with a sort of motionlessness that is so different from the furtive leaps with which he usually escapes' (p. 117, p. 120). The narrator's role is to be the 'conducting rod through which all the currents that charged the atmosphere were passing' (p. 139, p. 144). We might consider that the narrator possesses what are often thought of as 'feminine' characteristics. (We can perhaps go this far, while remembering that for Sarraute there are no fixed personalities or characters.)

The narrator is looking for 'tropisms' initially, trying to catch the movements of the father and his daughter, not to reduce them to characters. He does not consider identity as fixed, but as fluid. He looks for

the crack, the tiny crevice, the weak point, as delicate as a baby's fontanelle, at which I seem to see something that resembles a barely perceptible pulsation suddenly swell and begin to throb gently. I cling to it and press upon it. And then I feel a strange substance trickling from them in an endless stream, a substance as anonymous as lymph, or blood . . . And all that remains of the firm, rosy, velvety flesh of these 'live' persons is a shapeless gray covering.   (Sarraute, 1956, p. 69, p. 72)

In so far as she accepts anything of herself entering into the novel, Sarraute would identify with this narrator, the seeker of tropisms: 'In fact, I am rather this observer, who is passionately interested in the still unknown that is happening between the father and the daughter. . . . What I would be in this story would be the "seeker of tropisms".' The narrator gives up: 'Then the *déjà vu* comes back. The traditional novel invades everything. A "normal" character, the fiancé, appears' (Saporta, 1984, pp. 6–7). When he creates an ordinary novel, he is dissatisfied with himself. The old man is not, he knows, 'the cheaply manufactured puppet, the dime-store trash intended for the common herd, but as he was in reality, indefinable, without outlines' (Sarraute, 1956, p. 203, p. 216). Finally, however, he accepts a place among those – in fact, the old women of the neighbourhood – who see life simply, as a series of clichés. Thus, he differs from Sarraute: 'He finally treats his obsession as madness. . . . I have never considered that I was mad' (Saporta, 1984, p. 7).

The unnamed narrator of *Portrait*, in refusing solidity to others, in hesitating to attribute to himself any authority, in his confusion of witnessed and imagined scenes (so that the reader is never sure what has 'in fact' taken place – was there a grand scene between the old man and his daughter or not?), undermines any sense of security. The world is fluid, language cannot seize it, the undercurrents of emotion are also unstable and often seem to emanate from a childish world of malevolent witches. Such a vision, appropriate to the 'age of suspicion' as Sarraute has defined it, may be considered feminine in its refusal of authority.

In *Martereau* (1953), according to Sarraute, there is a contrary movement to that of *Portrait*. Rather than tropisms being abandoned for a conventional view of the world, Martereau is initially seen as a conventional character and is gradually dissolved into an amorphous being:

It's again a question of a literary experience, of a contrast between the monolithic character of Martereau as he fascinates the nephew at the beginning of their relationship and the same character as he is disintegrated by tropisms. (Saporta, 1984, p. 15).

The narrator of *Martereau* is another insecure, passive individual, who characterises himself as having an 'extreme self-effacement' (Sarraute, 1953, p. 2, p. 8). Like the narrator of *Portrait* he is thus in a good position to observe others and to discover what their behaviour may conceal beneath the surface. His lack of conventional aggressivity would seem to predispose him towards a less preconceived notion of other individuals, and also lead others more readily to drop their social masks, or at least, to be less than normally wary. Again, although Sarraute denies being interested in creating 'characters', 'personalities', she has chosen a narrator whose approach towards others leads him to a greater than normal ability to detect 'tropisms', a narrator who is conscious of what is

> expressed not in so many words, of course, as I am obliged to do now for lack of other means, not with real words like the ones we articulate distinctly out loud or in our thoughts, but suggested rather by certain sorts of very rapid signs . . . signs so brief and which slip so quickly through him and through me that I could never succeed in really understanding or seizing them, I can only recover them in bits and snatches and translate them awkwardly by the words these signs represent, fleeting impressions, thoughts, feelings, often forgotten. (Sarraute, 1953, p. 25, pp. 34–5)

The narrator's behaviour may often remind the reader of typically 'feminine' reactions:

> I try to make up for it, I should like to be forgiven. I resume our conversation in a slightly uneasy voice, I begin to ask questions. (p. 32, p. 42)

> I have often wondered what devil eggs me on at those moments . . . Some might say, a love of suffering . . . a morbid need to be humiliated, a vague desire to see that thing that has remained dangerously live under the ashes, finally burst into flame and devour me. (p. 33, p. 43)

Always, even when I feel their teeth about to sink delicately into
me, I am prepared to blame everything on myself.   (p. 68, p. 83)

Indeed, he compares himself to a 'hysterical woman' (p. 77, p. 93).
(Sarraute, of course, is not suggesting that either sex has a
monopoly of hysteria, but rather that the narrator sees in a
conventional way, and thus expects women to be more readily
hysterical.)
   In the narrator's aunt, Sarraute portrays typically feminine
behaviour: pleasure in her appearance and how it is judged by
others, pride in having accomplished things behind the scenes,
while always remaining soft:

'Well, that little woman with her air of not lifting a finger, is
all-powerful just now. That made your uncle very proud.' ... It
wouldn't need much to set her to twisting about with that
simpering, falsely innocent manner that certain precocious little
girls assume when they want to play the baby.   (p. 4, pp. 10–11)

If no moral judgement is intended, according to Sarraute, it is still
difficult not to read this opening scene of *Martereau* as a satire on a
type of bourgeois woman, playing a role, or rather several roles,
including that of the woman who gives up comfort to be independent. What is added, undoubtedly, to a typical portrait is the
awareness of fluctuations, changes in sensations beneath the overt
level of character.
   The description of the relationship between the aunt and uncle,
while showing the similar kinds of ploys for dominance, submission, role-playing engaged in by the two individuals, is also on one
level a picture of the battle of the sexes. Sarraute's tropisms may be
essentially identical for all individuals, but they still function with
particular force in a marriage; *Martereau* is a fine portrayal of the
tensions between man and wife in which, in spite of Sarraute's
own comments, the differences in male and female reactions are
evident. He is the wounded 'Samson' (p. 125, p. 149), she affects
the '"Woman Reading" pose' (p. 90, p. 108). He wants to be 'Lord
of creation' (p. 127, p. 151); she knows how to bring up topics, such
as a letter from her brother, that will soothe him.
   When he meets Martereau, the narrator already has a fixed
image in his mind. Martereau is not like his aunt and uncle; there
are no undercurrents in him: 'without the slightest crack through

which anything whatsoever that was suspicious might seep, nothing but sincere solicitude, the frankest sort of good-heartedness' (p. 76, p. 92). Martereau's life seems to be summed up in a series of photos of contentment, with troubles only 'like big thick, heavy, blocks with clear outlines, clearly drawn . . . clear and clean, in one block, like Martereau himself. Worthy of him. Made to his measure' (pp. 83–4, p. 101). Thus the narrator believes that for Martereau the world and language are consistent: 'Words are not for him what they are for me – thin protective capsules that enclose noxious germs – but hard, solid objects, from one casting, it's useless to open them up, make cross-sections, examine them, we should find nothing' (p. 112, p. 133).

When his doubts about Martereau begin, they are immediately connected to a memory of his doubts as a child about his mother's generosity, doubts aroused by remarks of the servants concerning the poor bits of meat she leaves for them. (The incident is a memory of Sarraute herself, which she recalls in *Enfance*.) Thus the destruction of the narrator's confidence in stable personality is linked to a child's awareness that his parents are not perfect. The narrator initially swings from a vision of a perfect Martereau to a vision of a scoundrel. Maturity of vision, it is implied, means giving up notions of good and bad characters.

Martereau is a series of narrative constructions, in which the narrator shows alternative versions of various events from what he imagines to be the point of view of various individuals, or different alternatives that might have been experienced by a single consciousness. None of the versions is authoritative. Each individual, at least in his reconstruction (for we are always aware that the words are filtered through his perceptions), uses words and gestures, often commonplace expressions – clichés and literary stereotypes – to 'establish an approved version of himself and the surrounding world' (Minorgue, 1981, p. 66). The narrator – and here, at least, he can be seen as similar to Nathalie Sarraute, his creator – is aware that words are weapons in a dangerous game of attack, in the world of society and especially of the family. This realisation of the undercurrents of all social discourse is, I would argue, particularly acute in marginal people – such as the narrator, a sickly young man dependent upon the financial support of his uncle – and thus also of such members of marginal groups as women, for, in the society that Sarraute depicts, as indeed in most societies, women are usually dependent upon the financial support of men.

Sarraute is not making moral judgements about this society. In showing how human discourse is a kind of war, and in portraying the reactions of the most vulnerable participants in this war, she makes, however, a deeper analysis of the psychological dangers of the roles of the dominating and dominated (or of the sexes) than might be found in explicitly polemical work. By its ironic unmasking of conventional behaviour, stereotypes, verbal simplifications of emotions, the novel makes fun of any attempts to categorise social roles, thus mocking assigning women to roles as victims or men to roles as masters, and showing the fallacies both of accepting societal gender constructions and of doctrinaire attempts to deconstruct gender roles. This refusal of easy categorisation might well be seen as a more profoundly 'feminist' vision of the world – if we accept that 'feminism' can include the recognition of the essential similarities of all human psychological reactions – than more overt polemics.

Martereau is often very funny; Sarraute uses humour in her exploration of the war games of social relationships, a weapon perhaps too often avoided by explicitly feminist writers. Her sense of the ambiguities, the mutations in human relationships, and especially of how each of us plays various roles (often based on literary stereotypes), leads her to see the comedy as well as the deceptions of life. The world presented in *Martereau* may be more easily made comic because it is essentially, of course, a comfortable bourgeois world; in her fiction Sarraute avoids problems of economics and politics.

In *Le Planétarium* (*The Planetarium*, 1959) there is still a timid, self-conscious character, similar to the narrators of *Portrait* and *Martereau*. He is Alain Guimier, who first appears as a narrator at a social gathering, telling the story of his aunt's problems with her new door. In *Planétarium*, however, this character is not a first-person narrator, and is not the only narrative voice. Rather, we have a 'polyphonic narrative', a multiplicity of voices.[3] In the earlier novels, the unreliability and the self-interest of the narrative voices were evident in their partial points of view. In *Planétarium*, Sarraute takes her criticism of the single dependable narrative voice still further. The idea that the multi-voiced text is 'feminine' appears in many feminist theories. In Sarraute's work, polyphonic voicing is not overtly 'feminine', but might be considered as a formal stratagem particularly appropriate to expressing the view of the marginal individual – either a self-conscious, alienated person aware of a vague guilt, or a member of a subordinate group in the dominant culture.

There is very little 'action' in *Planétarium*, but rather, as in the earlier novels, a focus on the underlying struggles of the characters to create worlds (all whirling in a planetarium) in their own image. It is at this psychological level, beneath the rather banal surface, that Sarraute considers that her characters are all similar, not differentiated by sex, or age (in moments of stress, they all often revert to images from childhood). While she never portrays at any length characters from social classes other than the bourgeoisie, one must assume that such characters would also engage in similar struggles to impose their views, and in similar feelings of inadequacy, although their choice of clichés and images might be different. The creation of one's own world is basically a process of narration, thus a matter of words; these words are weapons of attack against the worlds created by others. While the surface of *Planétarium* is somewhat calmer than that of *Portrait* – there is no violence quite to equal that of the father's possible attack on his daughter – or of *Martereau* – there is no illegal behaviour equal to that of Martereau's possible attempt at appropriating the property of others – the in-fighting and the implicit domination are just as great.

Planétarium also includes, however, a use of words not developed in Sarraute's earlier work – words for explicitly literary creation. Alain wants to become a writer, and seeks the approval of an established writer, Germaine Lemaire. It is a theme that will be developed in some of Sarraute's later works – *Les Fruits d'or*, *Entre la vie et la mort* – where the creation and reception of a book are of primary importance, where the book itself becomes the main character (an obvious rejection of gender!). *Planétarium* is particularly rich because the two uses of words – in battles within the sphere of social relations, and in battles within the creator struggling to find the right word – are interrelated. Since Germaine Lemaire seems a rather conventional novelist (though how can we judge?) and since Alain is only aspiring to write, literary creation in this novel is not a more important theme than the social creation of a world through the use of words.

There are no fixed values, no stable characters, no certainties, no truths. Everyone's opinions of everyone else vacillate. It is a frightening world, in which each individual seeks an illusory security by establishing a fixed persona, or by the possession of objects. The anguish that Sarraute's characters feel, and seek to overcome, is comic, because expressed in terms of the insignificant – Aunt Berthe's obsession with the vulgar fingerplate installed on her door, for instance – but it is finally tragic, as it reveals the instability of all human projects. Alain worries about the impression he makes on others, feels people are laughing behind his back. His mother-in-law worries about being judged as a meddling old idiot. Gisèle is aware of 'the old sensation she used to have, her own peculiar fear, still the same, the terror that had never left her' (Sarraute, 1959, p. 65, p. 66). Even Germaine Lemaire, surrounded by admirers, is aware of the precariousness of her situation, of the need to 'watch herself. Try to understand. Each time she must make the effort to tilt over towards them' (p. 190, p. 201).

Within this fluctuating world, the relations between the sexes are obviously unstable. Gisèle's stereotyped view of a perfect marriage, beginning with a perfect wedding, crumbles quickly. She hears two 'wicked fairies' (p. 67, p. 69) talking at the wedding reception about Alain's small income. (Such images from childhood literature – evoking a world of the clearly good and clearly evil – are frequently used in Sarraute's work to point to the fixed values to which people cling, and which have little to do with real life.) Gisèle is increasingly aware that 'Complete fusion exists with no one' (p. 75, p. 77), a theme similar to that of Colette. Often Alain and Gisèle see each other in conventional roles. For her, men are 'strong, intelligent' (p. 127, p. 132); for him, she is one of the 'tender little children' who need protection (p. 140, p. 146). But such stereotyped emotions are not stable. Gisèle's admiration for her husband, like that he feels for Germaine Lemaire, is capable of quick reversal. Germaine Lemaire's experiences as a writer offer a parallel to those of characters involved in more commonplace activities. She too tries to impose order on her world, and finds that it is instable. Narrative, like reality, can never be ordered. Sometimes her writing seems to have caught a 'vivid impression of reality'; a moment later she sees it as 'congealed', 'frozen', 'hollow' (pp. 181–3, pp. 190–2).

To see the tragedy of life in terms of the everyday, the trivial, may be to see from the point of view of someone whose assigned world is the private rather than the political, but also of someone whose alienation is not so extreme as to seem to require radical solutions – in other words, someone in the situation of a woman, both inside and outside the social and political sphere. Sarraute herself suggested that her characters' anguish can be linked to that of Samuel Beckett's characters, but that her characters don't talk about it.[4] Sarraute's characters avoid the grand gesture, but also even speculations about identity and purpose. They wait, not for Godot, but for the repairman, or for the chance to establish themselves momentarily through a cutting judgement on one of their acquaintances. Sarraute comically allows a character to equate her preoccupations with more 'serious' events. Gisèle's words, as she tells her mother she would rather have a *bergère* than a pair of leather armchairs, 'like those that once revealed heresy and led directly to the stake, showed that evil was still there, as alive and strong as ever' (pp. 49–50, p. 51).

In *Planétarium*, the absence of a first-person narrator, combined with the prominence of scenes set in social groups, produces more frequent juxtapositions of various clichés and incomplete sentences than found in Sarraute's earlier fiction. The style is thus even more fluid, sustaining the theme of instability, but also creating a poetic effect:

> 'Good heavens, it's awful, we enjoy ourselves so much at your house that we forget how late it is . . .' Noise of chairs . . . and he, scowling in his corner, ignored, almost forgotten already. . . . 'It was delightful. So when shall I see you? Oh, very soon. Don't forget to let me hear from you. One of us will telephone at the beginning of next week. I'll count on you, then, surely?' (p. 41, p. 42)

'Grated carrots', 'tender', 'finely chopped', 'well seasoned' (p. 115, p. 120) become poetic leitmotifs in a conversation between Alain and his in-laws. Images are drawn frequently from fairy tales, children's games, stories of American Indians. Occasionally, however, a more sinister note intrudes:

> Escaped prisoners, members of the resistance, Jews hiding under false names, were lolling in the sun, chatting on village squares, seated about fountains, drinking together in bistros, as though nothing had happened, cunning, disquieting prey, cunningly forcing the others, the pure who had done nothing, the strong who had nothing to fear from anybody, into loathsome complicity . . . until one fine morning, a man got up – after all

some one had to take it upon himself to do it – and hurried,
slinking along the walls, to denounce them.   (p. 220, p. 231)

This memory, or perhaps false memory, from Alain's childhood,
which he recalls as he considers how to get Aunt Berthe's
apartment, is as close as Sarraute comes to evoking her own
experience of the war years in her fiction.

Entre la vie et la mort (*Between Life and Death*, 1968), which Sarraute
considers her most important work, is a difficult book, a book
about writing, the hesitations and uncertainties of the writer, the
relation of the writer to the social milieu in which he or she lives,
the possibility of producing a work that lives. What is 'between life
and death' is not a person but a text. The writer, who is, along with
'his' work, the principal character of this novel, is a composite, not
really an individual. What little we know about him is often
contradictory. In what sense, even, beyond the use of the pronoun
'he', can we speak of this writer as male? He has no distinguishing
characteristics, except that he has a mother before whom he feels
shy and childish, is obviously middle class, and likes to drink tea.
This writer, however, and what we can intuit about the way he
works, bears striking resemblances to Sarraute herself and her
method. He is, from an early age, aware of the power of words, an
awareness which, initially, seems to him the mark of a poet, not
'someone who knows better than others how to look' but 'the man
who knows how to make a poem out of words' (Sarraute, 1968,
p. 26, p. 42). Later, however, he seems to consider that pure
word-play may indicate a divorce from the real world, that what is
important is capturing 'movements', neither images nor words,
but what Sarraute terms 'tropisms'. Like Sarraute, the writer in
Entre la vie et la mort is interested in platitudes, does not criticise but
describes, rejects rigid forms. He is of a more than ordinarily
'porous' material, soaking up the world around him. When he
comes to the moment of creation, he experiences great difficulties,
working slowly, often feeling himself divided between creator and
judge. In his attitudes towards the treatment of the writer by
literary society, he is also like Sarraute. He rejects classification in
any school, finds many of his readers insensitive to what he is
doing, is annoyed by attempts to make him a public figure, denies
that his work can be read as autobiographical. He even shares with
Sarraute a similar memory of the joy of writing his first school
composition on the death of an imaginary dog. Finally, what

matters is whether the work itself is living: 'Nearer to me, but not too near ... you my double, my witness ... there, lean over with me ... let's look together ... does it emit, deposit ... as on the mirror we hold before the mouth of the dying ... a fine mist?' (p. 183, p. 204). *Entre la vie et la mort* is therefore a book about how Sarraute feels that the artist works, but a book in which not only the author herself, but also her fictitious writer, are of secondary importance.

If we try to find a feminine perspective in this text, it is perhaps necessary to speak of the modesty and the self-effacement of the author behind the text, as well as the shyness, uncertainty and social insecurity of the writer as character. The record of creativity, in which the artist's ego doesn't finally matter at all, in which the product is all that counts, is in contradiction, for example, to the Romantic impulse, an impulse that seems to many critics particularly masculine.[5] Stephen Heath suggests that Proust and Sarraute are similar in seeking what lies beneath the superficiality of conversation, but that Proust seeks what is individual beneath the surface, and Sarraute seeks what is shared (Heath, 1972, p. 50). Is Sarraute's concentration on what every person shares perhaps feminine in its reduction of human experience to fundamental emotions, in its refusal to attribute supreme importance to a 'romantic' individual sensibility? She is, of course, creating a picture of an 'ungendered' writer and work. In spite of her stated intention, however, the work, even the fictitious writer 'himself', may well seem to the reader 'feminine'. His world, like that of many of her earlier characters, is a world of fear and solitude, a world in which he feels out of place but would like to be acccepted.

The basic preoccupation with states of consciousness and of awareness just below the level of consciousness, and of how such states are expressed or masked by words, exists in all Sarraute's writing from *Tropismes* through the novels to *L'Usage de la parole* (*The Use of Speech*, 1980), which combines elements of earlier works. It is in some ways closer to *Tropismes* as it dispenses with the sustained plot and characters of the novels; short sketches are related only in the most general thematic sense of showing how words are used. *L'Usage* also continues an examination of various themes from the novels. One theme is the recognition that beneath the surface meanings of conversation may lie words not used to communicate thoughts: words, for example, addressed to a friend 'so as to destroy those morbid cells in him in which his hostility, his hate proliferate' (Sarraute, 1980, p. 29, p. 32), words used to assert one's position, or to terrorise another. Another theme is an awareness of the impossibility of communication: 'he sees, facing him, his fellow man, endowed with an identical brain, capable of using an identical language.... Transformed ... an unknown being' (pp. 40–41, p. 44). Our perceptions of others are always far from the indefinable reality; they are rather 'a roughly-sketched form, a crude diagram, a robot-portrait ... a doll like the ones children cut out of cardboard' (p. 85, p. 85). The human personality, normally constructed according to social roles, is fragile and can crumble with terrifying results: 'a crevasse will open out between us ... we'll be wrenched away from one another, ejected from our broken shells ... two solitary souls errant' (p. 89, p. 88). Usually, however, the family tends to give individuals a socially constructed identity. This produces a loss of awareness of true individuality, but also a barrier against the terror of the void. In one family group we find: 'their soft, responsive contours melting and merging into one another, so that they no longer knew where one ended and the other began ... they are a living ball ... imbued with intimate, bland, sweet odours' (p. 51, p. 53). (So much for Plato's dream of the ball uniting lovers, a dream that, following Irigaray, we can see as an appropriation of the female into the male.)

If communication is impossible, it is both because of this unknown quality in any human being and also because of the vagueness of words, particularly abstract words: 'how rough and vague they are, how incapable of bringing out into the open and enabling us to see what might impel these people to take evasive action' (pp. 84–5, p. 84). Normally, however, we behave as if we understood others' language. The person who dares to say 'I don't understand' would break the hold 'of charlatanism, of terrorism, of conformism' (p. 150, p. 149). Such an action is perhaps only possible in a fairy-tale. Alexandra Sévin, writing in a politically radical magazine, uses Sarraute's work to attack the way the French Communist Party uses the language of power. She reads the *Je ne comprends pas* text, as the present-day revolt of women, since they are 'always dispossessed of the use of speech, reduced to repeating only words that are officially allowed'.[6] Perhaps she is too optimistic, since Sarraute talks of the fairy-tale ending of *Je ne comprends pas*; Sévin also finds a more overt political meaning than Sarraute's work would, I think, justify. Still, Sévin's article shows the extent to which Sarraute can appeal to militant feminist readers.

The language in *L'Usage* is more pared down and the perspective more readily comprehensible to the reader than in some of Sarraute's earlier work. The opening text, *'Ich sterbe'*, for example, addresses the reader directly: 'You'll see; be patient' (p. 7, p. 11); and explains the meaning of words: 'they come back (as people say: "It's coming back to me")' (p. 7, p. 11). This narrator uses the first person, directs the reader, anticipates our questions: 'What is there to look for in these signs that are so easy to read?' (p. 19, p. 22); 'What's so surprising about that, then? Nothing in that, of course, but just a moment . . .' (p. 27, p. 30). The narrator tells the reader how to respond not only to the text, but to the words of the dying Chekhov that lie behind the text:

> All we have here, as you see, are a few slight eddies, a few brief ripples captured amongst the infinite number that these words produce. If some of you find this game diverting, they may – with patience and time – amuse themselves by discovering others. At all events they may be sure that they are not mistaken, for everything they may perceive is really there, in every one of us: circles that continue to increase when, propelled from such a distance and with such force, these words fall on us and shake us to the depths of our being: Ich sterbe.   (p. 14, pp. 17–18)

Sarraute's suggestion that the reader cannot be mistaken might be seen as feminist, in so far as both reader-response theory and feminist theory reject the definitive, the authoritarian reading. Sarraute is, of course, speaking directly not of how to read her text, but of how to see the possible implications of Chekhov's last words – 'I die' – and thus of the universality of the experience of death. But her words are also applicable to the level of awareness that her own texts strive to reach, a level at which authority, the voice of reason or established truth, is of less importance than the subconscious reactions of each individual. Our personal awareness cannot deceive us; each individual's examples have an equal validity:

> You could easily, if you agree, add to them; or substitute others you may find amongst those in your possession. . . . Which of us has not stockpiled some of them in the limitless reserve funds which we never have either the leisure or the desire to inspect, to inventory, but which nevertheless nourish our existence.   (p. 35, p. 39)

Implicit in these appeals to the reader is a recognition that human beings, in spite of the difficulties of communication, share a common experience, that we are inseparable as well as separate.[7]

Each of the texts continues the appeal to the reader to enter into the creation of the experience, and gives this reader a clear orientation: 'We must observe that all the conditions are present that would justify us in assuming that we are witnessing a meeting of two friends' (pp. 20–1, p. 24); 'Here are two more interlocutors.... But here too, a little more patience is required' (p. 33, p. 37); 'and the whole of this story has been leading up to this dénouement' (p. 40, p. 43). *L'Usage de la parole* contains what Ellen Munley has termed a 'self-styled narrator–doctor of words who joins all of its loosely connected vignettes by virtue of her presence' (Munley, 1983, p. 238). There is even a certain tone of mockery, a suggestion that this narrator has written other, often misunderstood texts and that now, in a pedagogical fashion, she must clarify her intentions. Occasionally she mocks her own preoccupations, her own careful, meticulous examination of all facets of a word: 'no, don't be afraid, I'm not going to start again' (p. 110, p. 110); she realises that she herself might be the object of ridicule similar to that levelled at some of her characters. (If the narrator is a writer conscious of, and responding to, the criticisms sometimes levelled at Sarraute's work, we cannot, of course, identify the 'I' with Sarraute herself.)

In *'Ich sterbe'*, the description of Chekhov's last words, and therefore the text the furthest removed from the examination of minute movements between two unidentified speakers – the usual subject of these sketches – the narrator describes Chekhov as 'Wise. Modest. Reasonable. Always so undemanding' (p. 9, pp. 12–13), thus rather similar to the narrator of *L'Usage* in rejecting patriarchal authority. *'Ich sterbe'* contains an implicit criticism of the ability of language to fix experience. 'The unsayable will be said', but only at the moment of death. All is vacillating, trembling, an 'infinite disorder' (p. 9, p. 13), until it is immobilised, tranquillised in the words *'Ich sterbe'*, in which, finally, there is an order, but only the order of death. *'Ich sterbe'* speaks as well of how, in saying that he is dying, Chekhov would choose foreign words, those most removed from previous experience, thus without the breath of any passion. Sarraute, for whom Russian is the *mother* language (the language of the mother whose rejection she felt so bitterly in her childhood), writes in French, perhaps also a way of retaining a certain distance from passion. Chekhov's words are addressed to the German doctor, not to Chekhov's wife, for, it is implied, at the moment of death there is no more 'we': 'No, not our sort of words, they are too light, too limp, they would never be able to cross what is now opening, yawning, between us ... an immense chasm' (p. 12, p. 15). Perhaps in this rejection of the 'couple' there is another implicitly feminist theme.

The text most directly related to feminist concerns, however, is 'Your father. Your sister'. It is a strange piece, both in the uncertainty of the narrative tone and in the fluctuating perspective. The narrator wants to capture the force of the words 'Your father. Your sister' as indicating social roles, how the family is defined, how the mother, who speaks these words, sees herself as fixed within an identity. But the sentence chosen to embody these words – 'If you go on like that, Armand, your father will prefer your sister' – suggests more, 'an unnatural mother', 'a vile, vulgar person' (p. 60, p. 61). The narrator insists that this other resonance in the sentence is of no interest, that the sentence could as well have been 'You know, Armand, your father will take your sister to the doctor's'. But finally, the narrator is uncertain that the words 'Your father. Your sister' have in themselves, without the rest of the sentence, the force attributed to them. The element of doubt here may be considered, I believe, as Sarraute's reflection on the possible feminist import of her work. She says she is interested in how fixed family roles are perceived and how they influence speech and conduct, how both the mother and the father are enclosed in certain patterns of behaviour, even if the woman may feel their force more fully. The possibility that the mother's setting of son and daughter against each other, her assumption that the father *should* prefer the son, might reflect the patriarchal bias of society has never, according to the narrator, been a consideration. (The narrator, of course, does not use such terms as 'patriarchal'.) And yet, she wonders if perhaps she has been wrong not to consider such issues.

Enfance (*Childhood*, 1983) is Sarraute's only autobiographical work, and the story stops when she enters the lycée. The implication is that the later life of the author, like that of the writer in *Entre la vie et la mort*, is only, really, the creation of her work. Occasionally in interviews Sarraute has referred to harrowing experiences, and indirectly to her own bravery as a Jew in occupied France during the war, but she has denied the relevance of personal experience to an interpretation of her work. Her childhood, however, she is willing to recount, while suggesting that such a project may be a sign of creative sterility.

Enfance is of interest to the reader of Sarraute's fiction, as it shows some of the personal emotions and experiences that underlie her work ('all the memories that she has killed, all the childhood that was stolen from her' [Cournot, 1986]), but are never allowed to surface. In this respect, she is rather like Marguerite Yourcenar (or Samuel Beckett) and in considerable contrast to those women novelists, such as Colette and Marguerite Duras, whose 'I' is often confounded with fictional characters. It is an attitude, I would suggest, that is also 'feminine' in its origins. Either the boundaries between the self and the other become blurred (which Chodorow would attribute to the role of the mother in a daughter's childhood), or the self is rigidly kept in the background. It is interesting, in this regard, to remember that Marguerite Yourcenar's mother died soon after giving birth to her daughter, and that Sarraute shows, in *Enfance*, the trauma of being rejected by a beautiful and inaccessible mother, who in a letter calls her daughter a 'monster of egotism' (Sarraute, 1983, p. 229, p. 240); Sarraute had to choose to stay with her father and her difficult, uncaring stepmother. We may also consider Sarraute's work as in some ways related to that of her mother, as a reaction to her mother. This does not appear as a theme in her work, cannot be analysed directly as in the work of Colette and Duras. Nevertheless, her comments on her mother's own writing show both similarities and contrasts:

> My mother wrote 'romans-fleuves', children's stories and short stories. She wrote, in contrast to me, with great ease and much joy. She used a very rich vocabulary. The stories often took place in peasant settings. She wrote under a masculine pseudonym and was rather proud that no one – critic or reader – realised that her work was written by a woman.   (Cited in Saporta, 1984, p. 8)

If Nathalie Sarraute's style is very different from her mother's, there is a similar refusal to be identified by gender.

As a child, Sarraute is obsessed with the instability of her own family life, and attracted to those whose childhoods are spent with 'unified, fair and calm parents' (Sarraute, 1983, p. 233, p. 244). In spite of the traumas of her childhood, however, she often wants to assert, against the *alter ego* with whom she conducts her dialogue in *Enfance*, that she behaved 'in the same way as a lot of children do' (p. 16, p. 25). Even as a child, she rejected her own emotions, rejoiced when her mind seemed 'clean, flexible, healthy' (p. 119, p. 130). This control, this need to dominate the irrational, may explain to some degree Sarraute's insistence that she is writing about what all individuals share, and writing from an ungendered position, asserting a 'healthy' neutrality. *Enfance* also mentions another, more overt explanation for her refusal to consider her writing as feminine. In the intellectual discussions among her father's émigré friends in Paris, she is conscious that 'no one made the slightest distinction between men and women' (p. 177, p. 189). Her childhood world is thus one in which the sexes are united in intellectual pursuits, while widely differentiated in their expressions of emotion.

Enfance portrays a distrust of such abstract terms as 'happiness' and of emotional states – particularly irrational fear and sudden terror – that is shared by many of the characters in her novels. It also shares formal qualities with her fiction: a plurality of voices, with continual interruptions (there is Sarraute in dialogue with herself, and with her childhood self, who sometimes speaks directly in the present tense); a preoccupation with the need to find a word to pin down a feeling; a denial of any conventional interpretations. As a child Sarraute often read *The Prince and the Pauper*, important to her because of its theme of uncertain identity. While the book is obviously relevant to her own situation as a child without a clear sense of a 'home', it may also be seen as a prototype for the kind of fiction she creates in her maturity, in which characters have fluctuating, unstable qualities, and are haunted by fears of rejection.

An essential aim of Sarraute's work would seem to be to show a basic equality, the existence for both men and women of similarly banal conversations, a language filled with clichés, stereotyped reactions to the other sex, unstated emotions and sensations beneath the surface masks. The satiric element in her work thus functions finally toward a feminist end: a denial of any fundamental difference that might be used to prove the superiority of either sex. At the same time, these portraits of states of mind, because they exist within identifiable social situations, show the prejudices upon which relations between the sexes are based. There are no privileged characters in Sarraute's world. If women are not simply victims, neither are men naturally superior or inferior. Everyone is both aggressor and victim, just as everyone is unable to communicate with others.

What is the effect upon the reader of Sarraute's narrative technique and her preoccupations? First of all, it demands considerable co-operation from the reader, invites the reader to participate, in a manner that might be considered to undermine any air of authority, or any appearance of knowing the truth, on the part of the author. The reader is placed in a vacillating atmosphere where there are no rounded characters, no clearly discernible plot line, frequently no chronology. Expectations of stability in fiction are destroyed, and with them comes at least a questioning of stability in 'real life' beyond the novel.

Because of the very triviality of many of the situations, the reader may tend to find her or his own similarity to the reactions of the characters, see the fundamental common experiences that we all share, beneath our expectations of permanency, beneath our belief in such entities as 'love', 'respect'. This presumed reader is, finally, neither male nor female, but simply human. Sarraute's fiction describes a common store of human reactions underlying all gender determinations. Militants may discuss the political efficacy of such a vision in terms of political action, but in fiction it works as one way of breaking down categorisation, a method that may be as effective as either glorification of a female 'essence' or satire of socially imposed barriers.

6
Marguerite Yourcenar

Conscious identification with one's sex paves the way for
everything else. Even if we want to deny it and take the
opposite course, it determines our actions and thoughts.
(Bovenshen, 1985, p. 33)

The *partisanship* of feminist literary criticism must not be
allowed to take the form of voluntary sorting the sheep from
the goats, that is taking care of the goodies and leaving the
baddies to the mercies of male criticism.
(Weigel, 1985, p. 60)

If there is a 'feminine' aesthetic, as opposed to a consciously
'feminist' aesthetic, then it should be applicable in some way to the
work even of those who deny its existence. Marguerite Yourcenar
claims there is no feminine aesthetic applicable to her work, and
seems often to posit an essential androgyny. Her androgyny,
however, may seem essentially 'cooptation, the desire to ignore
and obscure differences – these are inherent in the claim that there
are no longer men and women, but just thousands of human
beings. Every woman has had countless experiences which render
such contentions absurd' (Bovenshen, 1985, p. 29). Yourcenar's
work makes us wonder why she takes her position, which is much
more radical than Sarraute's androgyny, since it often denigrates
female experience, or accepts conventional dualities in which men
are more forceful and thus more interesting. The anti-woman bias
in some of her explicit statements as well as in the surface themes
of much of her work is evident. But the strength of her rejection of
any possible feminine values may in the final analysis show
precisely a woman's reaction to her experience of being considered
part of the inferior social group, by seeking in some way to enter
the dominant group through the values and perspective of her
work. Yourcenar is a woman whose particular experience produces a pro-male perspective but one that is nevertheless essentially the perspective of a woman.

Yourcenar's work is largely based on historical subjects, many set in a rather remote past. Her 'autobiographical' books are essentially a history of her family that barely reaches her own birth (*Souvenirs pieux*, 1974, and *Archives du nord*, 1977). The subject matter thus entails a very conscious distancing of the author from the material recounted, almost the opposite of the outpouring of personal emotion often seen as the epitome of a woman's mode of expression.[1] Moreover, where there is any degree of identification with the characters in the narratives, it is almost always with male characters. Often Yourcenar's fiction is narrated in the first person and is thus, as she comments in the preface to *Alexis* (1928), 'the portrait of a voice' (Yourcenar, 1971, p. xi, p. 14). One consideration in examining possible feminine characteristics of Yourcenar's work will be to determine whether this voice is a strictly masculine voice, whether there are elements that suggest a woman's perspective beneath that of the male narrator.

That Yourcenar tends to identify to some extent with her narrators is evident from a comment in the 1963 preface to *Alexis*; thirty-five years after writing the novel she questions some of Alexis's opinions, but says they could not be changed for the new edition of the novel as they 'retain their value for characterisation' (p. xi, p. 15). The implication is that she would naturally tend to give her narrators views with which she would agree. In the preface she discusses Alexis's ideas about sexual pleasure and his explanations of his own homosexuality, and replies to them as if he were an independent person. The ideas presented in her fiction are considered as moral concepts worthy of discussion, it would seem, beyond their value for the portrayal of character or advancement of plot. The voice of a moralist is always present in Yourcenar's work. While commenting in the preface on the formal problems involved in finding the vocabulary to describe sensual pleasures, Yourcenar is very reserved about the sources of her themes, stating only that the 'quasi-Protestant atmosphere and the attempt to reexamine a sexual problem' (p. xiii, p. 16) did not come from the work of André Gide, to which *Alexis* bears both thematic and stylistic similarities.

Alexis is as much about the difficulties of expressing in language one's most profound sentiments, fears and desires as it is about the problems of coming to terms with one's homosexuality, though the two problems are closely intertwined. After twenty pages Alexis hints at his sexual preferences, without being able to name them. The novel is constructed as a long letter from Alexis to his wife,

Monique, whom he has left without warning, so that his embarrassment about finding the right words is heightened by his feeling of guilt. His hesitations, however, may remind us of feminist commentary on the inadequacy of the language of society to deal with all the qualities of life that cannot be neatly divided into dualities:

> Writing is a perpetual choice between a thousand expressions, none of which satisfies me, none of which, above all, satisfies me without the others.... A letter, even the longest, is obliged to simplify what should not have been simplified: one is always so much less clear the minute one tries to be complete! (Yourcenar, 1971, p. 3, p. 19)

Luce Irigaray has said that women want 'what is not yet fixed, frozen in a finished pattern' (Irigaray, 1985b, p. 297); Alexis may be said to share this desire. His description of the music that would express his soul – 'slow, full of prolonged reticences, yet truthful, clinging to silence' (Yourcenar, 1971, p. 13, p. 30) – is similar to some feminist descriptions of *l'écriture féminine*. Words are 'always too precise not to be cruel' (p. 13, p. 29); 'how can a scientific term explain a life? ... there are not two identical deeds in different lives' (p. 18, pp. 34–5). The continual preoccupation with language, and sometimes specifically with writing, tends to suggest an identification of the narrator (who is a musician, not a writer) with Yourcenar herself.

Alexis feels guilty towards his wife, unworthy of her. She is portrayed, through his eyes, as calm, understanding, generous. She has also brought her fortune to restore his family home and to support him. And she is several years older than he. The situation, like that of Chéri and Léa in Colette's novels, seems in some ways a reversal of the stereotypical gender roles. Alexis, as a homosexual hero in an eastern European noble family that has lost its money, but retained strict moral principles, and in an era (the beginning of this century, presumably, although no dates are given) in which his sexual preferences were highly suspect, thus suffers rather as a woman would suffer within that society. The point of view of his narrative, for all its 'masculine' orientation, is not that of an authoritarian father figure, but rather one with which a woman could more readily sympathise. Yourcenar's heroes are often outsiders, whether because of sexual orientation or religious and philosophical beliefs. One cannot, of course, deduce from this theme any feminist theory of women as natural outsiders. Yourcenar sees men as stronger, more capable of fighting social conventions. Her interest in the social misfit is perhaps nevertheless attributable to some extent to her own position as a woman.

Alexis is also implicitly a critique of marriage. Alexis, rather like the Chekhov of Sarraute's *'Ich sterbe'*, is aware of the unique nature of each person's identity, of how in crucial moments there can be no 'we', nor even any mutual understanding:

> Each of us has his own, unique life, determined by all the past about which we can do nothing, and which in turn determines, however little, all the future. His life. His life which belongs only to him. . . . Other people see our presence, our gestures, the way words form on our lips; only we see our life.   (pp. 17–18, p. 34)

Such a theme, though not in itself feminist, is congruent with a feminist vision, at least in its rejection of any concept of identity derived from socially defined, and especially family, roles:

> In family life, our role is fixed once and for all by its relationship to the roles of others. One is the son, the brother, the husband, and so on. This role belongs to us like our name, the state of health we are thought to have, and the deference we are, or are not, supposed to be shown. The rest is of no importance; the rest is our life.   (p. 43, p. 60)

If there are possible feminine themes, there is, on the other hand, a recurring anti-feminist tendency in Yourcenar's work, which often sees women as a group, a category of 'others' and attributes to them certain fixed, and less desirable, qualities:

> Women are rarely calm: either they are placid or else they are nervous.   (p. 77, p. 94)

> You cannot imagine how reassuring the calm affection of women was for an apprehensive child like myself. Their silence, their unimportant words which reflected nothing more than their calm, their familiar gestures which seemed to control things, their blank but tranquil faces which, somehow, resembled mine, taught me veneration.   (p. 21, pp. 37–8)

In contrast to Yourcenar's heroes who remember what is important in their lives, 'The memory of women is like those old-fashioned sewing tables they have. There are secret drawers; there are others, shut so long that they cannot be opened' (p. 56, p. 73).

We are seldom aware of any divergence between the narrator

and the author. Indeed his scrupulous analysis of his sensations and his moral reactions to his homosexuality are presented with great sympathy and with a presumption of reliability. We are aware of his hesitancy in naming his sexual nature, and of his snobbery with regard to the poor (whose song 'contained whatever soul they were capable of' [p. 48, p. 65]), but these traits are not treated with any satire, and in general there seems to be no screen between his voice and the reader. We may see this objective presentation of Alexis's voice, like that of later Yourcenar narrators, as part of her deliberate distancing of herself from her work. The tone of the fiction, however, frequently leads the reader to identify these self-analytical, extremely rational narrators, whose descriptions of their sensual passions are always reserved, with Yourcenar herself.

The style Alexis uses is marked by an abstract vocabulary, and by an abundance of maxims:

> Courage consists in accepting things when we cannot change them.   (p. 86, p. 104)

> What I hold against sickness is that it makes renunciation too easy. One believes one is cured of desire, but convalescence is a relapse; and one perceives, always with the same stupefaction, that joy can still make us suffer.   (p. 68, p. 85)

> The life of others always seems easier to us, because we do not have to live it.   (p. 88, p. 106)

> It is dangerous to expose oneself to emotions in art when one has resolved to abstain from them in life.   (p. 90, p. 108)

> While a fortune, my dear, does not give happiness, it often makes it possible.   (p. 97, p. 115)

There are many such examples. They indicate the analytical mind of Alexis, but also his method of self-justification, his need to impose his point of view. Although he intends to explain his decision to leave, and beg his wife's pardon, we often feel that he is lecturing her. Like other Yourcenar heroes, he is prey to many sensual desires, but at the same time capable of considering his behaviour from a distance, coldly, rationally but without self-condemnation.

The abstract vocabulary and prevalence of maxims is evident, as well, in *Le Coup de grâce* (1939), in which Eric von Lhomond, the narrator, a professional soldier, shares with the hesitant Alexis only poverty, a noble birth, homosexual tendencies, and this analytical turn of phrase:

> Danger brings out what is best in the human soul, but the worst, also. Since the bad usually predominates, the atmosphere of war is, on the whole, thoroughly debasing. (Yourcenar, 1971, p. 125, p. 228)

> There are periods in each person's life when a man really exists, and others when he is only an agglomeration of responsibilities, strain, and (for feebler heads) vanity. (p. 133, p. 233)

Le Coup de grâce is based on an actual occurrence; Yourcenar's work is essentially that of artistically transcribing what happened, not in inventing or imagining. Events are set in a less remote past than usual in her work (1919), but in the Baltic, thus 'giving to yesterday's events a distance in space that is almost equivalent to a distance in time', as she comments in her preface (p. 128, my translation). Her intention, she says, was to portray the 'psychological truth' of a particular tragic adventure, but as she believes that external events influence behaviour she was obliged to consult historical sources, to amass information about the civil war in the Baltic, in order to tell her story. The need to create an historically accurate background, to verify details, thus giving a setting to what is essentially a moralist's tale of human passions, will continue in her later work. This historical accuracy functions at least partly as a neutralising device, keeping the personality of the author at a distance. Similarly, Yourcenar says she chooses to use a first-person narrator because it 'eliminates from the book the point of view of the author or at least her comments' (p. 129). The assumption is that eliminating the personal is necessarily a good thing.

Yourcenar's 1962 preface to a new edition of *Le Coup de grâce*, from which I have been quoting, is a curious exercise in telling the reader how to respond to the story, and particularly in defining how the narrator's own words are to be interpreted. She instructs the reader in how to interpret the narrator's passions: 'Eric's attachment to Conrad is more than physical or even sentimental; his choice corresponds really to an ideal of austerity, to a dream of heroic camaraderie; it is part of a way of looking at life; even his erotic desires are an aspect of his discipline' (p. 132). Yourcenar is also anxious to defend her character from appearances of being sadistic and anti-Semitic, and to erase the impression on some readers that the work is a laudatory portrait of an aristocratic military class. The narrator served in pro-Fascist forces, but, as he was given a French name and French ancestors (these are rarely mentioned in the text of the novel), he is not, she says, an idealised portrait of a German officer. Yourcenar's defence is sometimes strangely naïve, as when she insists that the narrator cannot be sadistic since he is haunted by the memory of having caused suffering, or that he is not a 'professional'(?) anti-Semite because his anti-Semitic comments are part of his conformity to his class, and because he admires two individual Jews (although in the text the narrator, and therefore the reader, are always conscious that they are Jews, and although the narrator attributes to them such stereotypical characteristics as greed). The defence is not convincing, and one suspects that Yourcenar was rather embarrassed, in 1962, by the possible political implications of a story published on the eve of the Second World War. She also defends the 'nobility' of her character, a moral nobility which does not 'always' coincide with aristocratic birth, even though she knows she is going against current 'fashion' or 'convention' in her defence of nobility. She thus, at least partially, destroys the pretence of her objectivity as artist. The insistence on how to read the story, the authorially imposed interpretation, is at odds with Alexis's belief that no language can capture truth. There is a tension between Yourcenar's pedagogical tone in this preface, her assumption, here and in other texts where she speaks in the first person, that she is the correct authority, and the less 'patriarchal', more 'feminine' tone of such stories as *Alexis*.

There are, I feel, two sides to Yourcenar's work: a deliberately authoritative, perhaps extremely 'aristocratic' voice, that attempts to be more 'manly' than most men, that praises soldierly virtues and describes acts of violence and cruelty; and an undercurrent of awareness of the impossibility of establishing clear truths or living by authoritarian values. It is not easy to know on which side to place Yourcenar's preference for the homosexual hero. Is he representative of a complete rejection of women? Or is he the type of a refusal of conventional authority?

Le Coup de grâce is introduced by a simple framing device to establish what Eric has done between 1918 and 1938, and to set the occasion for his telling the story of his youth when, after the German defeat in the First World War, he joined a volunteer army fighting the Bolsheviks in Estonia. With the army officers, he is billeted in the half-destroyed family castle of his friend Conrad and Conrad's sister Sophie. There, amid the horrors of a civil war, a drama of unrequited passion is played out.

Eric's portrait of Sophie is biased by his inability to love her, and his misogyny (which Yourcenar does not defend in her preface as she does Eric's anti-Semitism). The portrait of Sophie is a mixture of admiration for her heroic qualities (or so he says, though he seldom shows such qualities in action) and a rather patronising tendency to reduce Sophie to a typical young girl. Sophie has been raped by a soldier and undertakes dangerous military duties; Eric nevertheless assumes she spent a night crying because he told her she is the last woman he could love: 'She must have passed that night before the white-framed mirror of her school girl bedroom wondering if it were true that her face and body could appeal only to tipsy sergeants' (p. 51, p. 173). In spite of living with and aiding the anti-Red forces, Sophie is sympathetic to Marxism. Eric assumes he can change her ideas, which in any case must really be those of her Jewish mentor, or which she must believe only as a challenge to the man she loves; he rejects the possibility that Sophie is capable of having her own ideas on social and political matters, that she is not always reacting to men:

> I tried more than once to prove her at variance with her principles, or rather with the ideas that Gregory Loew had implanted in her. But this was less easy to do than might have been expected; she would burst out with indignant protests. She seemed to feel obliged, strangely enough, to despise everything that I stood for, everything, that is, except myself.   (p. 49, p. 171)

For reasons that remain obscure, and in spite of his homosexuality, Eric decides at one point to marry Sophie. But he lets her leave the house to join the Bolsheviks, although he is aware that this will surely lead to her death. Months later she is one of the prisoners he captures and executes. Before the execution, their interview concerns not her political activities but with whom she has or has not been sleeping. Sophie is largely reduced to the role of a passionate creature, both in her love for Eric and in her courageous acceptance of her death. Yourcenar says that the two characters share 'their intransigence and their passionate desire to reach their own limits' (p. 132), but the reader is given only a very partial view of Sophie, from the perspective of Eric, who seems never to take her quite seriously as a rational being, and who believes 'nothing is important for women except themselves' (pp. 102–3, p. 212). Thus, although Eric deliberately shocks his listener by his final comment that Sophie got her revenge because he has sometimes felt remorse for killing her ('One is always trapped, somehow, in dealings with women' [p. 151, p. 248]), the story remains his; Sophie only exists as a creature to tempt his love or his hate. Yourcenar comments on the ending of the story: 'At the point they have reached, it doesn't matter which of the two persons kills or is killed. It even matters little whether they loved or hated each other' (p. 132). Perhaps, but it is Sophie who dies, Sophie who fulfills the traditional female role of beautiful, incomprehensible creature who must suffer for her passion.

Mémoires d'Hadrien (*Memoirs of Hadrian*, 1951) is again historical, based on extensive research, a first-person narrative (here a long letter addressed to Hadrian's successor, Marcus Aurelius), and another self-analysis by an erudite moralist with homosexual tendencies. The similarities to Yourcenar's earlier work are thus considerable. *Mémoires d'Hadrien*, however, is a much richer work, both in the portrait of the narrator and in the evocation of an era. It does not depend, as did *Alexis* and *Le Coup de grâce*, on any melodramatic elements, but rather builds, bit by bit, a solid structure that seems true to both history and psychology.

In what way might it show elements of a feminine perspective? *Mémoires d'Hadrien*, according to Yourcenar's 'Carnet de notes' published with the novel, is rather more than a richly detailed, subtly portrayed historical novel. She describes how she was steeped in the era of Hadrian, to the point of having visions, which she wrote down 'in almost automatic fashion' (Yourcenar, 1974a, p. 340, p. 326), and later destroyed. She compares herself to a 'sorcerer', hearing voices 'wiser and more worthy of attention than are his own clamorous outcries' (p. 341, p. 327). This concept of the artist as a medium, who in a sense disappears within the work, who is no longer creating an objective narrative so much as letting it create itself, leads eventually to the idea that Hadrian himself has taken over: 'At certain moments, though very seldom, it has even occurred to me that the emperor was lying. In such cases I had to let him lie, like the rest of us' (p. 340, p. 327). In *Alexis* and *Le Coup de grâce*, Yourcenar attempts to stay behind the voice of her narrators. Here, in *Mémoires d'Hadrien*, a much more successful work, she merges with the narrator. As she notes in the 'Carnet', this does not mean that Hadrian is Yourcenar, but rather that she tries to close the distance between them. She feels that 'Every being who has gone through the adventure of living is myself' (p. 342, p. 328). (Such an identification does not preclude, however, a feeling of superiority to the mass of humankind: 'Only a few students of human destiny will understand' [p. 339, p. 326].) Might we not see in the immersion of the author in the subject a rather feminine act, the rejection of firm ego boundaries analysed by feminist psychologists? It may seem strange to speak of a rejection of a clear self in relation to Yourcenar, and it is perhaps only with such a figure as an admirable, literate Roman emperor that she could feel herself identified. Nevertheless, there is, at least in the 'Carnet', a more 'feminine' description of the act of creation than we might expect.

The 'Carnet' is among the most personal writing Yourcenar has done. Besides describing this interesting process of creation, she speaks of her own life, even alluding to all the personal experiences that cannot be contained in these notes about the composition of the novel: sickness, anguish, joy, search for love. She also describes the great value of her friendship with Grace Frick. It is as if, having immersed herself in the portrait of an honourable man, having lost the 'I' more fully than previously, she can then let this 'I' speak more directly in the notes. She even addresses here the question of why she must choose a male hero, and answers it more realistically and with less apparent misogyny than in earlier writing:

> Another thing virtually impossible, to take a feminine character as a central figure, to make Plotine, for example, rather than Hadrian, the axis of my narrative. Women's lives are much too limited, or else too secret. If a woman does recount her own life she is promptly reproached for being no longer truly feminine. It is already hard enough to give some element of truth to the utterances of a man. (p. 327, p. 315)

One could, of course, advance arguments against this explanation. All Yourcenar is saying, finally, is that one doesn't know enough about the life of such a character as Plotine (the wife of the emperor Trajan) to write a realistic historical novel. It would be possible, one assumes, to write a novel about Plotine using fewer sources (Yourcenar is obsessed with historical accuracy at times), to make a more imaginative attempt to enter the mind of a Roman woman of the era. But Yourcenar obviously feels more affinity for a man's life. Women's lives are 'too limited', presumably too much in the private sphere. Her other argument, that if a woman tells her story she will be considered no longer a woman, obviously is specious applied to a twentieth-century novel about a second-century woman. Who will not be considered a woman? Plotine? Yourcenar? Nevertheless, the very fact that Yourcenar considers, in 1951, the possibility of writing about a woman, and feels obliged to give her reasons for rejecting such a project, shows that she is aware of the particular nature of her literary creations. That she is conscious of criticism of her treatment of women characters, and defensive about it, is also obvious from her postfaces to the three stories published together as *Comme l'eau qui coule* in 1982. Indeed the need to justify, to explain, is almost obsessive in Yourcenar's prefaces and postfaces.

Yourcenar makes of Hadrian both an emperor and a very human creature who, like her earlier heroes, believes that the body has greater 'assimilative powers' (p. 9, p. 14) than the mind. The theme might be seen as almost feminist. Although Yourcenar would probably have been surprised by the parallel, one could compare Hadrian's comments to those of Annie Leclerc:

All my life long I have trusted in the wisdom of my body; I have tried to distinguish between and enjoy the varied sensations which this friend has provided me.   (Yourcenar, 1974a, p. 283, p. 290)

To live is to be happy. To see, to hear, to touch, to drink, to eat, to urinate, to defecate, to dive into the water, to laugh and cry, to talk to those we love.   (Leclerc, 1974, p. 39)

Like Yourcenar's earlier narrators, Hadrian uses maxims frequently. The vocabulary, however, is less abstract than Alexis's or Eric's, the insights are more concrete, and, especially, the cynical view of human nature has been softened:

The mind of man is reluctant to consider itself as the product of chance, or the passing result of destinies over which no god presides, least of all himself.   (Yourcenar, 1974a, p. 26, p. 31)

Our great mistake is to try to exact from each person virtues which he does not possess, and to neglect the cultivation of those which he has.   (p. 42, p. 47)

I have come to the realization that few men fulfill themselves before death, and I have judged their interrupted work with the more pity.   (p. 86, p. 93)

Life is atrocious, we know. But precisely because I expect little of the human condition, man's periods of felicity, his partial progress, his efforts to begin over again and continue, all seem to me like so many prodigies which nearly compensate for the monstrous mass of ills and defeats, of indifference and error.   (p. 293, p. 300)

More than the tormented Alexis or the hardened Eric, Hadrian is a lover of life and of beauty:

I am not sure that the discovery of love is necessarily more exquisite than the discovery of poetry.   (p. 34, p. 40)

To build is to collaborate with earth, to put a human mark upon a landscape, modifying it forever thereby.   (p. 126, p. 134)

I am like our sculptors: the human contents me; I find every thing there, even what is eternal.   (p. 131, p. 139)

I was god, to put it simply, because I was man.   (p. 144, pp. 152–3)

The voice of Hadrian is, however, still close to that in Yourcenar's earlier work, and there are many similarities in theme: the discussions of the relation of physical sensations to love, the distrust of youth, the disdain of family and of marriage. Here is Hadrian's comment on his own marriage to the great-niece of the emperor Trajan:

Sabina, at that age, was not wholly without charm. This marriage, though tempered by almost continuous absence, became
for me subsequently a source of such irritation and annoyance
that it is hard now to recall it as a triumph at the time for an
ambitious young man of twenty-eight.   (p. 59, p. 66)

Like Eric, Hadrian is admirable partly for his physical courage,
partly for his literary sensitivity, and partly for his sensual passion.
Like Eric, he is often capable of grossly misogynist comments:

A man who reads, reflects, or plans belongs to his species rather
than to his sex; in his best moments he rises even above the
human. But my fair loves seemed to glory in thinking only as
women: the mind, or perhaps the soul, that I searched for was
never more than a perfume.   (p. 63, p. 70)

In the character of Plotine, however, Yourcenar portrays (though,
as usual, indirectly through a man's eyes) an admirable woman,
admirable in Hadrian's eyes partly because, unlike Sophie, Plotine
has no interest in sexual passions. Plotine, however, is a very
minor presence in the novel. While Hadrian says she was 'a mind
and a spirit with which mine had united' (p. 166, p. 174), this is a
simple assertion, not developed in the novel, where there are no
examples of Plotine's mental powers.

Mémoires d'Hadrien, like *Le Coup de grâce*, includes descriptions of
cruelty and torture, perhaps a reflection of Yourcenar's desire to
avoid any kind of feminine softness: 'I went so far as to send to the
dungeons of Antioch for a criminal intended for crucifixion, whose
throat was slit in my presence by a sorcerer in the hope that the
soul, floating for an instant between life and death, would reveal
the future' (p. 86, p. 94). More frequently, however, she shows the
humane intentions of Hadrian's reign, making of him a ruler who,
she says, is 'almost wise':

Most men are like this slave: they are only too submissive; their
long periods of torpor are interspersed with a few revolts as
brutal as they are ineffectual. I wanted to see if well-regulated
liberty would not have produced better results. . . . I was determined that even the most wretched . . . should have an interest
in seeing Rome endure.   (p. 114, pp. 122–3)

Occasionally Hadrian's reflections bear on matters contemporary to Yourcenar's readers, and seem close to her own opinions:

> I can well imagine forms of servitude worse than our own, because more insidious, whether they transform men into stupid, complacent machines, who believe themselves free . . . or whether . . . they develop a passion for work as violent as the passion for war among barbarous races.   (p. 115, p. 123)

> One part of our ills comes from the fact that too many men are shamefully rich and too many desperately poor.   (p. 117, p. 125)

He also comments on the new sect of Christians, whom he considers to have an impossible moral standard:

> I passed a whole evening discussing with him the injunction which consists in loving another as oneself; it is too foreign to the nature of man to be followed with sincerity by the average person, who will never love anyone but himself, and it is not at all suited to the philosopher, who is little given to self-love.   (p. 222, p. 229)

His ideas will have modern resonances for the reader:

> Chabrias fears that the pastophor of Mithra or the bishop of Christ may implant himself one day in Rome, replacing the high pontiff. If by ill fate that day should come, my successor . . . will differ from rulers like us less than one might suppose.   (p. 294, p. 301)[2]

Among the subjects of Hadrian's reflection is the condition of women. His opinions are applicable to the 1980s as well as to Rome, and are close to what Yourcenar herself expressed in *Les Yeux ouverts*. He sees the contradictions in the way women are regarded: 'The condition of women is fixed by strange customs: they are at one and the same time subjected and protected, weak and powerful, too much despised and too much respected.' He recognises the problem of deciding to what extent gender roles are determined by nature or by social conditioning: 'In this chaos of contradictory usage, the practices of society are superposed upon the facts of nature, but it is not easy to distinguish between the two.' He realises that most women will not want change, that 'they take their revenge by their strength in little things, where the power which they wield is almost unlimited'. Like Yourcenar, he wants especially to change the laws that relegate women to an inferior condition: 'The weakness of women, like that of slaves, lies in their legal status' (p. 116, pp. 124–5).

> If it is a question of fighting so that women with equal qualifications get the same salary as men, I will participate in this fight; if it is a question of defending their freedom to use contraception, I actively support several organisations of this kind and even abortion. (Yourcenar, 1980, p. 265)[3]

While Hadrian's meditations on the administration of the Roman Empire, on literature, art and philosophy are often fascinating, they occasionally read like catalogues of names, and presume an erudition few of Yourcenar's readers will have. The popularity of *Mémoires d'Hadrien* is surely based primarily on the love story, the love of the middle-aged emperor for the eighteen-year-old Antinous, a love which brought him a period of real happiness, a 'Golden Age'. Antinous commits suicide in Egypt; the narration of the final days of his life is the most fully dramatised part of the novel. Hadrian then seeks a possible explanation for the suicide that might absolve him from feeling responsible: 'In his dread of degradation, that is to say, of growing old, he must have promised himself long ago to die at the first sign of decline, or even before' (pp. 183–4, p. 192). But later he adds: 'I had not been loving enough to force the boy to live on. . . . A being deeply wounded had thrown this proof of devotion at my very face; a boy fearful of losing all had found this means of binding me to him forever' (p. 201, p. 211). He seems to accept that he could have 'obliged' Antinous to live, but also sees the death less as a personal act on Antinous's part than as an action directed against himself. His perspective, in other words, is always self-centred. He shares with other Yourcenar narrators an egoistic way of regarding his beloved, but it does not save him from grief. As emperor, Hadrian can command the apotheosis of Antinous, but even this cannot assuage his sorrow.

The love described in *Alexis*, *Le Coup de grâce* and *Mémoires d'Hadrien* is rather Proustian. The loved object is seen primarily in terms of his physical qualities, which are often described in minute detail: the curve of a shoulder, the shadow cast by eyelashes, the shape of a thigh. This can lead to rather brutal comments about the ageing of the loved one's body. The lover aims at a possession, if only sometimes momentary. There is seldom any suggestion of a meeting of minds. Hadrian does not understand Antinous's tears; enraged at some misbehaviour, he slaps Antinous. Eric treats Conrad as a child. Alexis, more radically, attempts to separate sensual pleasure from any sentiments. Lovers in Yourcenar's work obviously disdain conventional morality, and seek their own pleasure; they want at all costs to avoid conjugality and routine.

If pleasure is primarily physical in *Alexis*, love is deeper in *Mémoires d'Hadrien*; this love, however, is only analysed, and communicated to the reader, after the death of Antinous. Hadrian is very discreet in his evocation of his physical pleasure. The 'obscene' descriptions that Yourcenar says she wrote nightly, inspired by her research and produced almost automatically, have been completely eliminated from the finished work. As a result of concentrating primarily on Hadrian's grief, and also of presenting the story as a first-person narration, love can readily be portrayed as completely solipsistic. Antinous after his suicide, like *Albertine disparue*, is essentially a goad to the lover's imagination.

Why is this description of homoerotic love and grief so powerful, and so attractive to many readers? They probably respond to it as a tale of forbidden love, reading into the second century the mores of the twentieth. In *L'Œuvre au noir* Yourcenar recognises, through the reflections of Zeno, the particular eroticism of homosexuality:

It was the same for the complicated domain of sensual pleasures. Those which he had preferred were the most secret and most dangerous, in Christian lands, at least, and at the time when he happened to have been born. Possibly he had sought them out only because they were prohibited, and thus had necessarily to be concealed, making for violent sundering of custom, and a plunge into that seething realm which lies beneath the visible and licit world. (Yourcenar, 1976, pp. 178–9, p. 225)

This element of overcoming prohibitions adds to the eroticism of the story, for readers of both sexes, as does the vast difference in social situation between Hadrian and Antinous. What of the psychological effect of making the beautiful beloved object, often treated as a toy and never as an equal (especially, of course, when the lover is an emperor!) male rather than female? The possibilities of identification, substitution, projection, for readers of both sexes, are multiple. And the excitement of participating vicariously in what is proscribed can be balanced by an appreciation of the historical, even erudite nature of the work.

Yourcenar's other major historical novel, *L'Œuvre au noir* (*The Abyss*, 1968) is, like *Mémoires d'Hadrien*, set in a time of transition between two eras, in this case the Middle Ages and the Renaissance. It is similar to *Mémoires d'Hadrien* in its analysis of an historical period and of the philosophical and emotional problems confronting the hero, who is primarily homosexual (Zeno, a fictional creation, not based on a real person). Like *Mémoires d'Hadrien*, it is rich in descriptions and in discussions of philosophical ideas. Because Zeno travels often and engages in various religious controversies and alchemical experiments, the work has, however, a less focused centre than does *Mémoires d'Hadrien*, embracing a wide range of experience and relating incidents to which Zeno was not a witness. The most apparent difference of *L'Œuvre au noir* from Yourcenar's earlier fiction is its third-person narrative voice. The third-person narrative perspective permits a satiric tone less often found in the earlier fiction, a tone here used to describe especially two groups that are objects of Yourcenar's scorn: the weak and the fanatics. Yourcenar has an abhorrence of any kind of fanatical philosophy or behaviour. In *L'Œuvre au noir* the Anabaptists are particularly satirised.[4]

L'Œuvre au noir is the story of an individual of superior intelligence and courage, whose loves, it is implied, are also superior:

> I value most this delight rather more secret than any other, a body like my own reflecting my pleasure . . . it is born of desire, but passes with its passing, and if any element of love is mingled therein, it is not because I have been disposed toward it, in advance by the cheap songs of the day. (Yourcenar, 1976, pp. 117–18, pp. 152–3).

> Inclined by his tastes toward the sensuous passions least commonly felt, or least commonly avowed, requiring as they do concealment, and often lies, or, on the contrary, defiance. (pp. 27–8, pp. 39–40)

If he comes to realise that 'I should die a little less witless than I was born' (p. 123, p. 160), Zeno's search for love, like his search for knowledge, is self-centred; there is no observable reciprocity of emotion. Looking at the life of families, he thinks: 'These lives, so bound and limited, made the philosopher realise the value of an unattached existence' (p. 159, p. 201).

Zeno's story is highly theatrical. He is imprisoned because of false accusations, not because of his proscribed publications; he dies while calculating how long it will take the blood from the veins he has just cut to run under the prison door and avert his enemies of his suicide. (His cousin, Henri Maximilien, a similarly superior individual, who hoped for some glory from his poetry, dies in battle; his manuscript is buried with him in a ditch.) There is no salvation beyond the personal and limited:

> At the age of twenty he had thought himself freed of those routines and prejudices which paralyze our actions and put blinders on our understanding; but his life had been passed thereafter in acquiring bit by bit that very liberty of which he had supposed himself promptly possessed in its entirety. For no one is free so long as he desires, wants, or fears, or even, perhaps, so long as he lives.   (p. 177, p. 223)

Although most of the women portrayed in the novel are far from admirable, one could say the same of most of the men. Indeed Cyprien, whose lies cause Zeno's final imprisonment, is particularly weak and cowardly, even if his fear of torture is considered an excuse. It is the men whose fanaticism causes most of the suffering recounted in the novel:

> This teacher abandoning his humble profession, braving sword, fire, and sea in order to attest openly to his faith in the predestination of most of mankind to Hell, seemed to Zeno a goodly specimen of the universal dementia. But beyond such follies of dogma, he reflected, there doubtless exists among all restless human creatures certain repulsions and hatreds rising from the depths of their natures, feelings which, if a time ever comes when it will no longer be the fashion to exterminate each other for the sake of religion, will manifest themsevles otherwise.   (p. 273, p. 324)

Man, whose nature is the same everywhere, and whose faults and sufferings Zeno observes, is male, not generic man: 'Everywhere man has two feet and two hands, a virile member and a belly, a mouth and two eyes' (pp. 110–11, p. 144).

The women, although usually without power, are often especially superstitious and stupid, such as Divara, the Amsterdam prostitute who joins the Anabaptists and 'had the air of an indolent, healthy cow' (p. 70, p. 91); or Wiwine: 'Everything out of the ordinary frightened her' (p. 53, p. 71). Wiwine in old age is 'fat and foolish' (p. 345, p. 431), having been engaged to a soldier drowned in fight in Flanders, and never having recovered from the blow. Some seem primarily temptresses: Jeannette, who first seduces Zeno; Jacqueline, the wife of Henri Juste, who insists on nursing her child in front of nobility; Catherine, a servant who seduces Zeno (for whom she kills her master so that Zeno can inherit his money) but who, to Zeno, is merely 'comparable to the bread and ale of which one partakes with indifference, feeling neither distaste not delight' (p. 155, p. 195).

Idelette, the noble girl made pregnant by a young monk, is, on the contrary, less a temptress than a victim; the narrative is sympathetic to her, and strongly critical of the baker who appreciates her charms but is quick to condemn her when she kills her premature baby. There are several incidents, sympathetically presented, of women seeking abortions. Benedicte and Marthe, in spite of fanatical religious beliefs, are young girls aware of the limitations of their situation: 'Lying chastely embraced in each other's arms, they consoled themselves in weeping together. Then sheer youth gained the upper hand: they began to make fun of the small eyes and fat cheeks of the bridegroom' (p. 93, p. 120). Of Greete, an elderly woman who knew him in his youth, Zeno thinks: 'Between himself and a human creature a link had been formed, however slight, which was not of the intellect, as in his relations with the prior, nor, as in the case of the few sensuous connections which he still allowed himself, of the flesh' (p. 164, p. 207).

Yourcenar's attitude in *L'Œuvre au noir* is thus less a matter of continual misogyny than of a hard, cruel gaze on all human beings, allied both to an appreciation of the difficulties society places in the way of women, and to a strong preference for the more active, aggressive male role. For Marthe, Zeno's half-sister, he is 'the rebel that she had not dared to be; while he was wandering over the roadways of the world, her path had led her only from Cologne to

Brussels' (p. 323, p. 403). If Zeno spent a few years 'under a false name, hiding his vices and practicing his feigned virtues, as his enemies claimed, it was nothing compared to the lie she had lived all her life' (p. 324, p. 404). No more than Shakespeare's sister, described by Virginia Woolf, could Marthe have led the life of her brother.[5]

Nathaniel, the principal character of *Un homme obscur* (published with *Anna, Soror* and *Une belle matinée* in 1982 as *Comme l'eau qui coule* [*Two Lives and a Dream*]), is, like Zeno, a man who travels, this time to the New World, and who meditates on the meaning of his life. Although Yourcenar calls him an ordinary man, he is capable of carrying on a short conversation in Latin. She gives him adventures with an exotic Jewish prostitute and thief, who bears him a child; she establishes him as a servant in the household of a Dutch intellectual, thus allowing her to introduce some of her more usual speculations. Nathaniel shares Zeno's and Yourcenar's anger at religious intolerance, and their sentiment that there is no pattern to life: 'Everything seemed to happen as if, on some road that led nowhere in particular, you met successive groups of travelers, themselves ignorant of their destination and encountered for only one brief moment' (Yourcenar, 1985, p. 65, p. 142). Unlike Zeno or Hadrian, however, Nathaniel, 'the obscure man', is primarily heterosexual, although he has occasional homosexual experiences, and an open-minded attitude. Sexual activity is 'a few spasms' (p. 31, p. 108), not worth the disease or the unwanted children that might result. Nathaniel's loves are simple, physical.

Anna, Soror, an early work only slightly revised for republication in 1982, is another instance of Yourcenar's fascination with forbidden forms of love, in this case incest between brother and sister. The postface discusses literary precedents for this theme, as well as the reasons for its attraction: 'Perhaps, one could even say that for poets it quickly became the symbol of all sexual passions, which become more violent the more they are restrained, punished, and concealed' (Yourcenar, 1985, p. 239, p. 250). Another reason, only alluded to indirectly in the story, is that the woman in an incestuous union can escape the bondage of matrimony. At Valentina's death bed, Anna says: '"You will not see Miguel achieve fame, and me, you will not see me . . ."' She was about to say that her mother would not see her married, but suddenly the idea horrified her' (p. 170, p. 25). If Yourcenar can point to the occasional admirable female character in her work, there are no marriages – nor any long enduring relationships between men and women – that bring anything but suffering. (Relationships of any sort between individuals, in Yourcenar's work, however, produce nothing that could be termed happiness.)

Anna, Soror contains a more admirable female figure than in many of Yourcenar's stories. She is Valentina, the mother of the incestuous pair with whom the tale is primarily concerned. Valentina is praiseworthy because of her erudition (she reads Cicero and Seneca to her children), her charity towards the prisoners in her husband's fortress, and 'a singular gravity and the calmness of those who do not even aspire to happiness' (p. 156, p. 10). Valentina is thus passive, without the originality of intellect or energy of purpose of Hadrian or Zeno. She is also a rather minor character, and the reader does not enter into her thoughts directly. Nevertheless, in her postface Yourcenar is quick to point to Valentina as an example of an admirable woman in her work:

In what I pretentiously allow myself to call my *œuvre*, this serene Valentina seems to me an initial sketch of the perfect woman I have often dreamed of – at once loving and detached, passive out of wisdom rather than out of weakness – and whom I later endeavored to portray in the Monique of *Alexis*, in the Plotina of *Memoires of Hadrian*, and, seen from a greater distance, in that Lady of Froso who, in *The Abyss*, bestows a week of safe haven on Zeno. If I take the trouble to list them here, that is because, in a number of books in which I have sometimes been reproached for neglecting women, I have put into these women a good part of my ideal of humanity.   (p. 235, pp. 246–7)

Valentina is an ideal rather than a creature of energy. Anna is a stronger character, but the perspective shifts to Don Alvaro, Anna and Miguel's father, after Miguel's death. It is almost as though Yourcenar could not make Anna, a woman, the centre of the story.

A more convincing explanation of why the absence of strong female characters did not seem misogynist to Yourcenar herself is her contention that an indifference to the sex of the characters is common to all creators in the presence of their creatures. (She cites Flaubert as an example.) In *Souvenirs pieux*, she mentions the influence of her father:

In the eyes of that man [her father] who often said that nothing

human should be foreign to us, age and sex were only secondary
considerations in literary creation. Problems that later left my
critics puzzled were problems he never considered. (Yourcenar, 1974b, p. 284)

When she is not considering women as merely passive, self-
indulgent or superstitious creatures, Yourcenar bases her vision on
a universe of sensuality in which 'male' and 'female' are of limited
importance. Miguel thinks of the details of Anna's body – 'the
impossibility of recalling the precise curve of her lip, the special
shape of her cheek, or the beauty spot on the back of her pale hand
tortured him in advance' (p. 177, p. 33) – much as Hadrian thinks of
the body of Antinous. Nathaniel, in *Un homme obscur*, thinks:

> Ages, sexes, or even species seemed to him closer one to another
> than each generally assumed about the other: child or old man,
> man or woman, animal or biped who speaks and works with his
> hands, all come together in the misery and sweetness of
> existence.   (p. 117, p. 198)

A character in *Une belle matinée* cites Shakespeare with approval:
'"You're getting mixed up," said Humphrey. "Don't skip over the
best part. *As boys and women are for the most part cattle of this color*"'
(p. 137, p. 220; italics as in original). At the level of pure sensuality,
thus, there is for Yourcenar no distinction of sex. Her portraits of
desire also stress the similarity of mystic and carnal passions:

> the ardent, vague vocabulary of the love of God moved Anna
> more than that of the poets of worldly love. . . . Her head bent
> back and her open lips reminded Don Miguel of the languorous
> abandon of saints in ecstasy, whom the painters depict as almost
> voluptuously possessed by God.   (p. 176, p. 32)[6]

Besides a defence of her treatment of women, the postfaces to
the three stories in *Comme l'eau qui coule* also contain some of the
most personal comments Yourcenar wrote, alluding to her own life
with a directness not found earlier:

> I was twenty-one, precisely the age at which Anna has her
> passionate affair, yet I entered into a worn-out, aged Anna or
> into a declining Don Alvaro without the slightest difficulty. At

that time my sexual experience remained fairly limited; that of real passion lay just around the corner; but nonetheless the love of Anna and Miguel burned within me.   (p. 237, pp. 248–9)

Yourcenar also occasionally speaks of her aesthetic:

a few brief additions reveal my attempt to achieve a *local* reality – that is, one strictly tied to a place and a time, which is the sole reality that seems to me completely authentic.   (pp. 240–1, p. 252)

Every literary work is fashioned thus out of a mixture of vision, memory, and act, of ideas and information received in the course of a lifetime from conversations or books, and the shavings of our own existence.   (p. 224, pp. 259–60)

(The choice of 'shavings' here is of interest. Yourcenar never gives us more than 'shavings' of herself in her fiction.) Also interesting is the series of comments designed, under the guise of explaining what changes were made in the manuscript, to tell the reader how to read the work:

I have added a passage in which Anna, now widowed, lets herself be possessed one night during a journey by a virtually unknown man she quickly forgets; but this brief, almost passive, carnal episode only further emphasizes, in my eyes, her immutably faithful heart.   (p. 242, p. 253)

The essential point, in the present story, is that little Lazarus, sufficiently acquainted with a few Elizabethan or Jacobean dramas . . . lives in anticipation not only his own life but the life of every man.   (p. 227, p. 263)

One looks in vain in Yourcenar's work for relationships *between* women, the theme that various critics have noted is particularly lacking in writing by men. Nor is there any sustained description of a relationship by a person of either sex to a *mother*. Hadrian is not even sure when his mother died; Alexis sees his mother as a sort of angel, with whom he has little communication. Benedicte in *L'Œuvre noir* loved her mother, or, rather, did not know it to be even conceivable that she might not love her. But she had suffered from Salome's stupid and vulgar piousness, from her endless prattle about the neighbors, and even from her merriment, like that of an old nurse who likes to recall to grown children the days of their lisping, their chamber pots, and their swaddling clothes. (Yourcenar, 1976, p. 94, p. 123)

Zeno's mother, Hilzonde, is a more prominent character, but she 'would throw no more than a glance at her son, greedily suckling there at a servant's breast' (p. 19, p. 28). She is content to leave him behind to follow his fanatical Anabaptist stepfather, and the child Zeno 'struggled furiously to escape from his mother's hands, and from her rings, which hurt his fingers' (p. 23, p. 33). Later, in Munster, her fanaticism becomes more extreme than her husband's. Chosen as a mistress by the 'King' of the Anabaptists, 'She yielded now with disgust to the kisses of that wet mouth, but disgust changed to ecstasy; decency's last restraints fell from her like mere rags' (p. 69, p. 90). This degradation seems particularly unprepared. Hilzonde is *par excellence* the uncaring, stupid mother. In later life Zeno is more likely to evoke the memory of his stepfather than his mother.

Nathaniel has no ties to any family, his impressions of his mother being particularly judgemental, as is frequent in Yourcenar's work:

But, to begin with, who was this person he considered himself to be? Where did he come from? From the fat, jovial carpenter of the Admiralty dockyards, who liked to take snuff and deliver blows, and from his Puritan spouse? Not at all: he had only passed through them. (Yourcenar, 1985, p. 116, p. 197)

Nathaniel's son (in *Une belle matinée*) can take pleasure in having had a mother hanged in public for thievery, but he hardly knew her. Of his grandmother he thinks: 'No, she wasn't a bad grandmother. Still, he didn't love her enough to tell her he was going' (Yourcenar, 1985, p. 141, p. 224). Families are never sources of emotion in Yourcenar's work, including, of course, her memoirs of her own family. (She never knew her own mother. In *Archives du nord* she portrays her grandmother very unsympathetically.)

Yourcenar seems to fit into the category of *femme moderne* as defined by Verena Aebischer: the category of women who feel that intelligence has no sex, who have a taste for action, a preference for the masculine world, and a tendency to devalue the world of their own sex. They seek equality for themselves as individuals, and escape from the female ghetto through their own effort. When Yourcenar speaks of women as a group, one feels that she does not include herself among them:

> a great novel presupposes a free look at life which social custom has not hitherto permitted women to take; it also supposes, in the best cases, an opulence of creative power which women rarely seem to have had, or at least to have been able to manifest, and which till now has followed its free course only in physiological maternity.   (Yourcenar, 1984, p. 129)

Indeed she speaks of women's desire for achievement as being a false goal:

> Feminists are mistaken about the aims of human life: Social success is not the final goal. But I am profoundly feminist for everything dealing with sexual liberty ... equal salaries as well.... Success at any price, advancement, competition are outmoded ideas.   (Yourcenar, 1979, p. 27)

Presumably Yourcenar would not have said that success and advancement were inappropriate goals for a man, such as Hadrian. (In this interview it is obvious that she equates feminism with the fight for social advancement, not with the separatist, woman-centred culture of many French feminists.)

Mavis Gallant, although defending Yourcenar against many attacks on her attitudes, admits:

> Mme Yourcenar has said that one cannot write about women because their lives are filled with secrets. The visible and open aspect of women's lives must surely be the least appealing, if we are to take as just the dismal ranks of scolds, harpies, frigid spouses, sluts, slatterns, humorless fanatics, and avaricious know-nothings who people her work, and who seem to have been created for no other reason than to drive any sane man into close male company.   (Gallant, 1985, p. 22)

Of the five novelists I am discussing, it is clear that Yourcenar is the most difficult to discuss in terms of a feminine perspective or aesthetic. Elements that suggest such a perspective are combined with what often seems to be an attempt to be 'one of the boys'. Her style, with its use of maxims, abstractions, technical vocabulary, detailed descriptions, bears little resemblance to most definitions of women's style. Her syntax is controlled, clearly articulated, never obscure; she uses a great number of complex sentences, with many subordinate clauses. Mavis Gallant has described the style: 'The temperature varies between cool and freezing. The lightning is dramatic and uneven. Only the calm and dispassionate approach never changes' (p. 19). Another critic, however, has seen in Yourcenar the virtues of sympathy, patience, love of a simple life, and concludes that she 'is not far from believing that if this world merits saving, it will be saved by women' (Chaillot, 1980, p. 170). This comment is, however, based more on Yourcenar's attitudes expressed in her rare interviews than on her fiction. And yet, Yourcenar's very distinctive, individual style does not seem to me to be typically masculine, although it is difficult to say precisely why.

Perhaps it is the 'pedagogical' tone: the desire to explain behaviour and opinions, not simply to dramatise them; the frequent philosophical reflections; the references to the problems of 'the future', that is, the twentieth century, in her historical novels. It is undoubtedly because of this tone that critical discussion of her work so often centres on her view of life rather than on her literary talents.[7] Even in such a work as *L'Œuvre au noir*, where the narrative appears to leave certain ambiguities – the life of Zeno for many years 'was known vaguely' (Yourcenar, 1976, p. 57, p. 76) – the point of view seems always to be Yourcenar's own: 'Musing a moment, Zeno remarked, "It is strange that for Christians the supreme evil is constituted of so-called errors of the flesh. No one chastises savagery and brutality, barbarity and injustice with the same fury and disgust"' (p. 332, p. 414). While there are highly theatrical scenes, there are longer passages of abstract speculation. Yourcenar's talent, in spite of the detailed historical settings, is not that of the realistic novelist. If each book cannot be reduced to abstract ideas, it is as much the expression of her own way of looking at the world as a dramatisation of an era. Thus, while very different from the work of, for instance, Marguerite Duras, Yourcenar's work is also personal (and perhaps 'feminine'?).

7
Marguerite Duras

> Woman is desire. . . . We don't write at all from the same
> place as men. And when women don't write in the space of
> desire, they don't write. (Duras, 1977, p. 102)

Of all twentieth-century French women writers, it is Marguerite
Duras who is most often cited as an example of a feminine author.[1]
Hélène Cixous, for instance, does not see Nathalie Sarraute as
'feminine', places Monique Wittig a bit on the side, but finds that
Marguerite Duras produces exemplary texts (Cixous, 1976a,
p. 879). Duras has inspired, along with Cixous herself, the most
overtly feminine critical readings, if we accept that in feminine
readings the critic will be personally engaged, will not be primarily
giving a detached explication.[2]

Duras's works lend themselves to feminist analysis in their
themes (the emphasis on a passion that is all-powerful but never
fulfilled, the search for self-definition, a 'madness' that rejects
ordinary society, a consideration of politics in its relation to private
life), in their formal structure (the paucity of events in the plot, the
confusion of genres, the uncertainty of the narrative voice) and in
their style (the use of the passive construction, the disjunction
between what is said and 'objective' events, the confusion of
pronouns, the silences, ellipses, paradoxes, the provisional nature
of many of her sentences). She continually reworks certain obses-
sions; key stories and characters reappear from book to book, in
different perspectives, creating the feeling that there is no *single*
truth to be discovered about them. Her work also shows a
progression towards greater modernism, in the sense of ambiguity,
uncertainty, refusal of conventional plots – thus a modernism
allied to a feminine aesthetic.

As Duras's work is vast, I can discuss only a few novels: *Un
barrage contre le Pacifique* (*The Sea Wall*, 1950), *Moderato cantabile*
(1958), *Le Ravissement de Lol V. Stein* (*The Ravishing of Lol Stein*, 1964),
Le Vice-consul (*The Vice-Consul*, 1965), *L'Amante anglaise* (1967),

Détruire dit-elle (*Destroy, She Said*, 1969), *L'Amour* (*Love*, 1971) and *L'Amant* (*The Lover*, 1984). *Un barrage* is an example of Duras's earlier, more realistic manner, and begins a story carried through thirty-four years later in *L'Amant*. *Moderato cantabile* is a turning point in her work, both in being balanced between a realistic plot and a poetic evocation of passion and, she has said, in representing a transition towards a greater sincerity, as she recognised that she lived the experience of the woman who wants to be killed (Duras, 1974, p. 59). *Le Ravissement de Lol V. Stein* and *Le Vice-consul* are her own preferences among her works: 'I am very happy when I read "Lol V. Stein", but the strongest and most violent joy is "Le Vice-consul"' (Blume, 1985, p. 7). *L'Amante anglaise* is a particularly striking example of Duras's use of a crime story to explore basic emotions – a frequent technique in her work – and of the deliberate, literary destruction of any ideal of 'truth' in fiction. *Détruire* and *L'Amour* are typical later works, moving beyond any comprehensible plot, demanding a new (perhaps more 'feminine'?) kind of reading. *L'Amour* is also a new exploration of the story of Lol V. Stein. *L'Amant*, one of Duras's more accessible and presumably more autobiographical works, takes up again the childhood she explored in her first works.

Un barrage contre le Pacifique appears largely based on Duras's own life in French Indo-China as a child, although she has said that 'while her family was still alive she wrote around, rather than about them' (Blume, 1985, p. 7). It is largely a realistic work, in the sense that the setting, characters and events are clearly described in detail, the narrative point of view is straightforward. It is a 'full' text, without the ellipses, uncertain dialogues and paradoxes of the later work. Yet, in spite of the realistic setting and the depiction of the corruption of French colonial power in Indo-China, the theme of the novel is the intensity and destructive effects of passion, the foundation of all Duras's later work. In *Barrage* the passion is *described* as it is seen by the young girl, Suzanne, in its observable effects: the mother's passion to save her compound from the floods, the sexual passion of her brother and that of the wealthy man who courts Suzanne. The novel is *about* passion, rather than an embodiment of desire itself. Suzanne, in fact, seems cynically detached from any passion. This detached point of view will change, gradually, in the later works, but the importance of an *observer* will remain.

In *Moderato cantabile* (1958), there is still a setting, identifiable characters, a series of events. The effect, however, is closer to the enactment of passion than a description of it. The organisation is, as Duras herself has noted, similar to that of a poem (Knapp, 1971, p. 655); the emotional intensity of the characters determines the style and the tone of the book. The title, *Moderato cantabile*, indicates two opposing themes: moderation, restraint, routine, the life of Anne Desbaresdes in her bourgeois family; and singing, freedom, escape from normality, Anne's relationship to her son. Anne Desbaresdes seeks to escape from the asphyxiation of her world into a world of passion that she can only equate with death. Duras has commented Anne wants to be killed, and does not love Chauvin; the story is not a love story, but a sexual story (Duras, 1974, p. 59), a story about the most basic emotional level of the individual's development. Much of the power of the novel comes from the *disproportion* between what she does and what she seeks. All she accomplishes, on an objective level, is to drink too much in the company of a man of whom she knows little except that socially he is very different from her, and to discuss, endlessly, a crime of passion of which in fact she knows almost nothing except what Chauvin invents. Until the penultimate scene, the dinner party, little happens. Emotion is expressed in inadequate words and inadequate gestures. Critics have noted the frequency of passive constructions in Duras's work. Anne is a creature of great desire, but very little will.

Anne's husband exists only as representative of convention. Her child, on the other hand, seems to have become, until she meets Chauvin, the only means through which she can express any desire to escape. Of Chauvin we know little except that he, like Anne, is caught in a desire which transcends his ability to express it and his capacity to act upon it. Like Anne, he seems fragmented, his body distintegrated. He appears motivated, however, by a desire to dominate Anne, to make her a character in his story. In his version of the story of the murder, the man has dominated the women, broken down her sense of her own identity.

Moderato cantabile is about language, to what extent language is of necessity a lie, to what extent it can express the deeper subjective level of emotion. Silences constitute an implicit criticism of rational language, not as specifically male-dominated, but as incapable of expressing passion. For Anne, what can express emotion is the scream, the scream of the dying woman, her own screams during the birth of her child. These are two events outside social norms, which cannot be expressed in socially sanctioned language. Trying to talk about the murder they have not witnessed, Anne and Chauvin invent a story, use words to interpret and to lie. What their words express is not an objective truth, or even their interpretation of an event, but their own emotions: his desire to dominate, hers to submit, to die. The ability to find a language which, under the surface, is capable of expressing the passions is aided by the use of alcohol, a frequent theme in Duras's work. The reader must be aware of the fact that Anne is often drunk to appreciate the silences, incongruities and repetitions in her speech. (In later works, Duras's characters often use such speech without being drunk, but in *Moderato cantabile* there is still some conventional realism.)

The central event which triggers the action of the novel is absent; the murder takes place 'offstage', and can only be reconstructed through the dialogue of Anne and Chauvin. *Moderato cantabile* has, none the less, a dramatic scene in the dinner party, skilfully intermingled with glimpses of Chauvin outside, a scene which could still be placed within the perspective of realistic fiction. It is also, however, a violent reversal of the narrative structure of the previous chapter, changing the system of focalisation and introducing an ironic narrative voice. Thus its 'realism' is undermined by its inappropriateness to the preceding narrative (Borgomano, 1985, p. 23). Increasingly Duras will avoid the dramatic, the striking social event, to get closer to to the heart of passion behind or beneath all surface objectivity.

The tension between the themes of *moderato* and *cantabile* cannot, it would seem, be resolved dialectically; there can only be return to ordinary life, or death after freedom. (We are reminded of analyses of nineteenth-century novels, in which the heroine must either submit to conventions or die because of an illicit passion.) Duras suggests in her own interpretation of the novel that there is a kind of resolution: 'Anne Desbaresdes is the middle-class woman who suddenly feels and sees something else. . . . The change she undergoes is irreversible, but nothing, afterwards, is proposed for her. Even her child has been taken away. She has nothing left. As for me, I think she will probably go towards madness' (Micciolo, 1978–9, p. 63).

Critics, however, have suggested what may be a more positive resolution:

As she leaves the café, she has been able to transcend the opposition of *moderato/cantabile* and to accept an existence of

moderato cantabile: she will neither continue her bourgeois life,
nor has she succumbed to the deadly lure of passion. In her
identification with the other woman, she has discovered the
relational base of her own identity and has been able to transcend the separation imposed by the social roles of adult, of wife
and mother.   (Hirsch, 1982, p. 84)

Marianne Hirsch continues, however, to describe this resolution as
an 'affirmation of death and destruction . . . as a mean to other lives
which emerge after silence and emptiness have been reached'. In
what sense this is a positive transcendence for Anne herself is
unclear. George Moskos sees the murdered woman as a 'symbol of
the violence done to women in a culture that depends for its
existence (as subject) on their "elimination" '. Moskos sees Anne
refusing to accept the fiction of domination that Chauvin has
created, in order to be reborn 'in another place with another voice'
(Moskos, 1984, p. 42, p. 51). Duras suggests, rather ambiguously, a
possible social interpretation and a rebirth 'in another place':

During the time of the book, Anne Desbaresdes is suspended
between two worlds: that of pure annihilation, of madness, and
that of the bourgeoisie, asphyxiation. It begins like that, the great
mutation of humanity. . . . It is those who will come later who
will go further than Anne Desbaresdes. (Micciolo, 1978–9,
p. 63)

In what direction will they go, 'those who will come later'?
Towards madness or towards asphyxiation? Or towards a world in
which new possibilities will open? Duras said that Anne, caught in
the stagnation common to most bourgeois women, could not get
free through an intellectual or political experience, but only
through her emotions. To some extent, *Moderato cantabile* has as a
social theme a criticism of this bourgeois world, in which the
salmon and the duck at the dinner party seem more alive than the
people. There is in this novel and in other earlier Duras novels a
suggestion of a possible amelioration of the human condition
through political change, a suggestion found less and less frequently in her later work, or present there only in the sense that
destruction can be a form of liberation.
    If there is a dramatic event connected to *Le Ravissement de Lol
V. Stein*, it is a *pre-text*, the story of Lol's abandonment by her fiancé

years earlier. The novel itself is concerned not with that moment but with what it has produced later. (Often in Duras's work the echoes or repercussions of events are at least as important as the original events themselves.) Again, as in *Moderato cantabile*, the eroticism might be described as literary, since Lol's story is constructed, invented by the narrator, Jacques Hold, who informs his reader that he knows nothing, and yet who continues to tell his story, in which he is erotically involved: 'I know Lol Stein in the only way I can; through love' (Duras, 1985, p. 36, p. 46). His narration is not even logically consistent, as he often describes himself in the third person, sees himself from the outside, even sees Lol behind him. In this continual destruction of objective 'truth', this insistence that there can be no 'Oedipal' reading, lies the subversive element of *Le Ravissement* and perhaps of all Duras's later fiction.[3]

Lol is *par excellence* the female character without clear direction and individuation postulated by psychoanalysis. According to Michèle Montrelay: 'Lol no longer loves anyone. She has completely become love. She is "ravished", that is to say carried away in *jouissance* because suddenly her emptiness has been revealed to her' (Montrelay, 1977, pp. 15–16). She imitates 'the others, all the others, as many people as possible' (Duras, 1985, p. 24, p. 34). She is silent, or she lies. 'She thought that she had been cast into a mold, the identity of which was extremely vague and to which a variety of names might be given' (p. 32, p. 41). She seems only to have lived in the brief time when she was passionately in love with Michael Richardson; her identity, her life is thus dependent upon the existence of another. What is more, her life in the present of the novel is dependent upon Jacques Hold and his strange fascination with her story.

Lol's story is not that of the usual love triangle in which she loses a man to another woman, for, if we are to believe Jacques Hold (whose story is always, however, full of uncertainty) she does not suffer. Rather she enjoys the disintegration of her individuality, and reaches a kind of indifference. She then seems to reconstruct a situation like that of the ball where she was abandoned, by entering into a different triangular relationship with Jacques and his mistress Tatiana, by watching them make love, as she has dreamed of watching her fiancé Michael Richardson with Anne-Marie Stretter. The text suggests, however, that perhaps she sees nothing, when she is supposedly watching Jacques and Tatiana,

that perhaps her knowledge of this scene comes from what Jacques
tells her. Again, desire, eroticism, sensuality seem linked to a
fiction, a creation of words, which, as always in Duras's work,
signify to a large extent by showing what they cannot signify.
Again, as well, desire seems to be mediated through the vision of
another, just as Anne Desbaresdes needs Chauvin's version of the
story of the murder victim.

After being abandoned by Michael Richardson, Lol stopped
talking, she could not express the inexpressible:

> The only times she did speak was to say how impossible it was
> for her to express how boring and long it was, how interminable
> it was, to be Lol Stein. . . . The difficulty she experienced in
> searching for a single word seemed insurmountable. (p. 14,
> p. 24)

Later, she shows such detachment that Tatiana remarks that she
speaks of her own life as if it were a book. Jacques Hold is aware of
her lying: 'I desperately want to partake of the word which
emerges from the lips of Lol Stein, I want to be a part of this lie
which she has forged' (p. 97, p. 106). Lol describes to Jacques
seeing Tatiana in the hotel room with him: 'naked beneath her
dark hair, naked, naked, dark hair' (pp. 105–6, p. 115). The sentence, as Jacques hears it, conveys not information but emotion:

> The intensity of the sentence suddenly increases, the air around
> it has been rent, the sentence explodes, it blows the meaning
> apart. I hear it with a deafening roar, and I fail to understand it, I
> no longer even understand that it means nothing. (p. 106,
> p. 116)

If Lol cannot express in words the nothingness, the lack of a centre
in her life, the language of the novel also does not try to find any
clear meaning. Rather than constructing events, imagining 'obsta-
cles, accidents', Jacques Hold prefers to open holes:

> To level the terrain, to dig down into it, to open the tombs
> wherein Lol is feigning death, seems to me fairer – given the
> necessity to fill in the missing links of Lol Stein's story – than to
> fabricate mountains. (p. 27, p. 37)

Rather than truth, his language conveys emotion.

At the end of the novel, Lol goes with Jacques to revisit the ballroom where the original traumatic scene of abandonment took place, only to discover that almost nothing remains:

> One trace remains, one. A single, indelible trace, at first we know not where. What? You don't know where? No trace, none, all has been buried, and Lol with it.   (pp. 170–1, p. 181)

What is that single 'trace' that remains, and that a moment later becomes 'no trace'? An ambiguity subsists. Is there still something to discover? Lol earlier felt that if she could have discovered the right word, everything would have been changed at the end of the ball:

> that it would always have meant, for her mind as well as her body, both their greatest pain and their greatest joy, so commingled as to be undefinable, a single entity but unnamable for lack of a word. I like to believe – since I love her – that if Lol is silent in her daily life it is because, for a split second, she believed that this word might exist.   (p. 38, p. 48)

Could this word have been found, and could the meaning of the single 'trace' have been identified? Or is there no word for feminine desire (Borgomano, 1984, p. 64)? Duras is capturing a level of uncertainty that underlies any indifference that Lol may achieve. After the visit to the Casino where Michael Richardson abandoned her, Lol still must see herself as double – as both Lol and Tatiana – and still must wait outside the Hôtel des Bois to watch when Jacques goes to meet Tatiana.

The language of *Le Ravissement de Lol V. Stein* gains intensity from the frequent repetitions, a certain monotony of rhythm, a deliberate simplicity. The sentences are often short, simple:

> [she] leads her toward the French doors which open onto the grounds. She opens it. I see what she wants. I move forward, Keeping to the wall. There. I'm at the corner of the house. From this point I can hear what they are saying.   (p. 83, p. 92)

Or, alternatively, in attempting to catch the inexplicable, Jacques resorts to a convoluted syntax:

> It seemed as though she took everything for granted, and that

the infinite weariness of being unable to escape from the state she was in was not something that had to be thought about, that she had become a desert into which some nomad-like faculty had propelled her, in the interminable search for what? (p. 14, p. 24)

The physical setting is not, as it still was to some extent in *Moderato cantabile*, a background against which the drama takes place. Rather Lol makes of her world an empty space, in which words and their referents convey nothingness. She arranges her house with great care and precision so that it has nothing to do with her. The house and gardens have a glacial order, operate on a strict schedule. There is no life, no vivacity. Lol's mistake in planning the garden is an evident symbol of her detachment from normal life:

She wanted the garden paths to fan out evenly around the porch. But none of them intersected, and as a result they were unusable. John Bedford was much amused by the error. (p. 26, p. 35)

S. Tahla seems a place invented by a dreamer. Even the names – Hold, Tatiana, Lol, S. Tahla, U. Bridge – seem to refer to imaginary beings and places. This dream-like atmosphere is also conveyed through the many ambiguities, through the possibility that Jacques Hold is an unreliable narrator, especially through a structure in which the subject who orchestrates the dream-drama does not speak directly, is interpreted by another. Lol's story has been described as a 'wandering in space-time', in which nothing is fixed. Thus Lol doesn't grow older, and the novel doesn't end (Didier, 1981, pp. 281–2). Duras's work increasingly progresses towards a denial of any linear narrative.

In *Le Vice-consul* several stories are superimposed to create a poetic portrait of sorrow, desire, madness, alienation. First, there is the epic story of the beggar woman, chased from her home when she 'falls pregnant', who wanders across much of southeast Asia until she arrives in Calcutta. This woman is, like Lol, but in a more extreme fashion, a type of the indifference, the lack of individuation, of the female personality. She has no name, almost no physical attributes, no words beyond her plaintive song, which has been characterised as 'the cry of the woman perpetually out of relation to her maternal origin' (Willis, 1987, p. 103). She cannot speak. Thus it is not she, but a *man*, who tells her story. Peter Morgan, the narrator of her story, writes: 'How to put into words the things she never said? How to say what she will not say? How to describe the things that she does not know she has seen, the experiences that she does not know she has had? How to reconstruct the forgotten years?' (Duras, 1966, p. 55, p. 73). She is an embodiment of suffering. She is driven on by hunger, but also by a need to find her mother again, a mother whom she both loves and detests, and to whom she cannot return, a mother who has accepted social standards, for whom illegitimate pregnancy is a disgrace. In the extremity of her suffering, as she prostitutes herself for a bit of food, she is an epic figure of the sorrow of woman, for whom her mother and her own child are the only realities. She manages to give her child to a white woman, an act of unselfish love, but also a deliverance from an intolerable burden. In the description of her relation to her unborn child, Duras shows the ambiguity of maternal emotions: 'The child in her womb is growing more and more active. It is as though fish were snapping in her belly, or the insufferable infant were happily beating a drum' (p. 3, p. 12). As Monique Gosselin comments: 'Only a woman could write that or describe the resurrection of her own relationship to her mother when she experiences childbirth' (Gosselin, 1982, p. 159).

Another level of the story concerns the Vice-Consul, Jean-Marc de H., who presents a parallel to the beggar. His madness, however, takes the more active, masculine form of shooting at the lepers in Lahore, to call down the death he sees as the destiny of all humanity. While the beggar has had a number of children, unwanted products of her need to eat, he remains a virgin. Neither is able to reach any satisfaction of basic desires. His drama, like hers, is centred on his relationship to his mother, the basis, as Duras has noted, of all human emotion. In an interview she defines the movement of desire as an attempt to redress 'the definitive absence of this all-important presence, never replaced later, of my (the) mother' (quoted in Moskos, 1984, p. 37). The trauma of the child's inevitable separation from the mother is, perhaps, the central psychological event of human development, for children of both sexes. The beggar's mother has proved to be a cruel mother, forcing a second separation. Jean-Marc's mother abandoned him a second time when she remarried after her husband's death.

The Vice-Consul, who functions as an intermediary between the world of madness of the beggar woman and the world of the Europeans, is fascinated by Anne-Marie Stretter, wife of the French ambassador in Calcutta, and, incidently, the woman who seduced Michael Richardson away from Lol V. Stein in *Le Ravissement de Lol V. Stein*.[4] Anne-Marie Stretter recurs from one work to another; she is an obsession of Duras's; like the beggar, the character goes back to Duras's childhood. Anne-Marie Stretter was an adulterous woman, and someone had committed suicide because of her: 'for a long time she incarnated for me a sort of double power, a power of death and an everyday power'. Anne-Marie 'has gone beyond all prejudices . . . she is on a sure path to liberation'; 'she is an empty form . . . things are lodged in her'. 'Sometimes I tell myself that I have written because of her' (Duras and Porte, 1977, pp. 65–74).

Anne-Marie and the beggar are two faces of women: the desired, beautiful, rich woman with many lovers, mother of two daughters, whose life is nevertheless fundamentally empty; and the rejected, miserable outcast from a peasant family. Both are near madness and both, we learn, suffered from being rejected. Anne-Marie left her first husband: 'Even now, no one in Calcutta really knows whether she was living a life of shame or sunk in despair when he found her in Savannakhet' (Duras, 1966, p. 76, p. 99). Like the beggar, whom she met in Savannakhet, Anne-Marie is in exile in Calcutta after long wandering; unlike the beggar, she may have attempted suicide. The alternating scenes of the beggar's miserable existence and the luxury of embassy life finally suggest that beyond the social contrast lies a profound similarity between the lives of the two women, and also between them and the Vice-Consul.

We learn about these women through other voices, so that there is always a distancing. The technique emphasises the passive role of the two women. For Peter Morgan, the story is a way of throwing himself into the suffering of Calcutta, so that 'wisdom may start to grow out of bitter experience' (p. 18, p. 29). Although he learns about the beggar from Anne-Marie, he must substitute his own memories for those of the beggar to understand her madness.[5] The distancing narrative voice of Peter Morgan, and the uncertain narrative voices of the rest of the story, with which Morgan's tale is interspersed, permit the ambiguities, uncertainties at the heart of Duras's fiction. If we know that Peter Morgan must invent, we are not sure who is telling the story of Anne-Marie and the Vice-Consul. Perhaps Charles Rossett, a young attaché who has studied the Vice-Consul's dossier, and who is enamoured of Anne-Marie.

Peter Morgan's description of the wanderings of the beggar lends a legendary quality to her story, a story that becomes the opposite of a hero's search for his destiny:

> I need some signpost to lead me astray. Make your mind a blank. Refuse to recognize familiar land marks. Turn your steps towards the most hostile point on the horizon, towards the vast marshlands, bewilderingly criss-crossed by a thousand causeways. (p. 1, p. 9)

The language is, as often in Duras's work, full of repetitions, incomplete sentences, shifts from 'she' to 'I' in the middle of a paragraph. The characters are often unnamed, typical: *la dame, l'enfant blanche, la jeune fille.* Later *le directeur, les deux Anglais,* and so on, are used more often than proper names.

The scene of the dance at the embassy suggests a parallel to the never dramatised scene of Lol's abandonment at S. Tahla. It is in this artificial, conventional setting that the unconventional breaks through. Anne-Marie dances with the Vice-Consul. An indeterminate 'one', 'we', watches them dance, shocked at his social *faux pas.* Charles Rossett can only imagine that the pair are speaking of a new posting for the Vice-Consul, that he is using this opportunity to advance his shattered career. But in fact the conversation keeps turning around the edge of madness, around what cannot be expressed. Anne-Marie attempts to find 'the last word on the subject' (p. 96, p. 123). She wants to speak quickly, to avoid saying 'other quite different things, things much more remote, but which might just as well have been said. Why not? Don't you agree?' (p. 97, p. 124). He attempts a social conversation about leprosy because

> 'I have the feeling that if I tried to say what I really want to say to you, everything would crumble into dust' – he is trembling – 'for what I want to say . . . to you . . . from me to you . . . there are no words. I should fumble . . . I should say something different from what I intended . . . one thing leads to another.' (p. 98, p. 125)

Then, finally, he arrives at the essence, why he shot at the lepers:

'One other thing I can tell you, if you will bear with me: Lahore was also, in a sense, hope. You do understand, don't you?' (p. 99, p. 126). And she, from the depths of her own alienation, understands. The scene is remarkable for catching an emotional undertone in a conversation made up mostly of hesitations, half-formed thoughts, an undertone that has, as it rarely does in Duras's work, no immediate erotic connotations.

L'Amante anglaise (the title is word play, *la menthe anglaise* or *en glaise*, English mint, or mint in clay) is Duras's reconstruction of a real crime in the form of fiction. Although it is called a novel, it is in fact a series of conversations supposedly taped by a male 'novelist' (again, the female figure does not speak directly) with the presumed murderer, Claire Lannes, her husband Pierre and Robert Lamy, the proprietor of the Balto Cafe where Claire was arrested. The 'novelist' also has, and transcribes, an earlier tape, made by the police at the time the murderer confessed. How the novelist obtained this tape is perhaps the least of the puzzles.

From the beginning we are aware that discrepancies and ambiguities will exist. In the first tape the speakers are not always clearly identified. Robert Lamy, the first interviewee, inquires: 'How about the difference between what I know and what I say – what will you do about that?' (Duras, 1967, p. 3, p. 9). The 'novelist' replies: 'That's the part of the book the reader has to supply for himself. It exists in any book' (p. 3, p. 10). Commenting on the conversation with the detective in the bar, the evening of Claire's arrest, Robert says 'We were inventing a crime, we and he between us' (p. 11, p. 21). We are never sure what is invented, what took place, within the fiction. (The ambiguity is, of course, compounded by the fact that *L'Amante anglaise* is based on a real event.) The 'novelist', whom we tend, in spite of his sex, to identify with Duras, is also not trustworthy. At one point he says he is not sure who is the murderer. Later he tells Pierre Lannes that there is proof in Claire's fingerprints found on the dismembered body. He denies wanting to impose any interpretation of the book that is being done (*le livre qui se fait* – the use of the passive construction here serves to keep the writer from taking personal responsibility for establishing any 'truth', any 'Oedipal' interpretation). In any case, 'that's just words' (p. 60, p. 99).

While borrowing elements from detective fiction, and containing a mystery to keep the reader in suspense (the victim's body was cut into pieces and thrown from a viaduct into passing trains, but the whereabouts of the head is not known), the book is really about typical Duras characters – the dispossessed, alienated, those on the edge of madness, those who are, as the murderer terms them, on 'my side', as opposed to 'the other side', that of conventional society. The themes therefore centre on the personalities of the main characters, the moment of destruction, what pushes Claire into killing her deaf-mute cousin, Marie-Thérèse Bousquet, who has served for seventeen years as her housekeeper.

Duras's interest in the moment of madness, of crime, is like that of Anne Desbaresdes in *Moderato cantabile*.[6] The Duras criminal, however, is not a romantic, Byronic figure, but rather almost a passive victim of emotions beyond his or her control. Before she is identified as the murderer, Claire queries what the difference is between a madman and a 'natural' person (the term is the detective's and seems to mean for him someone not a professional killer, though it also suggests someone not bound by convention). Violence against another is often a displaced suicide, an irrational gesture of escaping routine: 'Perhaps because they were together in a situation that was too static and had been in existence too long. Not necessarily an unhappy situation in itself, but stuck, no way out, if you see what I mean' (p. 18, p. 32). The 'novelist' suggests that Pierre let the police get Claire because he wanted to end an intolerable situation, and that his act is comparable to hers. For the 'novelist', Claire is not so much mad as someone who has never adapted to life (though later, he tells the imprisoned Claire that she is mad). Pierre suggests that he, that most people, are capable of a crime. Robert refuses to answer when asked whether he would have protected Claire from the police. It is from this group of basically non-aggressive, misfit characters that Duras's criminals come.

There are two figures of the alienated female personality: Claire and Marie-Thérèse. Both are natural victims and both resemble Lol V. Stein. Marie-Thérèse Bousquet is without a family, without friends, without a place in society, a marginal being. Her name suggests a connection to nature rather than normal society. (*Bosquet* means 'grove' in French.) The forest is a symbol, in much of Duras's work, for the frightening density of human sexuality: 'the forest is for the mad, you see. . . . I have been afraid of myself since puberty. In the forest, before puberty, I was not afraid' (Duras, 1977, pp. 27–8). Claire's most persistent memory of her cousin is as a child joyfully playing with a cat. For Pierre, Claire is an empty space: 'It was as if she was closed to everything and open to everything at one and the same time. You couldn't get anything into her to stay, she retained nothing. Like a place without any doors, where the wind blows through and sweeps everything away' (p. 55, pp. 90–1). Claire is unable to become involved in normal life, and indifferent to most of what society considers important. Her love affair before her marriage, with the policeman from Cahors (he is never given a name), gives a sense to all her life:

> I've never been separated from the happiness I had in Cahors, it overflowed on to all my life. You mustn't think it was just the happiness of a few years: it was a happiness to last forever. It still goes on now, when I'm asleep. (pp. 99–100, p. 159)[7]

Claire is unable to use words normally. Robert Lamy describes her speech: 'Ten different things at once. Floods of words. And then suddenly silence' (p. 32, p. 55). His description seems to conform to a feminist psychoanalytic theory about how women seek to relate, rather than separate, phenomena: 'Before you knew where you were she was off in all directions, everything would connect with everything else' (p. 33, p. 56). Like Lol, Claire cannot find the right words: 'If I'd been asked the right question I'd have found the right answer' (p. 103, p. 165). She wishes she could have found *n'importe qui* (anyone at all) to whom to write about her love. Her ideas, her thoughts cannot escape what she describes as a leaden cover over her head: 'they just fell back again and stayed under the lid, swarming, and it hurt so much that several times I thought of doing away with myself so as not to have to suffer any more' (p. 100, p. 160). But, unfortunately, as she realises, 'I wasn't intelligent enough for the intelligence that was in me' (p. 102, p. 163); she is a creature of strong feelings, without the rational use of language to explain them.

Pierre Lannes seems typically masculine in his attitudes. He invents an 'understandable' crime: a worker who kills a woman who refused to follow him into the forest to make love. He questions whether such a crime should be punished as another crime would be. Pierre is interested in women, has had many adventures, and has divorced his sexual activity from any love. He is mainly worried about growing old, not having the energy to look for women. He feels that Claire would have committed a crime with any man, anywhere, thus that he can have no responsibility.

At the same time, however, he insists that she loved him, and refuses to place much importance on her previous love affair, which had led her to try to commit suicide. In his egotism, he seems to be more upset that his way of life has been altered, that he must find a new housekeeper, than that his wife has committed an extremely violent crime. At the end of the interview with Pierre, the 'novelist', who has tried to avoid interpretations, gives a clear one:

> I think you didn't only want to get rid of Claire – you wanted to get rid of Marie-Thérèse too. You wanted both of them to vanish out of your life so that you would be on your own again. I think you'd dreamed about the end of the world. (pp. 79–80, p. 129)

Thus *L'Amante anglaise*, a crime story, a psychological investigation, is based on a conflict between typically 'masculine' and 'feminine' personalities. There is, however, no resolution, no domination of the story.

In *Détruire, dit-elle*, the impulse towards destruction of *L'Amante anglaise* is given a more general, more political interpretation. The text of *Détruire* is a hybrid, moving between a novel or *récit* and a film script or play. It is a striking example of Duras's refusal to be limited to traditional genres. The three destroying characters – to some extent interchangeable – are Stein, Max Thor and Max's young wife, Alissa. Perhaps mad in the eyes of conventional society, they set out to destroy the bourgeois conventionalism of Elisabeth Alione and of her husband Bernard. The action takes place in a dream-like hotel which seems also to be a convalescent home, to which Elisabeth has come after losing a child at birth, but also after some unexplained relationship with her doctor. She is perhaps being isolated because of a moral transgression. The 'destruction' is subtle, at the level of gestures, small phrases, an invitation to Elisabeth to go into the 'forest' (an obvious symbol of the unconscious). The 'destruction' is also allied to 'love'. Alissa seems poised between loving and hating Elisabeth. At the conclusion, in spite of their attacks on the Aliones' way of life, the trio wants Bernard to stay with them, as they could love him. (This scene, Duras said, is the most important in the book.)

The life which they advocate is one in which Alissa can be loved by both the men, without jealousy, in which Alissa and Max leave the window open so that Stein can watch them make love (again the voyeur scene prominent in Duras's work), a world in which, as Alissa tells Elisabeth, one can act on one's own, not needing the advice of others, a world in which in the future there are only children. Max teaches a university course on the 'History of the future', where nothing is left, so that there is nothing to say, and the students can sleep. It is a world of innocence, of love without barriers, of a metaphysical breakdown of identity, a dream of 'revolution', symbolised by the music that enters in the final scene.

Détruire, dit-elle comes out of the events of May 1968. In an interview with *Cahiers du cinéma*, Duras speaks of the political implications of the work. It is a work about destruction of all police, all memory, all judgement; it is about falling in line with ignorance and perhaps with madness. Stein and Thor are 'German Jews' because 'We are all German Jews', all strangers to the systems of state and society (the slogan comes from May 1968). What Duras wants to encourage is a freedom at the level of the individual, a freedom that she relates to that of the 'hippie'. Duras realises that this may be a Utopian position; it is definitely one that the interviewers from *Cahiers du cinéma* cannot fully accept.

L'Amour takes up again, but in a very different manner, the basic situation of *Le Ravissement de Lol V. Stein*. It goes beneath or beyond descriptions or interpretations of the emptiness of lives such as Lol's (or Anne Desbaresdes's, Anne-Marie Stretter's, Claire's) to convey this emptiness poetically, largely through descriptions of light, sound, the sea, geometric movements. Scene, language, pure movement have practically replaced plot and character. The characters are: 'a man who watches' (the traveller: 'We will name this man the traveller – if by chance that is necessary' [Duras, 1972, pp. 13–14]), 'another man, who walks' (the prisoner/guardian), 'a woman', on a beach near a calm sea.[8] Their initial movements are described in a kind of balletic geometry, as they constitute three points of a shifting triangle. This triangle might be contrasted to the 'rectangle of sunlight' (p. 96) in the scene where the traveller says farewell to his wife and two children. *L'Amour* is thus a striking example of what Carol Murphy has described as Duras's later style: 'a *mise-en-œuvre* of the lack which is at the basis of all writing'; a 'pure musicality ... replaces the verbal, logical and ordered narrative of traditional prose' (Murphy, 1982, p. 14, p. 143).

All this movement, because of its abstraction in *L'Amour*, leaves a naked emotion as the only certainty upon which the reader can focus. Yet the text itself is deliberately unemotional, restrained.

There is a breakdown of individual identity, and a destruction of any social roles. Desire, linked to death, is all that remains. In *L'Amour* no one says 'I love you', no one takes responsibility for being a subject with desires. We are here in the presence of characters who are reduced to a level of reflecting the desires of others, whose life seems essentially without any normal supports. The quality of the novel is produced by a contrast between the emptiness, both the lack of emotion in the actual words, and their spacing on the page; and the intensity of the destructive impulses felt beneath the surface. Yet, in a sense, nothing happens; there is no moment of drama, no resolution. There is only a feeling of destruction, as if the only act of salvation is to go beyond identity or emotion.

Paradoxically, as the novel is less realistic than anything Duras wrote earlier, the physical setting is more important. It is not, however, a natural setting. The action takes place in S. Thala (the S. Tahla of *Le Ravissement?*), which extends, the woman says, as far as the stream. Later the prisoner agrees, but then adds that S. Thala also extends beyond the stream. One can neither go beyond S. Thala, nor enter S. Thala. It is thus, logically, an impossible place. Light in S. Thala grows, then suddenly 'stops'; there are noises of the sea and the seagulls, which also 'stop'. The seagulls 'devour the body of sand' (Duras, 1972, p. 23). There is a group of people in the background, whom the woman describes as 'my inhabitants of S. Thala' (p. 38). None of this is initially plausible. The atmosphere is poetic; S. Thala is a state of mind. Beyond is perhaps nothing, the end of the world (the world of Duras's play *Yes, peut-être?*): 'they were many: millions ... everything is devastated' (p. 30). When the traveller asks the prisoner/guardian to say something about the story (or history), he replies: '– In my opinion, the island emerged first – he points to the sea – from there. S. Thala arrived afterwards, with the dust – he adds – you know? Time . . .' (p. 49). If there is a 'story' it is a kind of 'pre-history', of the beginning or the end of the universe.

The woman is hardly conscious of anything; her eyes are shut initially. She is 'looked at' (*elle est regardée*, p. 10), rather than 'looks', but is not aware of being 'looked at'. Her actions are the result of another's will: 'She advances moved by the will of the person who stopped behind her' (p. 34). When asked who she is, she replies 'The police have a number' (p. 39). She expects a child, but does not know who the father is. The prisoner/guardian says she is 'angry with God in general, it's nothing' (p. 46). She is 'an object of desire, she belongs to whoever wants her' (p. 50). All 'ego', all willpower has vanished. As for the prisoner/guardian 'the absence of his gaze is absolute' (p. 16). And the traveller is uncertain whether he has previously been in S. Thala. He writes, to some initially unidentified correspondent, not to come to S. Thala. But, for himself, he realises 'I have difficulty going away from her' (p. 47).

All this is mystery, initially, to the reader. We are told, however, that the story has begun before the arrival of the traveller. It is as if a series of movements, looks, disconnected bits of dialogue were the surface beneath which something is happening, beneath which there is a pattern that the reader must create. Gradually some events seem to become clarified as they relate to the past, to a story that seems to be that of Lol's abandonment during the ball, so that we can 'read' the woman on the beach as Lol after her second breakdown, as Lol when she has become mad. *L'Amour* thus depends on a *pre-text*, *Le Ravissement de Lol V. Stein*. The traveller goes into the entrance hall of a hotel, where the woman meets him; she recognises the place and the man, but initially this seems only because she saw him on the beach. Eventually, the woman and the traveller go together to the ballroom, where she remembers nothing, realises the futility of trying to recapture the past. What she can remember is her marriage to a musician, and her two children by him, but neither the ball when she was eighteen, nor the fathers of all her subsequent children. She remembers, in other words, the inessential, that which has no profound charge, no connection to her 'madness'.

The two men have also abandoned any projects in a rational world. The prisoner/guardian seems intent on destroying the world, on setting fire to S. Thala. He is the guardian of 'nothing' (p. 136). The traveller seems to have come to S. Thala because he is dying or wants to kill himself. There is a somewhat more realistic scene of his final encounter with his wife and children, in which he abandons them. The wife reacts emotionally. The children, perhaps more in tune with elemental truths, accept their father's action calmly. The traveller will remain with the woman. Is this because of love? Does he see in her a kind of madness, of openness to the irrational, that attracts him? Increasingly the reader becomes aware of the impossibility of establishing any clear sequence of events, of envisaging a setting for what is described that might conceivably exist in the normal world. Rather the world of S. Thala appears a world of the mad, who have abandoned any relationship to normal life, who live in an absolute state of primordial realities.

The style of the text is simplified to an extreme. Words and phrases are repeated; there seems to be no connection between sentences:

He said:
– Colour is disappearing.
Colour disappears.
Then, in turn, movement.
The last sea gulls have left.   (p. 26)

Yet this simplicity leads to no clarity. Rather, the discontinuity from one phrase to another suggests the world of the mad in which any analysable comprehensibility has vanished.[9] The point of view is that of the camera eye, recording movements, conversation, almost no connections between events. Descriptions often read as directions in a film script. The shifts in scene are a kind of *montage* from which any narrative continuity has been banished. Occasional references to the passing of time are simple ('Three days') and do not orient the reader within any normal chronological development.

The reader must construct the book. We are invited to enter a world in which what are considered normal drives, aggressions, will, even normal desires, even the 'love' of the title, have no meaning. *L'Amour* might thus be considered as the quintessence of the female mode, defined as receptivity to the natural world, denial of self-consciousness, negation of rationality. The woman, who cannot die, is said to 'go back into the dead dog' (p. 104). The traveller is also 'nothing' (p. 136). If the text could be compared to some of Beckett's work, it differs in that the woman, unlike Beckett's heroes, has no wish to consider, to think about, to remember, her situation. She accepts. To what extent are this reduction of fiction to the creation of an almost abstract atmosphere and this insistence on the need for destruction linked to something definable as a 'feminine' sensibility? Or are both the form and the theme expressions of Duras's individual sensibility, going beyond considerations of gender? In various interviews Duras has suggested that what she is doing is essentially feminine (although not, she would increasingly say, 'feminist'). Her distrust of traditional forms and rational language she has linked to being female, not part of a literary or cultural tradition:

> Men don't translate. They begin from a theoretical platform that is already in place, already elaborated. The writing of women is really translated from the unknown, like a new way of communicating rather than an already formed language. But to achieve that, we have to turn away from plagiarism. (Husserl-Kapit, 1975, p. 425)

Duras has suggested that she writes 'to lessen my importance. Let the book be important instead of me. To massacre myself, squander myself, *to be swallowed up in the parturition of the book*' (quoted in Gosselin, 1982, p. 167). This movement is particularly evident in *L'Amant*, another reworking, reliving of the past – the author's past and the past as described in earlier texts. *L'Amant* tells of Duras's love affair with the son of a rich Chinese businessman, when she was fifteen. It is incidentally about the racial tensions which this relationship provokes from both sides, but essentially it is about writing, sexual passion and desire, and how they are related.

The text exists in the interplay between past and present. The book begins by posing the question of why Duras's face became old suddenly, when she was eighteen. There is no strict chronological order; the narrative shifts from Duras's childhood to the death of her mother years later in France, or to her own experiences in wartime Paris, before returning again to childhood. There is, strictly, no past; what exists is not history, but a recreation. *L'Amant* is the past of Duras as she can recreate it only after having explored the essential emotions in her other works. While the girl's frankness, her admission that she needs money, her fear of her brother, may remind us of Suzanne in *Barrage*, the young girl differs in the intensity of her desire, in her need as well to be humiliated, insulted. *L'Amant*, Duras told an interviewer, 'is much closer to *Vice-consul* or *Lol V. Stein* than *Barrage*':[10]

> Before, I spoke of clear periods, those on which the light fell. Now I'm talking about the hidden stretches of that same youth, of certain facts, feelings, events that I buried. ... if [writing] is not, each time, all things confounded into one through some

inexpressible essence, then writing is nothing but advertisement. (Duras, 1984a, p. 8, pp. 14–15)

L'Amant, in other words, is an exploration of how Duras writes, of how she finds the essential, going to the depths, realising that the mystery of her relationship to her family will always remain hidden. 'I've never written, though I thought I wrote, never loved, though I thought I loved, never done anything but wait outside the closed door' (p. 25, p. 35).

Is there a logical contradiction when she claims now to be free from her family?

Now I don't love them any more. I don't remember if I ever did. I've left them. . . . It's over, I don't remember. That's why I can write about her [the mother] so easily now, so long, so fully. She's become just something you write without difficulty, cursive writing. (pp. 28–9, p. 38)

One feels that in *L'Amant* Duras is saying everything she can, both her detachment, and the sense in which she is always still attached to the loved and hated mother, that the two contradictory attitudes exist together. She has described the book as a means of coming to terms with her mother:

I had written *Le Barrage* to tell the world about the injustice of which she was a victim. I had to write *L'Amant* to return her to ordinary humanity, and perhaps to expose her royalty to the promiscuity and the sexual pleasure of her child. (Costaz, 1984, p. 28)

It is perhaps a measure of the difficulty of this task that the text shifts frequently between 'I' and 'she', as if admitting to having been the young girl enjoying sex with a Chinese businessman is still frightening, as if she sometimes is the girl, sometimes wants to distance herself.

L'Amant is about passion, sexual passion and the passions of life in the family. It is not about love. In an interview, Duras is explicit:

It was not a love which declared itself there. It was an entrance into desire. Violent, stronger than I was. . . . When I speak of lovers without love that's what I'm speaking about in the book.

At the place where feelings don't enter, where happiness is the
happiness of suffering, of humiliation.   (Costaz, 1984, p. 29)

As soon as she steps into the Chinese limousine, the young girl
knows that she has made an essential choice. There is a feeling of
fatality: 'It's as if this must be not only what she expects, but also
what had to happen especially to her' (Duras, 1984, p. 36, p. 47).
With her first sexual experience, she realises both the power her
mother has held over the children and her mother's own ignorance
of sexual pleasure. In its combination of thoughts about her family
and her need for physical pleasure, the description of this first
scene of love-making is of a rare directness and emotional power.

The conflict that she feels from the beginning between family
and lover is especially intense because of her recognition of the
power of her older brother over her, and of her power over him. A
passionate desire to triumph over him, even to kill him, is also
present. She blames him for the death of her younger brother, a
death which changed her relationship to her mother:

Everything came to an end that day. I never asked her any more
questions about our childhood, about herself. She died, for me,
of my younger brother's death. So did my elder brother. I never
got over the horror they inspired in me then. They don't mean
anything to me any more.   (p. 28, p. 37)

Over and over again the text comes back to the constatation that
the older son, who steals from the mother, gambles, tries to sell his
sister, who later turns in Jews in occupied Paris, is the only loved
child. *L'Amant* is as much an evocation of the power of the family
as of the power of sexual desire:

I'm still part of the family, it's there I live, to the exclusion of
everywhere else. It's in its aridity, its terrible harshness, its
malignance, that I'm most deeply sure of myself, at the heart of
my essential certainty, the certainty that later on I'll be a
writer.   (p. 75, p. 93)

Family power is exercised as well by the Chinese father, who
refuses his son's pleas to accept the white girl, who would prefer to
see his son dead than with her.

The novel is filled with detailed indications of Duras's life at the age of fifteen, details which, she feels, make the reader see the young girl more clearly than any analysis. If the style is simpler than that of many of her novels, the structure is similar in its reliance on *montage*. Scenes of life with her mother and brothers are interspersed with scenes with her lover. Suddenly in the midst of the story of her early life, she moves to reminiscences about life in Paris during the war, about those she knew, both collaborators and resistance partisans. It is a world of shallow pretence in comparison to the world of her mother, brothers and lover.

Duras speaks of herself as a young white prostitute in the eyes of others, of her moral degeneracy, of her need to feel humiliated. Desire is accompanied by humiliation; it is also perverse. Of her friend, Hélène Lagonelle, more beautiful, more innocent, Duras says:

> I'd like to give Hélène Lagonelle to the man who does that to me, so he may do it in turn to her. I want it to happen in my presence, I want her to do it as I wish. . . . It's via Hélène Lagonelle's body, through it, that the ultimate pleasure would pass from him to me. A pleasure unto death. (p. 74, p. 92)

The voyeurism of Duras's work has an evident source here. In *L'Amant* she also describes the sources for two of the dominant female types in her novels and the reason for their prominence in her work. When she was eight years old she first encountered a mad woman, the source for the beggar of *Le Vice-consul*. She fears the mad woman because of the yet unacknowledged madness of her mother. Some years later, she realised that her mother's 'identity' might also disappear into madness. Is the beggar's abandoning of her children connected to Duras's feeling that her mother sacrificed her younger children to her eldest? A parallel is also suggested between the woman who served as a source for Anne-Marie Stretter and Duras herself; both cause the despair of their lovers, both are social outcasts. Perhaps the younger brother, whose death at twenty-seven made Duras feel she too was dead, is the source of the young, weak, unaggressive but sensitive men in her fiction: 'My younger brother had nothing to cry in the wilderness, he had nothing to say, here or anywhere, nothing. He was uneducated. . . . He was someone who didn't understand and was afraid' (p. 106, p. 129). Perhaps, as well, the attraction towards violence in her work has its source in her hatred of her elder brother. In its refusal to gloss over what may seem morally repugnant, in its denial of any excuses, as well as in its deep analysis of the relationship between mother and daughter, *L'Amant* may seem particularly feminine. There is no attempt at justification of a life, no moralising.

Duras's world is a difficult, almost unliveable world. Women are dispossessed, have no illusions, find that the slightest gesture requires an effort of will. Duras has said that all the women in her books have their source in Lol V. Stein, in a 'certain forgetting of themselves' (Duras, 1987, p. 32). They are always attracted towards love (often seem incapable of existing without a passionate attachment either in the present or, more often, in the past), yet love is linked to death. They are usually attracted to men who are also dispossessed, who are outside bourgeois coventionality – Chauvin, Monsieur Jo, the Vice-Consul – or share some feminine traits. Jacques Hold describes feeling, as he listens to Lol and Tatiana, 'similarly feminine voices which seem but one voice when they reach me' (Duras, 1985, p. 83, p. 92). As Xavière Gauthier has noted, there are hardly any fathers in all Duras's work, the exception being the father of Aurélia Steiner, and, as he is Jewish, he is 'marginal'.[11] Duras's families are filled with tensions, with a mixture of love and hatred. As she has said, 'There is always in relationships in the family something hateful.... We are not destined to live together' (Duras, 1984b, p. 93). As the novelist remarks in *L'Amante anglaise*, Claire and Marie-Thérèse got along well, without any quarrels for seventeen years, until Claire killed Marie-Thérèse.

The triangle set up by the three characters in *L'Amour*, which seems initially a spatial triangle, a series of balletic movements, is also a triangle of desire. Desire for Duras is almost always linked to the vision of another. In *Moderato cantabile* desire is mediated through the experience of another couple, but in the later novels desire is often expressed in a three-fold relationship: Lol, Michael Richardson and Anne-Marie Stretter, then Lol, Tatiana Karl and Jacques Hold; Anne-Marie Stretter, the Vice-Consul and Charles Rossett, or the beggar, Anne-Marie and Peter Morgan; Claire, Pierre and Alfonso, or Claire, Marie-Thérèse and the 'novelist'. There are, in other words, various permutations, but the emphasis is always on the need for one person's desire for another to be *seen*, *watched* by a third person. Perhaps the most explicitly erotic example is the narrator watching the man and the woman in

L'Homme assis dans le couloir (*The Seated Man in the Passage*, 1980). The psychology involved is a curious kind of voyeurism, as well as exhibitionism. The most intense emotions described are often those of the third person.

Is the triangular desire in Duras's work related to the mediated desire described by René Girard? For Girard, desire is not direct and spontaneous, but always develops in response to a mediator. A (the subject) loves B (the object) because he knows that C (the mediator) loves B. If A and C are not too far separated by physical or temporal or social distance, A will see C as a rival: 'As the distance between mediator and subject decreases, the difference diminishes, the comprehension becomes more acute and the hatred more intense' (Girard, 1965, p. 73). The mediated desire that Girard examines, in various works by Proust and Stendhal, for instance, seems competitive, aggressive, masculine in essence. Romantic passion, for Girard, is a 'war waged by two rival vanities' (p. 108). The triangular desire of Duras's characters is different, and, we might argue, particularly feminine, whether the desiring character is, in fact, male or female. Lol does not want to recapture Michael Richardson from Anne-Marie Stretter, but wants to imagine their love-making, wants to share an identity. The rival is not actively hated; in so far as there is a destructive impulse it is directed at the self, not at the other. The desire is to *see* the mediator with the object of desire – an emotion having less to do with rivalry than with a losing of the self.

As Toril Moi has shown, Girard's mimetic triangle is based on a rivalry with the father, and is basically concerned with masculine desire. There is no place for the infant's pre-Oedipal desire for the mother (Moi, 1982). A reading of Duras's work, and her own reflections on her mother and their love/hate relationship, shows the difference in female desire from Girard's model. Rather than desire being mediated by a rival who is also in love with the object, desire is mediated, for Duras, by the mother who is not the rival, but the body with whom the lover desires reunion. The imitative desire of Duras's heroines seems finally to be an attempt to share the erotic experience with the maternal figure. In *L'Amant*, in spite of the professed detachment from the mother, the girl's affair with her Chinese lover is a way of making up to the mother, at least financially, for her suffering. She would like to share more with her mother: 'We looked at each other for some time, then she gave a sweet, slightly mocking smile, full of so deep a knowledge of her children and what awaited them later on that I almost told her about Cholon. But I didn't. I never did' (Duras, 1984, p. 93, p. 114). For Hélène Cixous, Duras's work is menacing in its sense of impotence, but this impotence is, she feels, allied to 'an extraordinary quantity of love' (Cixous and Foucault, 1975b, p. 19), a love which is above all tactile, not visual. Desire then becomes the need to touch, to join – a need which would seem the contrary of the visual triangle of Girard's mediated desire. Desire and destruction, eroticism and violence, are always linked. This may be the essential key to the feminine perspective of Duras's work. Her heroines are basically passive, willing victims of aggression. They want to lose their identity, to merge with another in a moment of desire which is also a moment of death.

Duras's position might be related to Derridean deconstruction in that she wants to examine polarities in order to reverse them: 'Reverse everything. Make women the point of departure in judging, make darkness the point of departure in judging what men call light, make obscurity the point of departure in judging what men call clarity' (Husserl-Kapit, 1975, p. 426). This is not, however, a revaluation that says 'intuition' and 'emotion' are good, but a redefinition of terms. In the interview, Susan Husserl-Kapit attempts to read Duras's novels in terms of conventional masculine and feminine qualities and says that Duras's female characters are more 'masculine' than her male characters because they are more 'active'. For Duras the distinction is on another plane: 'activity' has been 'redefined' to imply an ability to occupy space, a willingness to talk. 'Power' is not authority: women 'have a power that is almost involuntary. That's it, it isn't directed. It *is*. It's the difference between "being" and "appearing". It is power that operates directly, that functions directly. The women go straight into action without any programming' (p. 427). Creation, for Duras, is the use of this power, a power that is not analytic:

> everything shuts off – the analytic way of thinking, thinking inculcated by college, studies, reading, experience. I'm absolutely sure of what I'm telling you now. It's as if I were returning to a wild country. Nothing is concerted. Perhaps, before everything else, before being Duras, I am – simply – a woman.   (p. 428)

The emphasis on remembering, on recreating the past, might also be seen as particularly feminine. Time does not progress in a linear fashion. but rather circles continually, is repetitive, spirals around a series of themes, of seminal events that cannot be recaptured. The need to *be seen* is also essentially feminine: the construction of the self as an object of desire for the gaze of the masculine other, a tactic used to gain material possessions by Suzanne in *Barrage*, becomes a way both of asserting a kind of identity and of merging that identity with the gaze of the other.

There is, at the *intradiegetic* level (where the narrator appears as narrator in the story) no female narrator in most of Duras's work: the detective in *L'Amante anglaise* is male, Peter Morgan tells the beggar's story in *Le Vice-consul*, Jacques Hold tells Lol's. Even the narrative *on* in several works (which is variously 'you', 'we', 'one') is unstable, fluctuating, does not allow us to place a narrator in authority. The first woman to write in Duras's work is Aurélia Steiner (whose mother is dead) (Borgomano, 1985, p. 83). The major exception to a male or an ungendered narrator, however, is *L'Amant*, where the narrative voice is variously Marguerite Duras as an older woman, Marguerite Duras as a fifteen-year-old, or an unidentifiable 'she'. It is as if she cannot fully assume the task of establishing an identity as narrator until *L'Amant* (after the death of her own mother, of course), and even here the voice shifts radically. If there is no clear narrative voice doing the telling, there is also no story prior to the *telling* of the story. We have not only the death of the author, but the death of the story. There is not even a setting. Duras says of the ball in *Le Ravissement de Lol V. Stein*, 'I see it occurring in two places'. If this is contradictory, 'What difference does it make?' (Duras, 1974, p. 130). All that remains is a voice, that may be interpreted as exposing the difficulty of a *woman's* entry into the realm of the dominant discourse, but also, more profoundly, as deconstructing any theatrical space, leaving only pure desire and pure horror.[12]

Duras has often spoken of her writing as allied to madness, to a loss of rationality: 'I never know very well where I am going: if I knew, I wouldn't write' (Duras, 1977, p. 37); 'When I write, I feel in an extreme state of concentration. I no longer possess myself, I am myself a strainer ... there are things I don't recognise in what I write' (p. 98). She has identified madness as a particularly feminine experience. Madness is a withdrawal into an imagined past. Madness is also a desire for destruction, whether of the self or of another – often the two are linked. In some of the later works, the desire for destruction extends to the world. This madness is apparent in the style of her work, at least from *Moderato cantabile* onward. The settings become increasingly unrealistic; if S. Thala in *L'Amour* is a state of mind, so is the Vice-Consul's India. The return to a kind of realistic detail in *L'Amant* is continually subverted by the interplay of past and present, real and imaginary photos. 'Madness' as Duras uses the term seems to indicate particularly an openness to the world resulting from a progressive loss of personal identity. There are always 'holes', 'blank spaces' in the ego, which is not a unified personality. The deliberate simplicity of syntax, the eliminations of accumulated detail, the 'silence' of the texts seem an attempt to capture the irrational, to move into a realm where a word, a simple gesture is all that is left as a handle on normality.

In an interesting analysis of Duras's style, Dominique Noguez speaks of the use of 'parataxis', a rhetorical device which is the opposite of ellipsis or resumé; every event is decomposed into a 'series of its phases, moment by moment'. Parataxis, Noguez says is 'the sign of a slow conquest of what is uncertain', though perhaps with Duras we might add that the uncertain is never completely conquered. Duras writes 'narrative texts that refuse closure through the instability of their narrating agency'.[13]

In a *Cahiers du cinéma* interview concerning *Détruire, dit-elle*, Duras speaks of her creative activity after *Moderato cantabile* as proceeding from a deliberate emptying of thought, in a state close to fear. As a result, there are elements in her work which remain obscure to her, incapable of rational interpretation. This plunging into obscurity is, however, only one side of the story. She is also, on another level, conscious of using certain kinds of techniques, of, for instance, creating an openness in the text, multiple possible readings, so that the reader has a more important role. Her various comments on how she works suggest that the subject matter comes from unconscious depths, but that at the same time at least minimal formal decisions are made at a more rational level.[14] Her comments on politics are similarly divided: on the one hand she wants to reach a destruction of all systems, a kind of vacuum from which individual sensitivity can emerge; on the other hand, she speaks in more rational terms of what amounts to influencing the readers and spectators of her work towards a rejection of society. In other words, the work remains political, or anti-political, but in any case purposeful, even as it is also about doing away with purpose. Duras frequently speaks of her need to go beyond rational analysis in order to write; in some of her interviews, where she castigates 'male' reliance on abstraction, she seems to show an increasing distrust of the intellect. It is always, however, only the creative impulse that needs to be liberated from rationality. In terms of her own life, Duras seems to value rationality. When, for example, she speaks of the fascination she felt at one time for the Communist Party, she criticises it as a mistake. The militant is lost. 'When you have lost your ability to analyse, your perceptivity disappears, then your identity' (Costaz, 1984, p. 29).

There is not, however, finally, any attempt on Duras's part to find an essential feminine essence, but rather to give voice to a specific way of existing as a woman, her way, with its particularities. As she says in *Les Parleuses*, 'I cannot believe that Lol V. Stein is *Woman*' (Duras, 1974, p. 160). And in *La Vie matérielle*, 'I don't even write for women. I write about women in order to write about myself, about only myself throughout the centuries' (Duras, 1987, p. 53).[15]

8
Monique Wittig

In order to find her own image she must liberate the mirror
from the *images of woman* painted on it by a male hand.
(Weigel, 1985, p. 61)

Humankind must find another name for itself and another
system of grammar that will do away with genders, the
linguistic indicator of political oppositions.
(Wittig, 1979, p. 121)

Verena Aebischer distinguishes four categories of how women
react to difference (Aebischer, 1985, pp. 68ff). The first two groups
believe in difference: *la femme traditionnelle* accepts a subordinate
role and finds it beneficial to her; *la femme nouvelle* lays claim to a
specificity that men have wanted to destroy, and wants to find a
feminine identity rather as Cixous looks for *l'écriture féminine*. There
are also two groups who deny difference: *la femme moderne*, who
feels intelligence has no sex, who wants equality with men, and
prefers the masculine world (a category into which, I have suggested, Yourcenar might fit); and the suffragette, a category which
seems appropriate to Monique Wittig, those whose aim is to
analyse oppression and fight against it, who refuse to accept an
essential biological specificity for each sex (in Wittig's case this
becomes praise of the lesbian as the individual who denies the
distinction masculine/feminine), but who also see any dialogue
with men as being impossible. For Wittig, what is particular to
women is not a style of speaking, but a project, a fight to change
the status quo. Wittig's work as a creative writer aims at portraying
women, not as they are seen by men, nor as they see themselves in
reaction to men, but as individuals whose identity does not
depend upon a concept of difference.

L'Opoponax (*The Opoponax*, 1964) is a *Bildungsroman* which recounts the life of a girl from early childhood until the age of about
eighteen, at the conclusion of secondary school. The narrator

164

registers various events in the life of a group of children in a small village. There are school lessons, games in the countryside, several deaths, many chances to observe the world of insects and animals:

> You realize that this is the sound made by all the insects who are flying at that moment, that it is a very loud noise completely separate from the sound of the people who are in the fields. You realize from this drone that there is a different world to which you can't possibly belong.   (Wittig, 1964, p. 120, p. 133)

Initially *L'Opoponax* is a portrait of childhood in which differences between the sexes are unimportant. From the point of view of the child narrator, there are little girls and little boys, but their behaviour does not differ fundamentally; little girls also like to urinate in groups and watch the puddles they form. They can be very cruel to an unacceptable new girl in the school. Their games consist of spider races, climbing trees, fights, feeding tadpoles to serpents, not playing with dolls. No one seems particularly interested in Robert, who wants to show his 'thing' (*quequette*). (Is it only by chance, however, that Robert dies?)

By beginning with very young children, Wittig bypasses to some extent the problems of how the adult woman's psychic life has been influenced by the society in which she has lived. Some incidents indicate that the women whom the children observe are oppressed, but from the children's point of view this sexually determined oppression is not evident. A mother complains about her sick husband: 'Last night he yelled because the soup was scalding hot, scalding he said I'm going to throw it in your face you do it on purpose, on purpose, me, on purpose, me' (p. 25, p. 28). But the narrator's reaction is: 'The lady has a funny smell. Like apples rotting under the tree' (p. 25, p. 28). She describes the pictures of Charlemagne in her school books, commenting on the lesson to be drawn from the juxtaposition of rich and poor children, and then remarks simply 'There aren't any little girls in the picture' (p. 94, p. 104). Thus Wittig is able both to indicate problems in the life of women and to avoid discussing their influence on the life of the girl children directly.

L'Opoponax is about love and its various manifestations. There are, to begin with, children who help the slow or disabled (although there are also children simply curious to see what is wrong). There are boys and girls who play together, helping one another with their projects. There are children who band together against adults, whether irate property owners or overly strict teachers. This love among children, which of course does not preclude much teasing and fighting, is hardly extended to the adult world. There are many lists of names of children. The only adults named are the teachers, who normally have religious names. (The exceptions are 'Mademoiselle' and 'Mme La Porte', no more personal than *'ma mère de l'enfant Jésus'*.) While Catherine stretches her hands as far apart as possible to show how much she loves her mother, the mother is not a character of any importance in Catherine's narrative.

The major love theme is the developing love between Catherine and Valerie Borge. Catherine's passion for Valerie is evident in her description of Valerie's hair as observed during a mass for the dead. The nuns are here, as Marguerite Duras observed, 'blind witnesses of a far more dazzling bliss than theirs' (Duras, 1983, p. 286). It is a love expressed most forcefully and physically through their fights as they greet each other at the beginning of a new school year:

> You see them rolling in the dust on top of each other, pulling each other, pushing each other, hitting each other trying to get away, Valerie Borge and Catherine Legrand are wrestling, Valerie Borge twists one of Catherine Legrand's wrists and Catherine Legrand twists her arm to make her let go. (p. 233, p. 256)

(This kind of fighting will be magnified immensely in the description of the lesbian lovers in *Le Corps lesbien*.) There is in *L'Opoponax* no physical sexual activity beyond this fight. Love is rather a slowly developing emotion, expressed through an exchange of notes in school, and through glances: 'Catherine Legrand wanders around the playground and wherever she is she never stops looking at Valerie Borge even when she is walking' (p. 207, p. 228). Especially important is Catherine's invention of her role as the opoponax. (The 'opoponax' is in reality a plant with yellow flowers. The correct spelling is 'opopanax' but the form Catherine chooses is a common error.) Her opoponax is an indefinable being:

> You can't describe it because it never has the same form. Kingdom, neither animal, nor vegetable nor mineral, in other words indeterminate. Humor, variable. (p. 162, p. 179)

And it's also him when you feel something run over your face when you're lying in bed in the dark. (p. 163, p. 180)

If you have trouble combing your hair in the morning you mustn't be surprised. He is everywhere. He is in your hair. (p. 208, p. 230)

The opoponax is thus a figure for someone beyond classification, the little girl who loves other little girls:

I began to write when I was about twelve or thirteen, when I had fallen in love with a little girl: I therefore had access to a double forbidden realm, not even named by those I knew: female homosexuality and writing. Besides, my language was the only way to give a reality to this experience that was denied, impossible. (Wittig, 1974, p. 24)

The love described in *L'Opoponax* – both the general love among the children and Catherine's love for Valerie – is at odds with the love that has been codified in the language and the culture that Catherine studies in school, based on a false conception of the sexes, a duality that does not correspond with Catherine's experience. As a very young child, she is told about a ghost who leaves his tomb to suck blood from the throats of his victims. The teacher swears it is a true story, as she knew a man who 'managed to escape because he was a man and because he didn't lose his self-control' (Wittig, 1964, p. 82, pp. 90–1). Another story, about how a fairy helps a princess go to the ball (a variant of Cinderella told by one of the children) is based on female passivity. Catherine reads *La Nouvelle Héloïse*, perhaps the epitome of stories of female sacrifice. Raphael is praised for 'madonnas glowing with youth, freshness and chaste motherhood' (p. 149, p. 166). The students present a dramatisation of a mediaeval story of stylised love (amusing as both male and female parts are played by girls, a fact of which Catherine is naturally aware). Latin texts that Catherine studies as she grows up are based on romanticisation of the female body:

Braided pearls bound to her temples fell to the corners of her parted lips, which were pink as a pomegranate. On her bosom there lay a variety of luminous gems that rivaled the scales of the muraena.   (p. 132, p. 147)

The 'parted lips, which were pink as a pomegranate' is a good example of the kind of metaphor for the female body that Wittig's *guerillères* want to suppress. Here, she indicates the falsity of the description by the sentence that follows: 'Catherine Legrand asks Vincent Parme what a muraena is. Vincent Parme says, Leave me alone.'

In Wittig's later texts she stresses that women must be aware of their bodies, and describes the female body very concretely: 'Indeed, one of the primary tasks of "lesbian writing" is to strip the female body of its heavy burden of metaphor and imagery imposed by male culture and to trace the steps necessary to restore the body intact to women' (Crowder, 1983, p. 119). In *L'Opoponax*, which is more traditional in structure and not so directly political in theme, the female body is described less technically and less forcefully than in *Les Guerillères* or *Le Corps lesbien*, but still concretely and without metaphors:

You rock your body back and forth. At first very gently then harder and harder. Finally it rocks so hard back and forth that your hands lose their grip and you fall face down into the nettles, bare arms, bare legs, bare thighs.   (Wittig, 1964, p. 74, p. 82)

Catherine Legrand sees Valerie Borge in profile with her hair lifted, she sees the descending arch of the left eyebrow the temple the cheekbone the cheek the line of the jaw the neck, Valerie Borge's hands are resting on the lowered window-pane.   (p. 245, p. 269)

The narrator says *'on'*. This *on* is not the general 'we' or 'everyone' of normal French usage, but a particular person (translated in the English version as 'you'): 'The Dies Irae takes up two pages in the missal. It is the first time you have heard it' (p. 171, p. 189); 'You look at Valerie Borge who is staring into space and who is far away, you don't know where. You ask Valerie Borge in a whisper where she is but she doesn't hear' (p. 196, p. 216). The identity of the narrative voice that says *'on'*, however, is not clear until later in the novel, when it becomes evident that she is

Catherine Legrand. She always refers to herself in the third person, even when also using first-person pronouns: 'Catherine Legrand has put the whip under her arm as she has seen [my] Uncle do' ('Catherine Legrand a mis le fouet sous le bras comme elle a vu mon oncle le faire') (p. 105, p. 117). Wittig has said that the *on* shows the passivity of women, the difficulty of assuming an identity (Wittig, 1974, p. 24). Luce Irigaray has suggested that in the development of the subject's use of personal pronouns, *on* is the 'refuge of subjectivity, the closest to the "zero" that establishes subjectivity, or to the unconscious that underlies it' (Irigaray, 1985b, p. 22). Wittig's use of *on* for the narrative voice of Catherine Legrand in *L'Opoponax* would seem at least partially a confirmation of such a theory. *On* is also, of course, a pronoun not specific to one gender, and thus may to some degree be a refusal of assignment to a particular sexual role.

Because *L'Opoponax* is told from a child's perspective, the style bears certain surface similarities to *l'écriture féminine*: organisation is fluid, one incident leading into another with no logical connection between them; there are no paragraphs, no signposts to guide the reader in a rational fashion. There are not, however, the multivalent layers of meaning found, for instance, in Cixous's work, nor the ellipses of the work of Marguerite Duras. Where there are seeming uncertainties, the reader can resolve them by putting herself in the position of a child, often by visualising a scene from a particular physical perspective:

> Reine Dieu is at the blackboard. She is making a mess of her multiplication. The board is behind Mademoiselle's platform, so that Mademoiselle turns halfway around in her chair and twists her neck to watch her. From the side you can see her bun and half of her glasses, one of the steel rims with glass in it. The sum is hooked behind her ear. (p. 57, p. 63; I have corrected the English translation here)

The child narrator is, in fact, a sort of natural Berkeleyian; what exists is what is perceived and, it seems, because it is perceived: 'When you look up there is a kind of flashing in the trees' (p. 203, p. 224). The outside world is not so much dominated by a narrator who sees herself at the centre (the theory of the masculine narrator as advanced by Claudine Herrmann) as fluctuating, unstable, only really there when one looks at it. Reality is not a stable entity, but a relation between subject and object. Spatial relations between objects depend upon where the observer is placed ('The sum is hooked behind her ear'), so that the validity of how one sees is never questioned. Similarly temporal connections are personal, memories following one another. Equivalent in value are the geography lesson of Madame La Porte, the marks she gives the students, and her pale gums and dripping saliva. Events cease to exist when the narrator is no longer there to observe, or when they are no longer of interest to her:

> When she turns around laughing and sees the looks on your faces she gets all red and you can't talk her into jumping up the wall again. Since the beginning of the history lesson Mademoiselle has been talking about Charlemagne who became emperor in the year 800.   (p. 93, p. 103)

We should hesitate, however, to term this a feminine point of view, since it is so clearly in *L'Opoponax* a child's point of view.

The style is full of simple repetitions; Catherine's way of looking at the world is conveyed through the use of a child's logic: 'The little fat girl whose name is Brigitte because she is fat' (p. 8, pp. 9–10); 'maybe they don't fly in this kind of a country. What is a country? It is where you are. Then where you aren't is not a country? No' (pp. 12–13, p. 15). There are frequent rather awkward constructions: 'All the water on them gets on your clothes so that your arms, your shirts, your legs and your thighs are all soaking wet' (p. 134, p. 149); 'The mass is sung slowly so that each prayer which is normally very short is repeated several times today and drawn out by the singing' (p. 170, p. 189). Especially prevalent in the latter part of the novel is this use of *ce qui* (more awkward than the English translation 'so that') to indicate why one event follows another, or to give an explanation. Another frequent stylistic device is the use of lists of nouns, whether names of the pupils, or names of flowers, and more rarely, a series of thoughts: 'you say', 'you say', 'you say' (p. 252, p. 276). This use of lists, as it continues in Wittig's later work, cannot be considered as peculiar to the child's style. Elaine Marks considers the use of lists of nouns as part of the deliberate provocation of Wittig's work (Marks, 1979, p. 376).

Les Guerillères (*The Guerillères*, 1969) is the story of a band of women who are fighting patriarchal society, and who are also establishing a consciousness of their own identity as a prerequisite for victory. Although it is not a novel, there is a progression in the short prose passages. It is a feminist rewriting of other texts, many of them listed at the end of the book. Thus as well as an attack on a society constructed according to sexual difference, it is an attack on the literature of difference and the vocabulary of difference:

> They say that in the first place the vocabulary of every language is to be examined, modified, turned upside down, that every word must be screened.   (Wittig, 1969, p. 134, p. 192)

Many of the stylistic devices of *L'Opoponax* are continued in *Les Guerillères*, especially the lists of names to produce an impression of fulness and continuity, rather than a division into logical categories. Indeed, an important theme is the distrust of logic and especially of binary divisions:

> I say that that which is is. I say that that which is not also is. When she repeats the phrase several times the double, then triple, voice endlessly superimposes that which is and that which is not.   (p. 14, p. 17)

(This thought is attributed to Phenarete, the mother of Socrates, and a midwife in fifth-century BC Greece. Socrates used the phrase 'give birth to minds' for his process of leading his disciples to find their own solution to problems, and attributed the phrase to the influence of his mother. Wittig, in recalling Phenarete, shows how little of the influence of women throughout history has become part of our cultural heritage.) Another important element of style is the use of precise vocabulary, especially in descriptions of the female body: 'They say that the clitoris is an erectile organ. It is stated that it bifurcates to right and left, that it is angled, extending as two erectile bodies applied to the pubic bones' (p. 23, p. 29).[1] This precision does not, however, preclude, especially in the first part of the text, an abundance of metaphors and symbols: 'They say that the clitoris has been compared to a cherry-stone, a bud, a young shoot, a shelled sesame' (p. 32, p. 42). The most prevalent female symbol is the 'O', the circle, the 'vulva ring' (p. 14, p. 16); the 'O' is an image of inclusion, a rejection of duality. Some descriptions rework classical mythology, such as pubic hair becoming the golden fleece. Other metaphors are less symbolic, but more striking: 'They say that the pubic hair is like a spider's web that captures the rays' (p. 19, p. 24).

But they also say that 'they have no need of myths or symbols' (p. 30, p. 38). They realise that metaphors cannot be used to glorify female genitalia, on a simple reversal of phallic worship.[2] Metaphors and symbols are for the first part of the battle:

> The women say that they perceive their bodies in their entirety. They say that they do not favour any of its parts on the grounds that it was formerly a forbidden object. They say that they do not want to become prisoners of their own ideology. They say that they did not garner and develop the symbols that were necessary to them at an earlier period to demonstrate their strength.   (p. 57, pp. 80–1)

Thus Wittig's text works to prevent any romanticisation of the female. The vulva is not a replacement for the phallus:

> They do not say that the vulva is the primal form which as such describes the world in all its extent, in all its movement.   (p. 61, p. 86)

> They say they must now stop exalting the vulva. They say that they must break the last bond that binds them to a dead culture.   (p. 72, p. 102)

Also rejected, finally, is a language resulting from drugs and irrationality, which in Wittig's description sounds rather like Cixous's *écriture féminine*:

> Around the tables, under the influence of the drugs, they engage in discourses which pile up paradoxes absurdities logomachies fallacies sophistries. At a certain point someone challenges the speakers, calling a halt, demanding reasoning devoid of error. Then the women all fall silent and go to sleep.   (p. 61, p. 85)

Another important feature of the style is the use of pronouns. There is a narrative voice, which uses *on*, frequently with the connotation of a first-person observer, as in *L'Opoponax*, and which comments on the women warriors, referred to as *elles*. Only at the end of the book does the pronoun *nous* occur, when the narrator is united with all women in singing the Internationale. This use of pronouns produces a certain distance between the action and the telling, a distance consonant with the epic works being retold, but a distance that also reminds us of the mythic nature of the story. The women fighters and their victory are still imaginary, not a realistic tale.

Although 'opoponax' is the name of a real plant, Catherine Legrand uses the word to refer to an imaginary being. Similarly in her later work Monique Wittig invents names for imaginary creatures, or uses words in unexpected senses. An important lexical remodelling is, of course, the title itself. *Guerrière* is a female warrior. *Guerillères* seems to be an invented female form of 'guerilla', the guerilla forces fighting a war of independence against an initially stronger entrenched power. The women read a *féminaire* (feminary), a book of their creed but without doctrinal closure. The feminaries have many blank pages and many pages with only a few words in capital letters (as does, of course, *Les Guerillères* itself). More radically, the feminaries may not all contain the same text. The world of the women warriors is a rejection of authority:

> These are either multiple copies of the same original or else there are several kinds. (Wittig, 1969, p. 14, p. 17)

> As regards the feminaries the women say for instance that they have forgotten the meaning of one of their ritual jokes. (p. 44, p. 60)

Eventually they even reject their own texts: 'the women say that it may be that the feminaries have fulfilled their function' (p. 49, p. 67).

Many of the tales the women tell are reworkings of classical history and mythology.[3] The women reread legends and fairy tales in terms of female meanings:

> They say it is impossible to mistake the symbolism of the Round Table that dominated their meetings. . . . There is the story of her who fell asleep for a hundred years from having wounded her finger with her spindle, the spindle being cited as the symbol of the clitoris. (pp. 45–6, p. 62)

Perhaps the most striking reinvention is the story of Eve, who becomes a naked black woman with snakes as hair, and who, through eating the fruit of the garden, gains knowledge that has been hidden from women: 'the woman of the orchard will have a clear understanding of the solar myth that all the texts have deliberately obscured' (p. 52, p. 73).[4] The women reclaim history. They remember their sufferings under male domination, when they were not passive victims but dangers to the establishment. And they remember a time prior to the patriarchy: 'There was a time when you were not a slave, remember that'. Matriarchy is an essential myth: 'Make an effort to remember. Or, failing that, invent' (p. 89, pp. 126–7).

Duality and authority are rejected. The women accept many goddesses: 'The women say that any one of them might equally well invoke another sun goddess' (p. 27, p. 35). 'Order' becomes a word without meaning: 'When they repeat, this order must be destroyed, they say they do not know what order is meant' (p. 30, p. 38). Commentaries on the stories that the women tell (for in spite of the 'feminaries' this is largely an oral culture) are not recommended; no one is to impose her interpretation (a comment as well on the fluidity of Wittig's text, perhaps). Wittig describes labyrinthian walks: 'Whatever the itinerary, whatever point of departure they choose, they end up at the same place' (p. 69, p. 97). The Pascalian definition of God becomes Wittig's image of a world without duality: 'It is virtually that infinite sphere whose centre is everywhere, circumference nowhere' (p. 69, p. 97). In contrast is mechanistic reasoning which leads to defining women in terms of opposition to man:

> It deploys a series of terms which are systematically related to opposite terms. Its theses are so crass that the thought of them makes the women start laughing violently.   (p. 80, p. 112)

The warriors play a game, mocking men's views of women. They reject the vocabulary of men; they look for the spaces in male language, 'all that which is not a continuation' (p. 114, p. 164).

Finally, however, if reworking myths, finding new metaphors and creating a new language are important, more important is political action:

> They say, let those who call for a new language first learn violence. They say, let those who want to change the world first seize all the rifles.   (p. 85, pp. 120–1)

The last part of *Les Guerillères* is more concerned with practical tactics; as well as using flame-throwers, the warriors lead men on seductively to entrap them:

> Then the women, at a signal, uttering a terrible cry, suddenly rip off the upper part of their garments, uncovering their naked gleaming breasts. The men, the enemy, begin to discuss what they unanimously regard as a gesture of submission.   (pp. 99–100, p. 143)

At the end there is a mixture of violence and non-violence, of armed revolt and the flower power of the late 1960s: 'The women cry out and run towards the young men arms laden with flowers which they offer them saying, Let all of this have a meaning' (p. 122, p. 176). After winning their war, 'They wish the survivors, both male and female, love strength youth, so that they may form a lasting alliance that no future dispute can compromise' (p. 128, p. 184). The references to young men with long hair who join the warriors, and the suggestion that Flora Tristan was right to see women's struggle as allied to the class struggle, remind us that *Les Guerillères* is a product of a particular era. The note of hope at the conclusion unfortunately contrasts with the 'hell' Wittig will describe sixteen years later in *Virgile, non*.

Le Corps lesbien (*The Lesbian Body*, 1973), likes *Les Guerillères*, is not termed a novel. Rather, it might be considered as a series of prose poems. It is thus a work of mixed genre, as is common to much women's writing, but also to much modernist or postmodernist work in general. In *L'Opoponax* there are boys with whom the young girls play as equals, not as enemies. In *Les Guerillères* men are explicitly the enemy until peace is attained. In *Le Corps lesbien* men simply do not exist. Mythological and historical figures are made female (Archimedea, Ulyssea, Christa) as are animals (*l'agnelle de lait, la serpente*). *Le Corps lesbien* is primarily about love, the love of equal partners, in a world in which there is no fundamental duality, no possessor and possessed. There is no linear plot, no chronological development in time. Especially, there is rejection of 'the stupid duality with all that flows therefrom' (Wittig, 1973, p. 145, p. 165).

Le Corps lesbien is the most poetic of Wittig's books, creating an atmosphere of strong bodies, aggressive love, in a world not defined in relation to the masculine. There is no tenderness, rejected from the beginning as a false, 'feminine' characteristic: 'say your farewells m/y very beautiful one m/y very strong one. . . . to what they, the women, call affection tenderness or gracious abandon' (p. 15, p. 7). Instead there are menstruation ceremonies, festivals of the lost and found vulvas, parades of great female figures. There are parody texts of Archimedes's discovery of the principle of the displacement of water, Icarus's flight, and Christ's agony on Golgotha. The Archimedea text cleverly mocks the pretensions of men's science, suggesting that women's practical experience needs no such confirmation:

> You cause m/e to observe that a body immersed in a liquid sustains a vertical thrust directed from below upwards, that m/y dearest is manifest to anyone who spends three-quarters of the day plunged in the water. (pp. 159–60, p. 182)

There are echoes of texts by male authors, such as DuBellay and Donne, now made feminine:

> Happy if like Ulyssea *I* might return from a long voyage. (p. 23, p. 16)

> *I* wait for the cold to overcome m/e so as to remain here with you m/y so adorable one in this cemetery in the open air m/y bones mingled with yours. (p. 156, p. 178)

There are also surrealistic games of pure sensation, such as the kaleidoscope of small coloured insects inserted under the lover's eyelid. Lyrical texts, in the manner of the 'Song of Songs' are addressed to Sappho:

> Sappho when *I* beseech her causes a violet lilac-smelling rain to fall over the island. *I* do not seek the shelter of the trees under pretext of escaping the moisture or to contemplate the diverse signs multiplying between earth and sky. (p. 114, p. 130)

The setting is an island. Images of water, boats, swimming, drowning, birds, fish abound. Because of this fluid atmosphere, Elaine Marks sees the narrator, *j/e*, as 'the most powerful lesbian in literature because as a lesbian-feminist she reexamines and re-designs the universe. Starting with the female body she recreates through anecdote and proper names a new aqueous female space and a new female time in which the past is abolished' (Marks, 1979, p. 376). The islands are intended, according to interviews Wittig has given, as symbols of an all-female culture:

> potentially in every society there are nuclei of an Amazon culture that could be reborn at any time, where women are defined in relation to themselves and no longer in relation to men. The Movement is made up of this kind of nuclei, that I will call 'islands'. Perhaps all women will not belong to these 'islands' but it is important that they exist. . . . because they can serve to support other women in their own fight. (Wittig, 1973b)

> The islands of women in *Le Corps lesbien* are not the islands of the classical past; they are our own islands (or rather islets) of culture, of life. Everywhere groups of women are forming who live among themselves and for themselves. (Wittig, 1974, p. 25)

The female imaginary mode of *Le Corps lesbien* includes both lesbian loves and the 'original imaginary dyad of mother-and-baby', with much oral, and thus infantile eroticism (Montefiori, 1987, pp. 156–7). It is an imaginary mode in which there is no father, no patriarchial rules or prohibitions, but also a mode without a developed narrative. Jan Montefiore has argued that the realm inhabited by *j/e* and *tu* exists before gender and is not specifically female. She then asks, how can one say that Wittig is avoiding gender since Wittig's work has such an obviously political purpose? We might reply the suppression of gender – of dichotomy, of the terms male and female – is exactly Wittig's political aim. If, after all, Baudelaire is a lesbian poet, then the lesbian body is not gendered as *woman*. Wittig is always conscious of the political purpose of her writing and of the political meaning of the very act of writing, as an attack on the male-dominated literary culture. Thus in *Le Corps lesbien* she marks the intrusion of a female 'I' into the male language by using a typographical slash each time the first-person subject occurs (*j/e, m/oi, I, m/y*, and so on). She also uses the typographical device of series of words (for parts of the lesbian body – muscles, organs, secretions, bones, sensations, and so on) in bold type, interspersed rather like a series of illustrations on separate pages throughout the book. These pages serve to 'burst the space of the book': 'I needed to name the places and the functions of the body' (Wittig, 1974, p. 24). This use of typography is similar in some ways to the blank spaces in Duras, as a means of constituting a message. Wittig, however, tends towards an exhaustive listing while Duras tends towards a reduction. Such typographical forms are not, of course, used only by women, but in both Wittig and Duras their use may indicate a need to find ways beyond linear discourse to express personal experience or the common experience of women.

In *Le Corps lesbien*, more radically than in *Les Guerillères*, aggressivity finds expression, but it does not turn murderous (as in some male homosexual writing), and is not based on a power relationship between the dominant and the dominated. Wittig also avoids the use of obscenity, common to homosexual writing by men, claiming that such language is expressive of a male way of looking at the human body. (The heterosexual women she will portray in *Virgile, non*, however, who accept the male point of view, frequently use obscenity.) Wittig's women are, however, not weak or pretty; their love is an expression of a savage passion. It often leads to an incorporation of one of the lovers into the other, a literal 'eating' of one another:

> you swallow m/e at once *I* enter into your immense red illuminated oesophagus, *I* fall against its wall, *I* find m/yself propelled from one point to another to the level of the arterial arch, *I* am utterly shattered by its throbbing.   (p. 92, pp. 101–2)

Such hyperbolic descriptions, often, as here, coupled with technical terms, create, according to Elaine Marks, 'images sufficiently blatant to withstand reabsorption into male literary culture' (Marks, 1979, p. 375). The descriptions of *j/e* and *tu* tearing themselves apart are a deliberate contrast to the pleasurable eroticism of much heterosexual love poetry.

In spite of the vast discrepancy of tone between *L'Opoponax* and *Le Corps lesbien*, between the child's slow discovery of her identity and the aggressive assertion of *j/e*, there are echoes of the first novel in *Le Corps lesbien*: 'I inform you that the wooden boats the windmills the bridges manufactured by little girls stud your suddenly closed eyes' (Wittig, 1973, p. 85, p. 93). The lovers *j/e* and *tu* play childish games similar to those in *L'Opoponax*: 'I recall your laughter m/y confusion when the bandage removed *I* have lost sight of you' (p. 77, p. 83). The lover *tu* shouts out the name of *j/e*. Catherine Legrand also shouted out names, but the names of all the pupils in the class except Valerie Borge's. In *L'Opoponax* lesbian love has only just begun.

Virgile, non (*Across the Acheron*, 1985) is the first work since *L'Opoponax* that Wittig has termed a novel. Yet it is not as traditional as *L'Opoponax*, where there is a clear progression in time, the development of a plot, and a number of characters with recognisable qualities. *Virgile, non* is a modern reworking of Dante's *Divine Comedy*. There is a progression, as the protagonist visits hell and reaches paradise at the end, but we are warned not to expect to see the circles of hell in order; and scenes of hell are interspersed with scenes of purgatory and paradise. The persona of the author herself, like Dante, is a major character. The direct entrance of the novelist as character is not like that in the work of Colette or Duras; in *Virgile, non* the intimately personal is avoided. Although the character 'Wittig', is a writer, 'Wittig', like Dante, is more a type than an individual. The theme is the search for paradise, not a particular love story. The novel recounts a voyage, 'which is both sacred and profane' (the French is *'classique'* rather than 'sacred' [Wittig, 1985b, p. 7, p. 7]), a voyage with classical models and with universal implications, but one based upon a secular and contemporary view of the world.

The paradise being sought is a paradise of lesbians, who have escaped from the bondage of the gendered world. *Virgile, non* is not, however, as was *Le Corps lesbien*, concerned simply with a world beyond men, since the hell in which most of the characters live is caused by the domination of men. It is not a hell of heroic suffering or of retribution for sin, but rather life in the everyday world of phallocentrism: 'The condemned souls ... are anonymous, and I challenge you to find any quality about them that clothes them in glory. In their case the horror and irremissibility of suffering are not caused by the ignominy of their deeds' (p. 8, p. 9). It is, however, often a chosen hell, not fully recognised by those within it who prefer it to following a lesbian: 'it's better to be fucked or screwed, balled or poked by an enemy who's got what it takes than by you who haven't' (p. 12, p. 13).

Manastabal, the guide (whose name is always followed by the epithet 'my guide') is a modern lesbian Virgil (her name comes from Mana, the ancient Roman goddess who presided over the spirits of the dead), and 'Wittig' (always Wittig, not Monique) is

Dante; the parallel to Beatrice is 'she who is my Providence' (p. 9,
p. 10), who is not named. By having two voices, 'Wittig' and
Manastabal, Wittig constructs a dialogue in which to discuss
various attitudes of the lesbian towards the heterosexual woman.
Manastabal argues for helping them: 'you can accost the damned
souls only with the aim of extricating them from Hell and succeed-
ing in the task, at whatever cost' (p. 33, p. 39). 'Wittig' is more
severe, seeing the woman oppressed by a man as better off dead:
'You can argue in vain. I believe it would be better for them to be
dead. Yes, death is a deliverance when degradation has reached
this level' (p. 34, p. 39). Later, 'Wittig' would like to rid women of
their 'appendages' (children)', but Manastabal reminds her 'we're
not in Hell to blame the damned souls but to show them, if
necessary, how to get out of it' (p. 46, p. 53). Manastabal and
'Wittig' also debate whether to fight small skirmishes or to work
towards a total revolution:

> You talk of gestures, clothing, bearing. You celebrate the shady
> beauty of the bandits and pride yourself on being one of their
> company. . . . Ah, Wittig, all this is guerrilla warfare. What can
> we gain from it when it's the whole world we have to
> repossess?   (p. 40, p. 46)

The discussions, however, do not lead to any simple answers.
'Wittig' wants to know if Manastabal has a plan for conquering the
world, but she is too busy saving one damned soul at a time to
reply!

The setting is contemporary San Francisco, with scenes in such
places as laundrettes, where 'Wittig', come to speak to the women
doing their laundry, and, attacked for being an unnatural creature,
strips between two rows of washing machines:

> [I] advance among them, not like Venus emerging from the
> waves, nor even as my mother bore me, but at any rate with two
> shoulders, a torso, a belly, legs and the rest. So I have nothing
> special to exhibit, only perfect human conformity with persons
> of my own sex.   (p. 14, p. 16)

The description is a good example of the mixture of the *classique et
profane* in the style of the novel:

But before I can take one step in this state of nudity they immediately begin to spin round, tearing their hair in the purest classical tradition, like tops or whirling derviches, uttering frenzied cries.   (p. 15, p. 17)

Virgile, non has more explicit, rational themes than *Le Corps lesbien*, since it is set not on an island of female culture but in a world inhabited primarily by men and heterosexual women, and is concerned with how the lesbian can function in this world as well as how she can reach paradise. Paradise itself is almost indescribable. 'Wittig' admits to difficulties in getting beyond such clichés as 'beauty'. Manastabal tells her, however, that finding the right words would not be enough: 'I can assure you, Wittig, that here you don't take to the air by using figures of speech' (p. 57, p. 65). As in *Les Guerillères*, language is an important weapon to use, but is not in itself sufficient for the fight.

Most of the novel is concerned, however, with the circles of hell. The central themes include the violent domination of women by men; the many ways in which women acquiesce in their own enslavement, including women's acceptance of and even advocacy of female circumcision, and willing participation in prostitution; the heterosexual's fear of the lesbian; and the unity, in spite of all problems of class, nation and economics, of all women:

There they are, then, each in the hands of a special gaoler who is prepared to set his own shanty on fire to stop them from getting away. Whether they live in a hovel or a palace, whether they do all the fatigues or have them done by others, the women are behind walls.   (p. 64, p. 74)

The portraits of men are largely undifferentiated; they are uncomprehending slave masters. The portraits of women are more varied, but they are all types, not rounded individuals. *Virgile, non* is a *conte philosophique* more than a novel. Some women enjoy being dominated: 'But I *like* being on a leash!' (p. 25, p. 28). Some are moralistic:

It's not long since an inspired prophetess railed at you and, with tears running down her cheeks, constantly prostrated in ardent prayer, crawling on her knees, implored that you should be stopped from corrupting children in the schools.   (p. 12, p. 14)

(This portrait seems drawn from Wittig's American experience!)
Some have accepted myths about lesbians, whom they consider to
be 'those monsters with hair all over their bodies and scales on
their chests' (p. 90, p. 105). Some, like members of other oppressed
groups, turn against themselves: 'Don't you know that the van-
quished, in their impotence at crushing their real enemy . . .
destroy each other mutually' (p. 63, p. 73). Some see too well two
sides to the problems of women.

> All their intelligence makes them tend equally to quit Hell and
> not to quit it. From the front, they have a total awareness of the
> functioning of Hell, they are capable of mastering its techni-
> ques. . . . From the back, they have a total understanding of the
> mechanism of domination that has reduced the majority of souls
> to the state of damnation. . . . At the front they believe it's better
> to remain masters in Hell in order to control events. At the back
> their belief is that it's better to escape from Hell without
> delay.   (p. 72, p. 84)

Some are, however, more intelligent than men, not because of any
innate quality, but because of their experience:

> The reason is this: Once they are aware of what is happening
> they set themselves the challenge of exercising their intelligence
> through all the laws that govern their world and immediately
> develop it in many more directions than is required in the
> dominant camp. Moreover, they have to act with a double intent
> and this duplicity sometimes leads them, as you have seen, to
> develop two heads.   (pp. 74–5, p. 87)

'Wittig' herself as a character tends to be more aggressive,
impulsive, less willing to forgive and understand than Manastabal.
We know little of her past except that she shares with Catherine
Legrand of *L'Opoponax* a religious education, which taught her that
women's sexual organs are invisible. The character of 'Wittig' is
treated lightly and humorously. She compares herself to Christ,
but in a sentence that cannot quite be taken seriously: 'My task is
to chase them out of the temple of love, as they call it' (p. 97,
p. 114). The 'as they call it' introduces a note of levity, as does the
slang of the following sentence: 'If I'd been brought here to cut off
tails I'd have been given a butcher's knife'. More often than in

Wittig's earlier work there is self-mockery. 'Wittig' is criticised by the 'ulliphant' for having a view of paradise 'of pure imagination conceived in flashes' (p. 21, p. 25, perhaps an allusion to *Le Corps lesbien*?). The *bourlababu* makes fun of 'Wittig's' attempt at stopping a tempest; Manastabal mocks her naïveté about the use of drugs in San Francisco. In an obviously ironic reference to the mixed form of *Virgile, non* itself, Manastabal says, when 'Wittig' thinks of getting a horse: 'What will you do with a horse in Hell, Wittig? Remember, we're not in a western. Your confusion of styles is sometimes quite barbaric' (p. 55, p. 63). When 'Wittig' says that she is saved at the last moment, 'a near miss, by my beard, by the skin of my teeth' (p. 43, p. 49), is this an amusing way of denying duality (everyone can have a beard)? A mockery of male language? Or more self-mockery? Even the style, a mixture of the vulgar and the noble, is treated with self-conscious irony: 'I remember in time that I have adopted the noble style to lend a little glamour to our enslaved sex, for it's better to leave our enemies the job of dragging it through the mud' (p. 13, p. 14).

The mockery of character, the mixture of registers and genres, the unresolved discussion of such problems as how to save heterosexual women, all contribute to a lightness of tone not so frequently found in Wittig's earlier work. Wittig seems not to want to be seen as a heavy-handed prophet, and is perhaps reacting against the praise of some of her commentators: 'She [j/e] is, in fact, the only true anti-Christ, the willful assassin of Christian love' (Marks, 1979, p. 376). Self-mockery, a sense of the comic, a use of classical models, a style based upon such diverse registers as formal invocations to the gods, precise technical vocabulary, slang, vulgarity – such a range of expressive means raises the work to a level well above the didactic. These are not, of course, characteristic traits only of women's writing. The most overtly anti-masculinist of the five novelists I am examining is as little 'feminine' in style and language as is Marguerite Yourcenar, whose work often appears to present a masculine view of the world.

Wittig's work is especially a refusal of what is often considered 'feminine'. Her characters are aggressive, often violent. They carry guns and are proud of their muscles. Her language is often precise, or often highly imaginative and poetic, but never vague or 'flowery'. She has spoken of women's language (the language women use daily, not literary language) as being more 'concrete' than that of men (Wittig, 1973b). There is a constant tendency in her work to use precise words. Even the poetic descriptions of erotic activity in *Le Corps lesbien*, or of paradise in *Virgile, non* are based largely on a proliferation of names of individual beings and things. When Wittig speaks of women taking possession of language, she is often speaking of the political act, not of changing the way of writing. In her own work, the problem of writing as a woman was, particularly at the beginning, one of finding the right pronoun (Wittig, 1974, p. 24).

My comments on the 'unsexed' quality of Wittig's style may seem at variance with analyses by critics who stress ways in which Wittig's techniques convey the power of lesbian writing:

> the use of the present tense to abolish time distinctions; the passive voice; a concrete vocabulary; repetition; multiplication of the female subject; the transformation of intransitive into transitive verbs; and the elimination of grammatical forms preempted by the masculine gender.   (Crowder, 1983, p. 130)

However, with the exception of avoiding grammatical forms suggesting the masculine (and therefore maintaining a system of duality) these techniques seem to me ways of asserting female power, and not ways of expressing a specific 'femininity' of language. Wittig has stated that she feels thought and language go beyond sexual distinctions: 'In your reading as in your dreams, when you think of yourself you see yourself as beyond the two sexes' (Wittig, 1985c). This attitude underlies her style; it is a militant style, screening vocabulary and grammar for possible sexist attitudes, but within a rational perspective. Wittig is highly critical of the exclusion of women from male-dominated language, of their relegation to the category of objects rather than subjects; she attacks the language of the dominant culture, however, not by an acceptance of a fluid, multivalent poeticism, but through sharp, often ironic analysis. If some of her own transformations of language might seem at first similar to those advocated by Cixous and Irigaray – particularly the concept of 'lacunae', absences which signify – she is aiming at filling in what has been missing, what is censored in heterosexual culture. When she leaves men out, it is to make their absence felt: an aggressive act, not a psychological defence nor a method of trying to express what is inexpressible in rational language.

Wittig's style, however, includes a good deal of poetic imagery,

some of it surrealistic. The imagery of *L'Opoponax* is largely
concrete, related to the child's gradually developing awareness of
the world around her; the poetic effects are rather a result of the
juxtaposition of radically disparate events and perceptions. With
Les Guerillères, however, surrealistic imagery appears with increasing frequency.

> At a certain point they collide with the floating decaying carcase
> of an ass, at times the swell of the sea reveals sticky shapeless
> gleaming lumps of indescribable colour.   (Wittig, 1969, p. 10,
> p. 11)

> Sometimes it rains on the orange green blue *islands*. Then a mist
> hangs over them without obscuring their colours. The air one
> inhales is opaque and damp. One's lungs are like sponges that
> have imbibed water. The sharks swallow the necklaces that are
> thrown overboard to be got rid of, the strings of glassware, the
> opalescent baubles.   (p. 49, p. 68)

In *Le Corps lesbien*, the most radical images are those of the violence
of lesbian love. Often they are images of mutual devouring or
dismembering:

> Through m/y vagina and m/y uterus you insert yourself breaking
> the membrane up to m/y intestines. Round your neck you place
> m/y duodenum pale-pink well-veined with blue.   (Wittig, 1973,
> p. 37, p. 33)

> m/y mouth fastened on your mouth your neck squeezed by m/y
> arms, I feel our intestines uncoiling gliding among themselves,
> the sky darkens suddenly, it contains orange gleams.   (pp. 51–2,
> p. 53)

The body turns into various aggressive animals, or is attacked by
animals:

> Then harassed at every point I launch m/yself into a furious
> gallop, m/y hooves violently hammer the ground, I neigh
> incessantly.   (p. 56, p. 57)

> I discover that I am absolutely covered over m/y entire naked

body with great black spiders from the feet to the hair m/y skin all eaten away creviced full of bites of purplish swellings vile. Your fingers rest on m/y mouth brushing away several of the creatures to prevent m/e from crying out.   (p. 79, p. 85)

But the lover transformed into an animal can bring pleasure:

m/y lips shoot, they become an elongated gutter, . . . it is a sucker a very narrow trunk, *I* apply it lightly to your throat your shoulders your nipples your belly your vulva, . . . m/y trunk palpates you searchingly, clinging to you thus by m/y six feet *I* begin m/y delectable one to flap m/y wings against your back.   (p. 152, pp. 172–3)

One scene of violent sharks as symbols of eroticism is particularly reminiscent of Lautréamont:

One of m/y legs comes in contact with the water, it is brutally torn off by the open mouth of one of the sharks. M/y other leg is bent at a right angle. Well-braced against the side of m/y boat you throw m/e down, you cast both m/y arms to the sharks which devour them.   (pp. 106–7, pp. 119–20)

In *Virgile, non*, surrealist scenes of violence are no longer erotic, but express the aggressive domination of women by men:

The damned souls have their thoracic cages opened, their sawn ribs exposing the heart, for it is at this beating organ itself that the patrons of the shooting-galleries fire. The women stand without flinching, supported on one leg with one knee bent, and they are hardly shaken when a bullet, an arrow or a knife perforates their thorax.   (Wittig, 1985b, p. 77, p. 90)

The animals, however, are somewhat gentler: a robot eagle that attacks 'Wittig' with words; a giant butterfly; the ulliphant, 'motionless, ochre in colour, the folds at the back of its thighs visible in its silky flesh. . . . starting from the Cartesian assumption that one can conceive only that which exists, deduces the absolute physical reality of Paradise' (p. 21, p. 24). While the many dragons in hell, fought by changing into Saint George in shining black armour, are an obvious phallic enemy, we are warned not to look for symbolic meanings in the imagery:

It doesn't matter much that, with my laser-beam, I appear as the figure of the exterminating angel from the Last Judgement here, for I distrust symbols, I believe in the literal and, angel or not, I flatten every enemy in a minute or two, so breaking a record for prowess in this type of narrative.   (p. 87, p. 102)

Wittig's style is also aggressive in her use of obscure words, long lists of synonyms that tend to disorient or simply bore the reader, such repetitions as 'Manastabal, mon guide', which become an annoying mechanism. There are also a number of awkward sentences, in which the abnormal word order slows down the reader: 'Bringing you a finger-bowl and crystallised fruits the women inform you of what and of whom you have eaten' (Wittig, 1973, p. 105, p. 118). The intent seems both a deliberate rejection of 'fine writing' and a means of making the reader constantly aware of language, thus reinforcing the theme of the sexist assumptions of normal language.

Colette's intense emotional relationship with her mother is her model for a lesbian relationship: 'What is involved is someone younger needing protection, someone older offering a refuge and caring' (Marks, 1979, p. 364). The lesbian relationship is thus not between equals, and can often be described in terms similar to those used for a heterosexual relationship, with a stronger and a weaker partner. Wittig, however, who seldom speaks of mothers, attempts to describe the emotions linking two lesbian lovers without recourse to images of either domination or mothering. Thus her lovers in *Le Corps lesbien* take turns devouring each other. When she feels rejected by her lover, *j/e* may describe emotions similar to those of a weaker partner in a heterosexual union: '*I* begin to dance very clumsily with the jerky movements of a puppet, you do not see m/e. *I* sing a song which is known to you, *I* throw my/self flat on m/y face in your path, you step over m/e and continue' (Wittig, 1973, p. 110, p. 124). But neither *j/e* nor *tu* is consistently the weaker or stronger partner.

Marguerite Yourcenar makes mothers a handicap to most of the characters in her work. If Wittig does not paint quite such a critical picture of mothers, she seems to consider having children as part of the oppressed role women are made to play in patriarchal society. In *Virgile, non*, children are 'appendages', who tear their mothers apart: 'Sometimes even they are dragged in the opposite direction and torn apart as a result' (p. 45, p. 52). The mothers don't know what to do without their children, however, and find it hard to let them grow up. If 'Wittig' realises that the problem of motherhood is not easily resolved ('It's like the Gordian knot, only you're cutting through living flesh' [p. 45, p. 52]), the fact that heterosexual reproduction is necessary to populate the world is never considered directly. In *Le Corps lesbien*, reproduction is $XX + XX = XX$. Even in *L'Opoponax* there are more mentions of uncles than mothers, and the major adult female characters are unmarried teachers, usually nuns. (When Josiane admits to having little love for her mother, however, she is severely punished by the nun, since love of one's mother is socially expected.)

If ignoring reproduction and motherhood may seem one weakness of Wittig's position, one socialist feminist critic finds another weakness in *Virgile, non*:

> The wrongs against women are straight out of Adrienne Rich and Mary Daly, but they have no class, racial or cultural inflection or specificity, as if the crucial political debates within feminism in the late 1970s and 1980s have passed Wittig by.   (C. Kaplan, 1987, p. 21)

Monique Wittig is nevertheless both the most radical in theme among the five novelists I have studied and, along with Yourcenar, the furthest from any identifiably 'feminine' style. The 'feminist' in literature cannot be easily defined in terms of language, except in so far as it is a rejection of a phallocentric perspective.

9
Is There a Conclusion?

I think maybe the time we're going through now is more perverse, or if you like more baroque, a play with the psychic space, which supposes that these distinctions between X and Y [mother and father] are not so sharp, and which supposes that there are contaminations between them. This gives to the modern psychic space something that resembles the medieval, the fact that people don't have fixed identities. . . . For me the feminist movement has several positive points particularly on the liberation of women. But maybe one of its most unexpected achievements at the moment will be to contribute to the creation of this baroque space . . . this ambiguisation of identities. (Kristeva, 1984, p. 23)

Feminist criticism is devoted to the liberation of the ideal of beauty and aesthetic pleasure from its bondage to the patriarchal logic, which usually attaches these values to the representation of women as other. Thus feminist criticism is and is not literary criticism. It is an effort to preserve what literature and criticism can and ought to be against what they have become. . . . feminism is unfinished business. It is in the process of producing its meaning. Therefore, it cannot be comprehended by any set of fixed principles. Our interest in feminist criticism is grounded in the belief that the literary and critical enterprise is a crucial arena for the production of the meaning of feminism. (Schweickart, 1982, p. 175)

We have to be aware of the paradox that there cannot be any certainty about what is feminine in art but that we have to go on looking out for it. (Ecker, 1985, p. 21)

Woman is the subject of a good portion of the literature written by men. The image of woman created by the male artist is also often the image to which men expect or want women to conform. This image, because it is imposed from the outside, cannot coincide with a woman's image of herself. How, in writing, does the female artist present an image of herself or another woman? In terms of an ironic mimicry of the image man has created? By reversing the values of the male-inspired image, glorying in, for example, the parts of the body usually ignored or suppressed? By creating an authentic picture of woman as defined within her own perspective, without reference to male norms? But, in the latter case, can we discuss such images directly as critics, without considering 'difference' from these norms, without using the usual vocabulary? Is it possible to discuss writing by women without thinking of difference?

The problem is similar to that raised in the critical discussion of 'new', non-metropolitan literatures, where criticism begins by establishing 'differences' from the art of Paris, New York, London. Criticism of new literatures can move beyond such preoccupations, taking as its norm of comparison other works written in new centres of culture, defining its own aesthetic without direct reference to the standards of older literatures. Can such a detachment exist for critical reading of literature by women? Women, of course, have no territory as do the Australians or the Québecois, and thus no obvious way of separating a culture. Women are, as well, defined by other variables – nation, race, social class – which make gender less obviously prominent than is, say, nationality in a newly independent nation. And, defining a new national literature does not in itself challenge the hierarchy of patriarchal norms to such a profound extent, is not, in the final analysis, as revolutionary as an independent women's literary criticism would be. We have only to consider the number of prominent women artists who object to being classified as women artists, seeing this as being relegated to a ghetto. One can hardly imagine a Senegalese or Jamaican author insisting that she or he not be classified as part of a national literature.

How then can we discuss the images of women in literature written by women, while avoiding continual comparisons with male norms? And how can we evaluate women's writing (for there must still be some critical standards, obviously) without relying on the aesthetic tenets of the dominant culture? Perhaps it might be possible simply to make comparisons with other works by female authors, to establish critical distinctions only within a body of women's writing? Or must we consider that 'a reinterpretation of female experience when reading women's literature can only succeed if the detour via the male idea is taken into account' (Weigel, 1985, pp. 63–4)? For some critics, the male image of woman has so influenced woman's view of herself that it is *not yet* possible to have an 'authentic' sex, one not defined in relation to man (p. 79). If an authentic sex is not yet possible, how much less an expression of that sex in writing? The novelists I have discussed have not, of course, arrived at the expression of authenticity we might project for the future or imagine in some Utopian state. Already, however, they have subverted anticipated male images and described the reality of women's lives, without the need to reincorporate them into the dominant social order.

Arthur C. Danto, reviewing an exhibition of Frank Stella's work, speaks of the tendencies of women's art and of what he considers 'feminine' elements in Stella's recent work, in terms that often recall those of critics of women's writing: 'Women artists, in the name of women's art, aimed at a kind of impurity instead, messy, often shocking, with an openness to rejected materials and crazy forms and provocative juxtapositions and illogical sequences . . . at the destabilization of accepted categories.'[1] A woman artist, Mary Kelly, speaks of the woman's loss of her imagined closeness to the mother's body, and then speculates about the particularity of women's desire, in terms that may recall Danto's: 'pleasure, then, would be produced in the representation of exactly that which was assumed to be outside of language, unspeakable, invisible, unrepresentable'.[2]

While such rejections of accepted forms exist in literature as well as in the plastic arts, it is difficult to say, looking at the varied styles of the five novelists I have discussed, that a 'woman's sentence', a 'woman's form', could be defined in any objective fashion. The texts, however, would seem to confirm some theories of what is present in women's writing: the theme of the search for identity, the theme of the relationship to the mother (or the glaring *absence* of the mother), the less clear-cut characters, the lack of well-defined linear plots, the mixture of genres. Obviously, most of these characteristics are a part of twentieth-century modernist and postmodernist literature and are not limited to writing by women. But often they are particularly appropriate to express a twentieth-century woman's vision of the world. (The larger question of their prevalence in earlier work by women would require another book.)

The search for identity is particularly important for women, and is often linked to the conflict between desire for love and desire for independence – a conflict felt, obviously, more acutely for women than for men in any existing society. Even such an independent and creative woman as Colette lives this conflict at a level of 'obsession'; it is an emotional tension that cannot be readily resolved in theme, plot or character, any more than it can be resolved in life. If love remains an important theme of much women's writing, it is not necessarily linked, however, to a story of a couple – either as equal partners or as desiring subject and desired object. Those two of the five authors I have discussed who are most directly concerned with heterosexual love – Colette and Marguerite Duras – are also adamant in attacking the life of the couple, seeing it as a bondage, an enslavement of one partner to the other.

One particularly feminine characteristic may be a refusal to attribute any 'authority' to the writer's voice. Duras speaks in *La Vie matérielle* of how the reader of *Le Ravissement de Lol V. Stein* participates in Lol's madness, and calls such a reader a 'reader-author' (Duras, 1987, p. 32). A true reading is immersion in this madness; her books can only be understood in this sense: 'It is a question of a personal relationship between the book and the reader. You complain and you cry, together' (pp. 119–20). Related to this refusal to be the 'voice of the master' is an identification of author with character (perhaps explicable to some extent by Chodorow's theory of 'permeable ego boundaries'?). Thus Marguerite Yourcenar becomes one with Hadrian. Yourcenar also judges her characters as if they were flesh-and-blood creatures, who could have (often should have) done something else.[3]

Another feminine trait may be an openness to the non-traditional, in subject-matter and in form. Colette's exploration of what lies beneath the surface of Renée's statement to Jean in *L'Entrave* – 'I do not agree with you' – is similar to Nathalie Sarraute's exploration of the undercurrents of language in *L'Usage de la parole*. Both authors are primarily interested in what slight emotions and thoughts lie hidden beneath the surface of conversation. Both explore as well the underlying significance of gestures. Like Marguerite Duras and Monique Wittig, Colette and Sarraute are distrustful of analytic psychology. If Yourcenar seems a more traditional novelist in terms of psychology, she is similar to the others in a rejection of conventional morality. Duras speaks of the 'nobility of the ordinary' shared by some of her female characters. When she defines a possible 'moral' for her own work, is she not speaking as well of what is most valuable in women's writing, of a moral that might be said, for instance, to exist also in the work of Colette, Sarraute, Yourcenar and Wittig?

> Morality consists in rectifying a sort of faulty situation of writing, perhaps, the deceitful situation of writing in general, when it deals with love, desire, the world, the self in relation to the world. (Lamy, 1981, p. 62)

The theme of the relation of mother to child may seem the quintessential woman's theme. It can be approached from two sides: the adult woman in relation to her *child*, or in relation to her *mother*. Women writers often stress one of the two sides. Colette, whose attachment to her own mother was profound, abiding and uncritical, seldom speaks of *being* a mother. Indeed, none of her major female protagonists is a mother. In her writing, the relationship is largely that of the unworthy daughter seeking a nurturing mother. The mother to whom Julia Kristeva assigns a privileged role because she combines the semiotic and the symbolic functions in her relation with her child is the mother seen from her own perspective. When discussing how a daughter sees her mother, on the other hand, Kristeva speaks almost exclusively of the semiotic realm. The woman artist, as daughter and creator, is exiled from the pre-Oedipal, archaic territory of the mother in so far as she is normally attached to a man as sexual partner. (For the male artist, a woman can be ersatz mother and muse.) The mother seems a rival, an object at the same time of intense love and hatred. This love/hate, usually suppressed, can, Kristeva feels, produce hysteria, or can be a powerful motive for symbolisation (Boucquey, 1975, p. 26).

Duras speaks of both sides. She creates characters whose deepest attachment is to their children (such as Anne Desbaresdes). She has said that having children is for women the full use of life, that maternity is a 'bursting of the ego', a 'mad love', and that 'My son brings me more than myself'.[4] But she also creates characters whose ambivalent relationship to their mothers motivates their behaviour (such as the beggar in *Le Vice-consul*) and relates this ambivalence about the mother to her own life. For

Duras's mother, there seems to have been no 'bursting of the ego', at least with regard to her daughter:

> My mother obviously preferred her sons, she never hid that. Psychiatrists have told me that this preference was decisive in my life. . . . I was apologising for being born, and my exams as well as my books, were meant for her, brought to her to be admitted into her kingdom.   (Horer and Socquet, 1973, p. 174)

On Duras's part, however, is this apology not a form of love? As Julia Kristeva says, the mother in Duras's *L'Amant* is 'the archetype of the mad women who people the Durassian universe'; Kristeva continues: 'out of fear of maternal madness, the novelist eliminates the mother ... but ... she actually takes her place, substituting herself for maternal madness' (Kristeva, 1987, p. 146).

If the mother in Duras's fiction is mad, there is none the less an attempt, through the portrayal of many 'mad' characters, to represent her, much as Colette attempts through the portrayal of her mature female characters to represent Sido. On the other hand, of course, the theme of mother and daughter is dismissed by Yourcenar, is mostly ignored by Wittig, and is transferred to father-daughter relations by Sarraute in *Portrait d'un inconnu*. If the woman novelist cannot identify with a mother, she may need to eliminate her in a deliberate manner.

The act of writing is, as Duras terms it, 'this unnamable transgression' – the ability to filter personal experience and raise it to a poetic level, without worrying about how it will be received. Duras considers that she does not know what 'indecency' is, and adds 'That's perhaps the only feminist point to which I can allude' (Faucher, 1981, p. 50). (We may be reminded of Colette's statement that 'purity' has no intelligible meaning.) Women's writing, when it goes beyond the sociological or historical interest of, for example, diaries, letters, theory or militant criticism (what Duras terms 'literature of information') is perhaps of value for its ability to use the *female* personal, the experience of the marginal, the 'Other', often repressed by civilisation, without worrying about 'decency'. Duras believes that women can now express libidinal energy better than men can, because this energy has been preserved during their long silence.

An observation frequently made by both male and female critics is that women's writing expresses personal experience more directly than men's writing. Sometimes, of course, this is a way of denying its universal value, of relegating it to a sphere less significant than what Boisdeffre, in criticising Colette, called 'the nobility of man'. Sometimes, with recent feminist criticism, it is a way of asserting that 'the personal is the political', that social values which ignore the importance of the individual emotion have falsified reality and that expressing the most intimate experience is a political act. Colette and Sarraute largely ignore in their fiction what is usually called the political – the realm of government, of established institutions of public power. Limiting their work to the realm of the private is a deliberate choice, a commentary on the greater importance of relationships between individuals. Duras reaches out to the political, incorporating into her own being the trauma of the Holocaust. Since Auschwitz, she said, 'no matter what I do, what I write, I have never completely left this territory, that of the Jews, of their massacre' (Duras, 1986, p. 115). The public realm, however, is largely absorbed into personal anguish.[5] The two novelists whose work is least in tune with theories of feminine difference – Yourcenar, who aspires to be part of the masculine world, and Wittig, who would like to eliminate the very distinction masculine/feminine – are also those whose work seems the most overtly concerned with public issues. Both, however, show a rather Utopian desire to reform the public world so that it is less hostile to individual experience.

Modern feminist literary criticism came to the forefront at about the same time as newer literary theories and as the literature of postmodernism, for it is part of an era in which old, established forms and perspectives seem irrelevant. While feminist critics often adopt such postmodern tenets as a rejection of distinctions between form and content, they are frequently more 'political' than most of their male contemporaries. There is a continual reference from the world of the literary text back to the world of non-literary reality.[6] Feminism leads beyond the pessimism of many of the male theorists on whose work its concepts are often based: 'The feminist thinkers have added a Utopian edge to their thought. For if Derrida, Foucault, Lacan and others leave room for difference to be thought, and thought differently, the envisaging of this difference heralds an unrepressed future that remains speculative. Only feminists seem to think that this perfectly unoppressive world is possible' (Duchen, 1986, p. 96).

While optimism is not common in their work, the five novelists I am studying might be said to have an indirect political aim: the rejection of rigidly defined gender identity and of patriarchal moral standards. They all accept the radical individuality of each human being and her or his sexual specificity. Allied to a refusal to categorise and to judge, there is an acceptance of some form of bisexuality in all their work: in the eroticism of Colette, Duras, Yourcenar, all of whom deny any superiority to the male body; in Sarraute's androgynous tropisms; in Wittig's individual interpretation of lesbianism. Sharon Willis suggests that increasingly Duras's 'narrative strategies seem aimed at disclosing the mobility of gender positions'. She cites as examples of Duras's moving away from gender-binding the characters of the Vice-Consul and of the traveller in *L'Amour* (Willis, 1987, pp. 117, 120). Might we not see a similar movement away from gender-binding in the strong women and beautiful, unassertive men of Colette's work, the insecure, androgynous narrators of Nathalie Sarraute, the equal and assertive couples of Wittig, even Yourcenar's choice of male homosexuals to express the realm of desire?

At the end of *The Daughter's Seduction*, Jane Gallop speaks of how Hélène Cixous and Catherine Clément evoke in *La Jeune née* an 'other bisexuality', 'neither the fantasmatic resolution of differences in the imaginary, nor the fleshless, joyless assumption of the fact of one's lack of unity in the symbolic, but an other bisexuality, one that pursues, loves and accepts both the imaginary and the symbolic, both theory and flesh' (Gallop, 1982, p. 150). It is this bisexuality that is given life in the imaginative works of the five women writers.

Notes

Notes to Chapter 1: Ideas of Difference

1. French feminism also includes, however, many practical, concrete movements. See Carolyn Greenstein Burke, 'Report from Paris', *Signs*, 3 (1978) pp. 843–55; Dorothy Kaufmann McCall, 'Politics of Difference', *Signs*, 9 (1983) pp. 282–93; Duchen, 1986; and Dorothy McBride Stetson, *Women's Rights in France* (Westpoint, Conn. Greenwood Press, 1987).

2. Dorothy Kaufmann McCall ('Simone de Beauvoir, *The Second Sex*, and Jean-Paul Sartre', *Signs*, 5 [1979] pp. 209–23) has suggested that Sartre's obsession with the horror of nature and the flesh influenced Beauvoir.

3. Linda Gordon has shown how considering women in terms of androgyny – demanding equality – has alternated historically since the eighteenth century with considering women as possessing unique qualities (Gordon, 1986, pp. 26–7).

4. Sarah Kofman's attack on *Le Fait féminin* as a Rousseauist discourse founded on 'nature' does not seem to me justified. (See proceedings of Séminaires des femmes, Paris, 15 March 1985.)

5. See Carolyn Burke, 'Rethinking the Maternal', in Eisenstein and Jardine, 1980, pp. 107–14, for a good discussion of Freud in France and America.

6. Several good analyses and critiques of the work of Cixous, Irigaray and Kristeva are available in English; see, among others, Cameron (1985), Duchen (1986), Moi (1985), Montefiori (1987), Suleiman (1986).

7. Some critics have said that the horror and contempt suggested by, for example, Céline's description of the female body during childbirth may 'generate a subliminal defense of the maternal which then reemerges in Kristeva as an idealized category' (Russo, 1986, p. 220). Gayatri Chakravorty Spivak makes a radical criticism of Kristeva's use of the concept of the mother, and of the political implications of her work (Spivak, 1987, pp. 126ff).

8. A number of theorists have, in fact, reacted against the idea of a feminine specificity (see Gelfand and Hules, 1985). Cora Kaplan has said: 'If feminist criticism is to make a central contribution to the understanding of sexual difference, instead of serving as a conservative refuge from its more disturbing social and psychic implications, the inclusion of class and race must transform its terms and objectives' (C. Kaplan, 1985, p. 149).

9. She also, in contrast, for example, to Adrienne Rich, seeks a political alliance with male homosexuals against the socially approved norm. Wittig sees lesbianism as 'the refusal of the economic, ideological and political power of a man' (Wittig, 1981, p. 49), but does not consider to what extent the homosexual man may hold that power, and repre-

197

sent oppression. Wittig also says that male homosexuality is often considered with respect 'because the fascination that masters exercise on masters is justified', but that lesbianism is incomprehensible, as why would one dominated creature desire another (Wittig, 1979, p. 120)? Marguerite Yourcenar reads the relative acceptance of male and female homosexuality in the opposite fashion. In *L'Œuvre au noir*, lesbianism is more acceptable because 'it is better . . . for a woman to assume the role of a man than for a man to play a woman's part' (Yourcenar, 1976, p. 42, p. 56). Yourcenar attributes this comment to an historical source, Brantome (p. 369, p. 463), but presumably quotes it with approval. Undoubtedly these two interpretations are primarily reflections of the psychology of the two authors: Wittig reacts constantly against the patriarchy; Yourcenar wants to be part of it.

Notes to Chapter 2: Theories of Language

1. Interestingly, however, George Eliot felt that, in her time and previously, the best works by women were those in French. 'With a few remarkable exceptions, our own feminine literature is made up of books which could have been better written by men' ('Women in France', in Thomas Pinney (ed.), *The Collected Essays of George Eliot* (New York: Columbia University Press, 1963) p. 53). This, she felt, could be explained by the fact that French women were more in contact with ideas, less isolated in domesticity.

2. Robin Lakoff, *Language and Woman's Place* (New York: Harper and Row 1975). Empirical studies have indicated, for example, that among working-class English communities women tend to be more careful, more 'correct' in their use of language (P. Trudgill, 'Sex, convert prestige and linguistic change in the urban British English of Norwich', *Language in Society*, vol. 1 (1972) pp. 179–95). Verena Aebischer suggests that this hypercorrectness is a manifestation of the hyperadaptation of those outside the dominant group, and thus cannot be explained by sexual roles (Aebischer, 1985, pp. 42–3).

3. One study found that in single-sex groups men talked more about themselves, women more about human relationships (Elizabeth Aries, cited in Spender, 1980, p. 127). A study of grammatical cases tended to verify a greater female concern with human relationships (Nancy Barron, cited in Barrie Thorne and Nancy Henley (eds), *Language and Sex: Difference and Dominance* (Rowley, Mass.: Newbury House, 1975)). Another study also found that women used more words implying feeling and emotion; men more words implying time, space, quantity. These differences tended somewhat to disappear among the more highly educated (Gleser, *et al.*, cited in Thorne and Henley). What was clear from a number of studies was that in many social situations men tended to dominate the discussion. Such an observation is, of course, more valuable as a commentary on social power than on language use. Verena Aebischer (1985) suggests that most linguistic studies of women's language (includ-

ing Lakoff's) are founded on a presupposition of a feminine nature; what is studied is, in fact, how an observer describes language, not the language used by a speaker. Almost all those Aebischer interviewed (both men and women) thought that women chattered about trivial matters (which they saw as negative), so they found this stereotypical trait and did not observe women's actual speech impartially. Michèle Kail suggests that much research has only served to legitimise social stereotypes and that differences between the sexes are usually much weaker than variations within each group ('Le Sexe parle-t-il?', paper at Colloque *Femmes – Féminisme – Recherches*, Toulouse, December 1982, pp. 5–6).

4. *Sorcières* published an issue on women's writing (no. 7, January 1977). In her introductory comments, Xavière Gauthier makes it clear that positions she expressed in *Tel quel* were not doctrinaire, that no one can define women's writing: 'The links between body and writing [*corps et écriture*] are multiple, twisted or coiled, and many other factors – especially history – come in. Everything or almost everything is still to be discovered and explored – and in many directions' (Gauthier, 1980, p. 9). Nevertheless, she does suggest that use of time, rhythm, *'économies pulsionnelles'*, will be different for the two sexes.

5. Issues no. 12, June 1976, and no. 13, October 1976. The contributions include a pragmatic introduction by Françoise Collin, one of the editors, about women's exclusion from language and culture; satiric lists of terms used to define women and their place in the world; a moving essay by a daughter visiting her mother in a psychiatric hospital; Luce Irigaray's 'Quand nos lèvres se parlent', addressed to her mother; interviews with immigrant women in Belgium about their problems with learning French; an interview on how fascists used language to attract women; an essay by and interview with Hélène Cixous, an article by a typist on how she has no right to speak to those who bring her work. In other words, a wide variety of pragmatic and a few more theoretical studies of women and language. The perspective seems healthily down-to-earth. Even the questions asked of Cixous keep her speaking of concrete topics.

6. The female text, as Cixous defines it, is *not* a text necessarily written by a woman. Indeed her examples are often drawn from male writers – Kleist, Joyce, Genet – although recently she has turned her interest more towards Clarice Lispector: 'What it means to be a man, "being-a-man", consists first of all in eradicating femininity. But in writing – particularly in writing, much more so than in any other domains where they can be found – there are men who transmit femininity' (Makward, 1976, p. 22).

7. Chantal Chawaf makes similar points about woman's writing as a way of reaching the physical and spiritual source of life (Marks and Courtivron 1980, p. 178). For a criticism of Cixous for not considering how the excessive quality of female sexuality is related to women's social domination, see Michèle Richman, 'Sex and Signs', *Language and Style*, 13 (1980) pp. 62–80.

8. The distinction between metaphor and metonymy has occasionally been evoked as a possible site of gender-related differences in language use. But while some see metonymy (contiguity, touch) as female and metaphor (comparison, vision) as male, others have taken the opposite view, considering metonymy as hierarchical and male, metaphor as analogy, harmony and female. At this point, we have perhaps reached a realm of metaphysical speculation too abstract to be meaningful for practical literary criticism.

9. While Alice Jardine, the translator, calls this 'one of the more explicit references to the mass marketing of "l'écriture féminine" in Paris over the last ten years', the comment is more devastating than that, as it would seem to include such writers as Cixous and Chawaf.

10. Cited in Bruno Vercier and Jacques Lecarme, *La Littérature en France depuis 1968* (Paris: Bordas, 1982) p. 236. Duras has also denied being really interested in feminism (Blume, 1985, p. 7).

Notes to Chapter 3: Forms and Themes

1. Irma Garcia, in a two-volume work, *Promenade femmilière* (Paris: des femmes, 1981) has attempted an analysis of themes and imagery from many women's novels, from a perspective similar to Cixous's (from whose work she draws many examples). In spite of some interesting insights, Garcia unfortunately tends to large generalisations, frequently taking quotations out of context (thus, for example, missing the satire of some of Yourcenar's comments about women, which must be read as criticism, not praise), and attributing to women many features found equally in men's writing.

2. This is not, unfortunately, a problem only of the past. See Renate Mörhmann, 'Occupation: Woman Artist', in Ecker, 1985, p. 157.

3. See Adrienne Rich, *On Lies, Secrets and Silences* (New York: Norton, 1979) p. 39.

4. Interestingly, when citizen's groups wanted to clean up homosexual pornography, photos depicting two women together were considered not lesbian, but normal male pornography – what Wittig has termed 'harem lesbianism', for the benefit of the male.

5. For another analysis of how women's writing both runs counter to and shares in postmodernism, see Evans, 1987, esp. pp. 220–8.

6. Christiane Makward has distinguished a number of styles in Cixous's work, in 'Structures du silence / du délire', *Poétique*, 35 (1978) pp. 314–24.

7. See Giovanna Pezzuoli, 'Prisoner in Utopia', in Gabriela Mora and Karen S. Van Hooft (eds), *Theory and Practice of Feminist Literary Criticism* (Ypsilanti, Mich.: Bilingual Press, 1982) pp. 36–43.

8. Giles Marcotte in *Le Roman à l'imparfait* (Quebec: La Presse, 1976) has applied Robert's insights to the work of Marie-Claire Blais, which he sees as utilising the Foundling story.

9. Didier, 1981, p. 39. Agreed, but not the relation of a woman to her

mother, or to her body. Colette effectively showed the weaknesses of Proust's view of lesbianism, in *Le Pur et l'impur.*

10. A confirmation of this formulation of a male perspective that may inform many narratives by men can be found in Carol Gilligan's discussion of Daniel Levinson's *The Seasons of a Man's Life*, Erik Erikson's *Childhood and Society* and George Vaillant's *Adaptation to Life.* See Carol Gilligan, *In a Different Voice* (Cambridge, Mass.: Harvard University Press, 1982).

11. As Kathleen McLuskie has shown, such a Shakespearean text as *Measure for Measure* 'focuses the spectator's attention and constructs it as male'; see Kathleen McLuskie, 'The Patriarchal Bard', in Jonathan Dollimore and Alan Sinfield (eds), *Political Shakespeare* (Ithaca, N.Y.: Cornell University Press, 1985) p. 96. See also Elizabeth A. Flynn and Patrocinio P. Schweickart (eds), *Gender and Reading* (Baltimore, Md: Johns Hopkins University Press, 1986). Whether men can 'read as women' is another question. See Segal, 1985, p. 4.

Notes to Chapter 4: Colette

1. See the English translation, 'The Laugh of the Medusa', *Signs*, I (1976) p. 877 (published in French 1975), and the interview of 1976, in Stambolian, 1979, p. 82.

2. Indeed one critic has considered that Chéri is the only successful male character in Colette's novels, 'the only man whom one can conceive existing beyond the confines of the book; and it has been observed, and rightly that Chéri has something feminine about him' (Richardson, 1984, p. 231).

3. See Françoise Mallet-Joris, 'A Womanly Vocation', in Eisinger and McCarty, 1981a, pp. 7–15.

4. See Mary Ann Doane, 'Film and the Masquerade', *Screen*, 23 (1982) pp. 74–87.

5. See Marilyn Yalom, 'They Remember Maman', *Essays in Literature*, 8 (1981) pp. 73–90.

6. For a good commentary on the novel, see Didier, 1981, pp. 211–21.

7. Colette, 'Comment est née Claudine', in *Paris* (1 April 1949).

8. There are, however, parallels between Renée's career and Colette's own, as Martha Noel Evans points out in *Masks of Tradition* (Ithaca, N.Y.: Cornell University Press, 1987) p. 40.

9. Colette exaggerates the extent of Léa's ageing at fifty-six. (Colette herself was fifty-three when *Fin de Chéri* was published, and was not behaving like an old woman.) Realistically it is hard to imagine that six years would change beautiful arms into arms 'too fat to touch her body at any point', that Léa would have renounced so completely any 'feminine allurement' (p. 172). While we would imagine Léa ageing more slowly, the exaggeration and the foreshortening of time are needed in order to give full weight to the onset of Chéri's disillusionment, shortly after the end of the war.

10. See Mieke Bal, 1977, p. 48. Critics in 1933 often thought that the novel showed a distinct prejudice against Camille, as have some more recent critics.

Notes to Chapter 5: Nathalie Sarraute

1. Cited in Marion Scali, 'Sarraute, promenade', *Libération* (24 July 1986) p. 30.
2. Christiane Makward, 'Corps écrit, corps vécu', in Suzanne Lamy and Irene Pages (eds), *Féminité, subversion, écriture* (Quebec: Éditions du Remue-Ménage, 1983) pp. 127–38. Makward finds in Robbe-Grillet's work a great distance between the subject and the world, a distance which makes his work evolve towards sado-masochism, the contrary of 'l'écriture féminine'. See also Ann Jefferson, 'Representation in the Novels of Nathalie Sarraute', *Modern Language Review*, 73 (1978) pp. 513–24: 'the texts specifically deconstruct both the more tradition-al realist reading whereby the language of the text behaves as if it were a copy, and the more radical anti-representational reading implied by pure scriptural activity, in order to produce as much meaning as possible. In this respect Sarraute occupies a somewhat anomalous position among her contemporaries' (p. 524). For a quite different reading of the contrast between Sarraute and Robbe-Grillet, see Lucien Goldmann, 'The *Nouveau Roman* and Reality', in *Towards a Sociology of the Novel*, trans. Alan Sheridan (London: Tavistock, 1975) pp. 132–51. Goldmann sees Sarraute as still believing in a human reality which writers can explore, whereas Robbe-Grillet fits into a later historical stage, accepting, as does Goldmann, the lack of any immutable reality. Goldmann's reading seems to accept the import-ance of the political and economic world, an importance that Sar-raute, in fact, discounts. Perhaps this is another 'feminine' character-istic?
3. Minorgue suggests, however, that Alain is the narrator, who gives up the privileges of his role and displaces himself (Minorgue, 1981, pp. 87–8).
4. This is similar to Marguerite Duras's remark that a man would intervene, where she doesn't.
5. Dorothy Wordsworth, for example, wrote 'I should detest the idea of setting myself up as an Author'. See *The Letters of William and Dorothy Wordsworth, The Middle Years, 1806–1811*, ed. Ernest de Selincourt, rev. Mary Moorman (London: Clarendon Press, 1969) p. 454.
6. Alexandra Sévin, 'Nathalie Sarraute ou le piège des mots', *Elles voient rouge*, no. 4 (1980) esp. pp. 38–9.
7. Ellen Munley sees in *L'Usage de la parole* a positive message: 'With enough give and take, we can not only mutually understand but contribute to each other's development' (Munley, 1983, p. 246). This is perhaps overstating the case.

Notes to Chapter 6: Marguerite Yourcenar

1. See Jean-Bernard Vray, 'Le Chant du ventriloque', *Sud*, no. 55 (1984) pp. 37–59, for an interesting analysis of how Yourcenar uses the third person in writing her memoirs, in order to make her own birth part of a universal pattern, and how the characters in her fiction seem to her more real than herself.

2. What, however, should we make of Hadrian's frequent judgements on the Jews as the the most fanatic of his subject peoples? Surely he could have made a similar comment about the Christians? The prevalence of anti-Jewish comments in *Mémoires d'Hadrien*, although undoubtedly accurate historically for Hadrian, leaves the reader feeling that Yourcenar was, to say the least, rather insensitive in a work written shortly after the Second World War. There is no reason why a woman writer should not have the same racial prejudices as a man, obviously. Indeed, Claudia Koonz, *Mothers in the Fatherland* (New York: St Martin's Press, 1987) has shown the virulence of pro-Nazi, anti-Semitic women in Hitler's Germany. But lack of sympathy for one minority group may go with lack of sympathy for another, or for women as subordinate.

   Mavis Gallant defends Yourcenar against accusations of anti-Semitism, saying she in no way held the same opinions as Eric in *Le Coup de grâce*. Gallant admits, however, that Yourcenar seemed to know little about Jews, observing them as figures out of the Old Testament, and makes the excuse that in her milieu as a young person she may never have met any Jews: 'Whenever she is questioned on this subject, Mme Yourcenar replies that she has a great number of close Jewish friends' (Gallant, 1985, p. 19). Some of my best friends ... Hardly an adequate reply! Undoubtedly Yourcenar was not actively anti-Semitic, and was genuinely opposed to racism, but there is little doubt that she regarded Jews as fundamentally 'other'.

3. Jacques Lovichi, 'Note sur les *Mémoires d'Hadrien*', *Sud*, no. 55 (1984) pp. 8–12, considers that the narrator isn't Hadrian, but Yourcenar herself, who speaks of her philosophic preoccupations and her encyclopaedic culture.

4. In a note to the novel Yourcenar again explains some of the issues of theme and form she confronted. Much of the note is concerned with historical documentation, giving in some detail the sources of characters, incidents, ideas, and stating the reasons for any deviation from historical accuracy. All this survey of her documentation assumes a reader knowledgeable about the history of the sixteenth century, one who might like to consult documents in a number of languages, one who might be curious about slight inaccuracies of dates. Yourcenar addresses this learned reader in a somewhat pedagogical fashion, explaining both her historical sources and how the earlier versions of the text of the novel were used in revision. She explains in some detail how the novel developed from a shorter earlier text, and then explains why she has felt such an explanation necessary.

5. Yourcenar's attitude towards women was not, however, simple. While she seemed to denigrate the typical role that women play, she often, consciously, praised the work of individual women artists, using her own prestige to bring them to the attention of a wider audience, as in the case of Hortense Flexner, Amrita Pritam, and Marie Métrailler. *Presentation critique d'Hortense Flexner, suivie d'un choix de poèmes, traduit par Marguerite Yourcenar* (Paris: Gallimard, 1969); 'Traduction de dix poèmes d'Amrita Pritam', *Nouvelle revue française*, no. 365 (1983) pp. 166–78; Marie Métrailler, *La Poudre de sourire* (Monaco: Édition de Rocher, 1982), with prefatory letters by Yourcenar. Women are not in her view innately inferior, but rather normally put into social roles that limit them; thus she is quick to praise those who have escaped these limitations.

6. Speaking of Hindu sculpture, Yourcenar praises its 'art of mixing characteristics of the sexes', and its mixture of sensual and religious ecstasy. *Sur quelques thèmes érotiques et mystiques de la Gita Govinda* (Marseilles: Rivages/Cahiers du sud, 1982).

7. See the avant-propos to the special issue of *Sud*, no. 55 (1984) devoted to Yourcenar, where the editor, Christiane Barodie, comments that most contributors analyse Yourcenar's work in relation to their own interests, reading her mostly for opinions with which they agree or disagree.

Notes to Chapter 7: Marguerite Duras

1. Several years ago, at conferences in New Zealand and Australia, I read a paper on female style and asked the audience to try to identify the sex of the authors of four passages from French novels of the 1950s and 1960s, by Duras, Robbe-Grillet, LeClézio and Wittig. Only with Duras were readers to a large extent sure of the sex of the author.

2. See particularly Marcelle Marini, *Territoires du féminin* (Paris: Minuit, 1977).

3. See Susan Cohen, 'Phantasm and Narration in Marguerite Duras' *The Ravishing of Lol V. Stein'*, *The Psychoanalytic Study of Literature*, ed. Joseph Reppen and Maurice Charney (Hillsdale, N.J.: Analytic Press, 1985) pp. 255–77.

4. It is not, however, completely certain that she is the same; the name of her lover is changed from Richardson to Richard. Anne-Marie Stretter reappears in *India Song*; the Vice-Consul whistles *Indiana's Song*, another link to *India Song*.

5. See Bal, 1977, esp. p. 68 for an analysis of how Peter Morgan's attempt to write the beggar's story questions not only the authenticity of literature but also the moral problem of whites in India. The beggar's story is subordinated to the story of European society.

6. Duras shocked many readers in France by her articles seeking to understand why 'le petit Grégory' was killed by his mother while the matter was *sub judice* in 1985.

7. There is an evident parallel here with the German lover in *Hiroshima, mon amour*.

8. As Christiane Makward has remarked, however, it is even impossible to say clearly how many female characters there are in the book. ('Structures du silence / du délire', *Poétique*, 25 (1978), p. 314. See Duras, 1974, pp. 68 and 199, where she first says she is not sure whether a 'woman in black' exists in *L'Amour*, and later says 'there are not two women in the novel'.) Of the woman whom the traveller is seeking it is said 'Where she goes, everything comes apart' and 'death becomes useless' (Duras, 1972, p. 81); this woman thus seems radically different from the woman with a cigarette in a bourgeois house. Duras said that *L'Amour* was written with what wasn't in *Le Ravissement* (quoted by Deborah Gaensbauer, 'Revolutionary Writing in Marguerite Duras' *L'Amour'*, *French Review*, 55 (1982) pp. 633–9, esp. p. 634). It is impossible, however, to say that the woman is Lol, or that the prisoner is Jacques Hold, or that the traveller is Michael Richards (or Richardson).

9. Luce Irigaray's analysis of the language of schizophrenics, in *Parler n'est jamais neutre*, might well be applicable to the language of *L'Amour*, as well as to that of *Le Ravissement de Lol V. Stein*.

10. M.A., 'Duras à l'état sauvage', *Libération* (4 September 1984) pp. 28–9: 'Everything stops there, after the year of the lover. In writing, everything that I lived afterwards serves for nothing' (p. 29). Duras also said that *M.D.* (Paris: Edition de Minuit, 1983), a work by Yann Andréa describing Duras's battle with alcoholism, showed her clearly her own 'brutality' and 'savagery' and contributed to this return to herself that is *L'Amant*.

11. Xavière Gauthier, 'Marguerite Duras et la lutte des femmes', *Magazine littéraire*, 158 (1980) p. 19. One should, of course, add Monsieur Andesmas.

12. See Régis Durand, 'The Disposition of the Voice', in Michel Benamou and Charles Caramello (eds), *Performance in Postmodern Culture* (Milwaukee, Wis.: Center for Twentieth Century Studies, University of Wisconsin, 1977) pp. 99–110. In *La Vie matérielle* (1987), p. 14, Duras speaks of her distrust of theatre, of acting, which takes away from the text.

13. Dominique Noguez, 'La Gloire des mots', *L'Arc*, 98 (1985) pp. 26–9. Also Willis, 1987, p. 120. See also Pierre Fontanier, *Les Figures du discours* (Paris: Flammarion, 1968) p. 424, for a nineteenth-century discussion of *chronographie*, a rhetorical device to characterise time, that is basically similar to Noguez's parataxis. Noguez's analysis of Duras's use of adjectives linking the abstract to the concrete ('colonial river', 'blond disorder') is also of interest.

14. 'Afterwards, when I reread my words, I reassemble them into sentences. I construct a sort of syntax, although a poor one' (Duras, 1986, p. 116).

15. See Kristeva, 1987, for an analysis of the particularity of Duras's vision. Also see Borgomano, 1985, for an interpretation of Duras's *fantasmes*.

Unfortunately, I cannot discuss here Duras's films, which suggest interesting comparisons to her novels. Some of the techniques of Duras's fiction, such as the cross-cutting between the dinner party and Chauvin in *Moderato cantabile*, are similar to those of more conventional cinema. Many of her films are, like her later fiction, deliberate reworkings of traditional genres to disrupt the normal responses of her reader or spectator. This is evident in the break between images and sound track in *India Song*, so that the characters appear on the screen without speaking and the voices commenting on the action seem to be offering only one possible interpretation. More radically, the sound track may be telling a story with no direct relation to the images, as in *Aurélia Steiner*. Another possibility is the reduction of the film to a reading of a film script, as in *Camion*. In each case, not only are the normal expectations of the audience disrupted, but the whole 'suspension of disbelief' on which most representational works of art have been based is subverted.

Notes to Chapter 8: Monique Wittig

1. These detailed descriptions thus mock male images of women: 'the knife without a blade that lacks a handle', thus, of course, 'nothing' (no phallus) (p. 23, p. 30). See Duffy, 1983, p. 402.
2. See Duffy, 1983 and Wenzel, 1981.
3. It would be interesting to compare Wittig's use of references to the classical world with that of Marguerite Yourcenar. In spite of great differences between them, both use the classical world to comment on the present. If Monique Wittig, more radically, turns the male heroes into female ones, is this not perhaps similar to the way in which Yourcenar projects herself into male heroes such as Hadrian? Both methods posit an absence of sexual specificity.
4. See Crowder, 1982, pp. 163–6.

Notes to Chapter 9: Is There a Conclusion?

1. *The Nation* (21 November 1987) p. 604. See also the discussion of Stella's ideas on the relationship between the baroque and the modern – ideas similar to those of Kristeva quoted at the beginning of Chapter 9 – in Adam Gopnik, 'Stella in Relief', *New Yorker* (4 January 1988) pp. 70–3.
2. Mary Kelly, 'Woman – Desire – Image', in Lisa Appignanesi (ed.), *Desire* (London: Institute of Contemporary Arts, 1984) pp. 30–1.
3. Marguerite Yourcenar says in *Archives du nord* (Paris: Gallimard Folio, 1977, p. 75): 'I would like to have had as an ancestor the imaginary Simon Adriansen of *L'Œuvre au noir*', again suggesting a lack of clear separation between fictional characters and real people. Marguerite Duras sometimes makes similar judgements of her fictional charac-

ters. She also tends to treat real people, such as the mother of 'little Grégory', as if they were characters in her novels.

4. Duras, 1987, p. 137; Husserl-Kapit, 1975, p. 433; and Lamy, 1981, p. 66.

5. Kristeva sees as early as *Hiroshima, mon amour* an 'implosion of love into death and death into love' and considers that this film contains the union of 'socio-historical realism' and 'the X ray of depression', the two currents of Duras's work. In *Hiroshima* 'private pain absorbs political horror' (Kristeva, 1987, pp. 142–3).

6. See Christiane Makward, 'Corps écrit, corps vécu', in Suzanne Lamy and Irene Pages (eds), *Féminité, subversion, écriture* (Quebec: Éditions du Remue-Ménage, 1983) pp. 127–38.

Bibliography

Abel, Elizabeth, *Writing and Sexual Difference* (Brighton: Harvester, 1982).

Aebischer, Verena, *Les Femmes et le langage* (Paris: Presses Universitaires de France, 1985).

Albistur, Maïté and Daniel Armogathe, *Histoire du féminisme français* (Paris: des femmes, 1977).

Arnette, Jacques-Pierre, review of *Disent les imbéciles*, *Le Point* (4 October 1976).

Bal, Mieke, *Narratologie* (Paris: Klincksieck, 1977).

Barrett, Michèle, 'The Concept of Difference', *Feminist Review*, 26 (1987) 29–41.

Beauvoir, Simone de, *The Second Sex*, trans. H. M. Parshley (New York: Alfred A. Knopf, 1953).

Benjamin, Jessica, 'A Desire of One's Own', in Lauretis (1986) pp. 78–101.

Besser, Gretchen R., 'Colloque avec Nathalie Sarraute, 22 avril 1976', *French Review*, 50 (1976) 284–9.

Biolley-Godino, Marcelle, *L'Homme-objet chez Colette* (Paris: Klincksieck, 1972).

Blau du Plessis, Rachel, 'For the Etruscans', in Showalter, 1985, pp. 271–91 (1985a).

Blau du Plessis, Rachel, *Writing Beyond the Ending* (Bloomington: Indiana University Press (1985b).

Bleier, Ruth, *Science and Gender* (New York: Pergamon Press, 1984).

Bleier, Ruth, 'Lab Coat: Robe of Innocence or Klansman's Sheet?', in Lauretis, 1986, pp. 55–66.

Blume, Mary, Interview with Marguerite Duras, *International Herald Tribune* (22 March 1985) p. 7.

Borgomano, Madeleine, 'Une écriture féminine?', *Littérature*, 53 (1984) 59–68.

Borgomano, Madeleine, *Duras: une lecture des fantasmes* (Petit Roeulx, Belgium: Cistre, 1985).

Boucquey, Eliane, 'Unes femmes' [*sic*] (avec Kristeva), *Les Cahiers du Grif*, 7 (1975) 22–7.

Bovenshen, Silvia, 'Is there a Feminine Aesthetic?', in Ecker, 1985, pp. 23–50.

Britton, Celia, 'The Self and Language in the Novels of Nathalie Sarraute', *Modern Language Review*, 77 (1982) 577–84.

Brulotte, Gaëtan, 'Tropismes et sous-conversation', *Arc*, 95 (1984) 39–54.

Cameron, Deborah, *Feminism and Linguistic Theory* (London: Macmillan, 1985).

Cardinal, Marie, *Les Mots pour le dire* (Paris: Grasset, 1975).

Cardinal, Marie, *Autrement dit* (Paris: Grasset, 1977).

Carter, Angela, 'Notes from the Front Line', in Wandor, 1983, pp. 69–77.

Carter, Angela, 'Magical Mannerist', *Literary Review*, 77 (1984) pp. 37–8.
Chaillot, Nicole, 'Marguerite Yourcenar', in *Femmes et littérature*, tome 2 (Paris: Éditions Mortinsart-Romorantin, 1980) pp. 133–73.
Chodorow, Nancy, *The Reproduction of Mothering* (Berkeley, Calif.: University of California Press, 1978).
Cixous, Hélène and Catherine Clément, *La Jeune née* (Paris: Union Générale d'Éditions, 1975a).
Cixous, Hélène and Michel Foucault, 'À propos de Marguerite Duras', *Cahiers Renaud-Barrault*, 89 (1975b) 8–22.
Cixous, Hélène, 'The Laugh of the Medusa', trans. Keith Cohen and Paula Cohen, *Signs*, I (1976a) 875–93.
Cixous, Hélène, 'Interview with Jean-Louis de Rambures', *Le Monde* (9 April 1976b) p. 20.
Cixous, Hélène, 'Interview avec François Coupry', *Libération* (22 December 1981a).
Cixous, Hélène, 'Castration or Decapitation?', trans. Annette Kuhn, *Signs*, 7 (1981b) 41–55.
Colette, *Renée, the Vagabond*, trans. Charlotte Remfry-Kidd (Garden City, N.Y.: Doubleday, 1931).
Colette, *Short Novels of Colette* [various translators] (New York: Dial Press, 1951) (includes *Chéri, The Last of Chéri, The Cat*).
Colette, *Earthly Paradise*, ed. R. Phelps, trans. Herma Briffault and Derek Coltman (New York: Farrar, Straus and Giroux, 1966).
Colette, *The Pure and the Impure*, trans. Herma Briffault (London: Secker and Warburg, 1968).
Colette, *The Complete Claudine*, trans. Antonia White (New York: Farrar, Straus and Giroux, 1976a).
Colette, *The Shackle*, trans. Antonia White (New York: Farrar, Straus and Giroux, 1976b).
Colette, *Flowers and Fruit*, ed. Robert Phelps, trans. Matthew Ward (New York: Farrar, Straus and Giroux, 1986).
Collin, Françoise, 'La Lecture de l'illisible', *Cahiers de recherches*, 13 (1984) 7–10.
Conley, Verena Andermatt, *Hélène Cixous: Writing the Feminine* (Lincoln, Neb.: University of Nebraska Press, 1984).
Cornillon, Susan Koppelman (ed.), *Images of Women in Fiction* (Bowling Green, Ohio: Bowling Green University Press, 1973).
Costaz, Gilles, Interview with Marguerite Duras, *Le Matin* (24 September 1984) pp. 28–9.
Cournot, Michel, 'Nathalie Sarraute', *Le Monde* (23 July 1986).
Crowder, Diane Griffin, 'The Semiotic Functions of Ideology in Literary Discourse', *Bucknell Review*, 27 (1982) 157–68.
Crowder, Diane Griffin, 'Amazons and Mothers? Monique Wittig, Hélène Cixous and Theories of Women's Writing', *Contemporary Literature*, 24 (1983) 117–44.
Culler, Jonathan, *On Deconstruction* (Ithaca, N.Y.: Cornell University Press, 1982).
Delphy, Christine, 'Proto-féminisme et anti-féminisme', *Les temps modernes*, 346 (1975) 1469–500.

210   *Bibliography*

Didier, Béatrice, *L'Ecriture femme* (Paris: Presses Universitaires de France, 1981).
Doane, Mary Ann, 'Film and the Masquerade', *Screen*, 23 (1982) 74–87.
Donovan, Josephine, 'Feminist Style Criticism', in Cornillon, 1973, pp. 341–53.
Dranch, Sherry, 'Reading Through the Veiled Text', *Contemporary Literature*, 24 (1983) 176–89.
Duchen, Claire, *Feminism in France* (London and Boston, Mass.: Routledge and Kegan Paul, 1986).
Duffy, Jean, 'Women and Language in *Les Guerillères* by Monique Wittig', *Stanford French Review*, 7 (1983) 399–412.
Duras, Marguerite, *Le Vice-consul* (Paris: Gallimard, 1966); *The Vice Consul*, trans. Eileen Ellenbogen (London: Hamish Hamilton, 1968).
Duras, Marguerite, *L'Amante anglaise* (Paris: Gallimard, 1967); trans. Barbara Bray (London: Hamish Hamilton, 1968).
Duras, Marguerite, *L'Amour* (Paris: Gallimard, 1972).
Duras, Marguerite and Xavière Gauthier, *Les Parleuses* (Paris: Minuit, 1974).
Duras, Marguerite and Michelle Porte, *Les lieux de Marguerite Duras* (Paris: Minuit, 1977).
Duras, Marguerite, 'Une oeuvre éclatante', Postface à *l'Opoponax* (Paris: Minuit, 1983) pp. 283–7.
Duras, Marguerite, *L'Amant* (Paris: Minuit, 1984a); *The Lover*, trans. Barbara Bray (New York: Pantheon, 1985).
Duras, Marguerite, 'L'Inconnue de la rue Catinat', *Le Nouvel Observateur* (28 September 1984b) pp. 92–4.
Duras, Marguerite, *Le Ravissement de Lol V. Stein* (Paris: Gallimard, 1964; Folio Edition, 1985); *The Ravishing of Lol Stein*, trans. Richard Seaver (New York: Grove Press, 1966).
Duras, Marguerite, Interview with Pierre Benichon and Hervé Le Masson, *Le Nouvel Observateur* (14–20 November 1986) pp. 114–17.
Duras, Marguerite, *La Vie matérielle* (Paris: POL, 1987).
Ecker, Gisela (ed.), *Feminist Aesthetics* (Boston, Mass.: Beacon Press, 1985).
Eisenstein, Hester and Alice Jardine (eds), *The Future of Difference* (Boston, Mass.: G. K. Hall, 1980).
Eisinger, Erica and Mari McCarty (eds), *Colette: The Woman, the Writer* (University Park: Pennsylvania State University Press, 1981a), 'Introduction', pp. 1–4.
Eisinger, Erica and Mari McCarty (eds), *Women's Studies: Charting Colette*, 8 (1981b), 'Introduction', pp. 255–6.
Eisinger, Erica, '*The Vagabond*: a Vision of Androgyny', in Eisinger, 1981a, pp. 95–103 (1981c).
Elshtain, Jean Bethke, 'In the Grand Manner', *Women's Review of Books*, IV (1987) 13–14.
Evans, Martha Noel, *Masks of Tradition* (Ithaca, N.Y.: Cornell University Press, 1987).
Faucher, F., Interview with Duras, in Suzanne Lamy and André Roy (eds), *Marguerite Duras à Montréal* (Montreal: Spirale, 1981) pp. 43–54.

Fauré, Christine, 'Absent from History', trans. Lillian S. Robinson, *Signs*, 7 (1981) 71–86.

Féral, Josette, 'Du texte au sujet', *Revue de l'université d'Ottawa*, 50 (1980) 39–46.

Francis, Claude, 'Entretien avec Simone de Beauvoir', in Claude Frances and Fernande Gontier, *Les Écrits de Simone de Beauvoir* (Paris: Gallimard, 1979) pp. 568–76.

Furman, Nelly, 'Textual Feminism', in Sally McConnell-Ginet and Nelly Furman (eds), *Women and Language in Literature and Society* (New York: Praeger, 1980).

Furman, Nelly, 'The Politics of Language', in Greene and Kahn, 1985, pp. 59–79.

Gallant, Mavis, 'Limpid Pessimist', *New York Review of Books* (5 December 1985) 19–24.

Gallop, Jane, *Feminism and Psychoanalysis: The Daughter's Seduction* (London: Macmillan, 1982).

Gallop, Jane, 'Quand nos lèvres s'écrivent', *Romanic Review*, 74 (1983) 78–83.

Gardiner, Judith Kegan, 'On Female Identity and Writing by Women', in Abel, 1982, pp. 177–91.

Gardiner, Judith Kegan, 'Mind Mother: Psychoanalysis and Feminism', in Greene, 1985, pp. 113–45.

Gauthier, Xavière, Selection from 'Existe-t-il une écriture de femme?', in Marks and Courtivron, 1980, pp. 161–4.

Gelfand, Elissa D., 'Albertine Sarrazin: a Control Case for Femininity in Form', *French Review*, 51 (1977) 245–51.

Gelfand, Elissa D. and Virginia Thorndike Hules, *French Feminist Criticism: Women, Language, and Literature: An Annotated Bibliography* (New York and London: Garland, 1985).

Gilbert, Sandra and Susan Gubar, *The Mad Woman in the Attic* (New Haven, Conn.: Yale University Press, 1979).

Girard, René, *Deceit, Desire and the Novel*, trans. Yvonne Freccero (Baltimore, Md: Johns Hopkins University Press, 1965).

Gordon, Linda, 'What's New in Women's History', in Lauretis, 1986, pp. 20–30.

Gosselin, Monique, 'Voyage au bout de la féminité', in Jean Bessière (ed.), *Figures féminines et roman* (Paris: Presses Universitaires de France, 1982).

Greene, Gayle and Coppelia Kahn, 'Feminist Scholarship and the Social Construction of Women', in Greene and Kahn (eds), *Making a Difference* (London and New York: Methuen, 1985) pp. 1–36.

Gubar, Susan, '"The Blank Page" and the Issues of Female Creativity', in Abel, 1982, pp. 73–93.

Heath, Stephen, *The Nouveau Roman: A Study in the Practice of Writing* (London: Elek, 1972).

Heath, Stephen, 'Difference', *Screen*, 19 (1978) 51–112.

Heilbrun, Carolyn, 'A Response', in Abel, 1982, pp. 291–7.

Herrmann, Claudine, 'Women in Space and Time' (extracts from *Les Voleuses de langue* [Paris: des femmes, 1976]), in Marks, 1980, pp. 87–9 and 168–73.

Hirsch, Marianne, 'Mothers and Daughters', *Signs*, 7 (1981) 200–22.
Hirsch, Marianne, 'Gender, Reading and Desire in *Moderato cantabile'*, *Twentieth Century Literature*, 28 (1982), 69–85.
Homans, Margaret, *Women Writers and Poetic Identity* (Princeton, N.J.: Princeton University Press, 1980).
Horer, Suzanne and Jeanne Socquet, *La Création étouffée* (Paris: Pierre Horay, 1973), 'Marguerite Duras Interview', pp. 172–87.
Husserl-Kapit, Susan, 'An Interview with Marguerite Duras', *Signs*, 1 (1975) 423–34.
Irigaray, Luce, *Spéculum de l'autre femme* (Paris: Minuit, 1974).
Irigaray, Luce, 'And the One Doesn't Stir Without the Other', trans. Hélène Vivienne Wenzel, *Signs*, 7 (1981) 60–7.
Irigaray, Luce, *Ethique de la différence sexuelle* (Paris: Minuit, 1984).
Irigaray, Luce, *This Sex Which is Not One*, trans. Catherine Porter (Ithaca, N.Y.: Cornell University Press, 1985a).
Irigaray, Luce, *Parler n'est jamais neutre* (Paris: Minuit, 1985b).
Irigaray, Luce, 'Présentation', *Langages*, 85 (1987) 5–8.
Jacobus, Mary, 'The Question of Language', in Abel, 1982, pp. 37–52.
Jardine, Alice, 'Interview with Simone de Beauvoir', *Signs*, 5 (1979) 224–36.
Jardine, Alice, 'Pre-texts for the Transatlantic Feminist', *Yale French Studies*, 62 (1981) 220–36.
Jardine, Alice, *Gynesis: Configurations of Woman and Modernity* (Ithaca, N.Y.: Cornell University Press, 1985).
Jehlen, Myra, 'Archimedes and the Paradox of Feminist Criticism', *Signs*, 6 (1981) 575–601.
Jones, Ann Rosalind, 'Writing the Body', *Feminist Studies*, 7 (1981) 247–63.
Jones, Ann Rosalind, 'Inscribing Femininity', in Greene, 1985, pp. 80–112.
Kaplan, Cora, 'Speaking / Writing / Feminism', in Wandor, 1983, pp. 51–61.
Kaplan, Cora, 'Pandora's Box', in Greene, 1985, pp. 146–76.
Kaplan, Cora, 'Journeywomen to Grief', *New Statesman* (24 July 1987) pp. 21–2.
Kaplan, Sydney Janet, 'Varieties of Feminist Criticism', in Greene, 1985, pp. 37–58.
Ketchum, Anne Duhamel, 'Colette and the Enterprise of Writing', in Eisinger and McCarty, 1981a, pp. 22–31.
Knapp, Bettina L., 'Interview avec Marguerite Duras', *French Review*, 44 (1971) 653–9.
Koch, Gertrud, 'Ex-Changing the Gaze', *New German Critique*, 34 (1985) 139–53.
Kolodny, Annette, 'Some Notes on Defining a "Feminist Literary Criticism"', in Cheryl L. Brown and Karen Olson (eds), *Feminist Criticism* (Metuchen, N.J., and London: Scarecrow Press, 1978) pp. 37–55.
Kristeva, Julia, 'femme / mère / pensée', *Art Press International*, 5 (1977a) 6–8.
Kristeva, Julia, 'Interview avec Jean-Paul Enthoven', *Nouvel Observateur*, 20 June 1977b, pp. 98–133.
Kristeva, Julia, *Desire in Language* (New York: Columbia University Press, 1980).

Kristeva, Julia, 'Women's Time', trans. Alice Jardine and Harry Blake, *Signs*, 7 (1981) 13–35.
Kristeva, Julia, 'Conversation with Rosalind Coward', in Lisa Appignanesi (ed.), *Desire* (London: Institute of Contemporary Arts, 1984) pp. 22–7.
Kristeva, Julia, 'The Pain of Sorrow in the Modern World', *PMLA*, 102 (1987) 138–51.
Kroker, Marilouise, *et al.* (eds), *Feminism Now: Theory and Practice* (Montreal: New World Perspectives, 1985).
Lamy, Suzanne, Interview with Duras, in Suzanne Lamy and André Roy (eds), *Marguerite Duras à Montréal* (Montreal: Spirale, 1981) pp. 55–72.
Lauretis, Teresa de, *Alice Doesn't* (Bloomington, Ind.: Indiana University Press, 1984).
Lauretis, Teresa de, 'Aesthetic and Feminist Theory', *New German Critique*, 34 (1985) 154–75.
Lauretis, Teresa de (ed.), *Feminist Studies / Critical Studies* (Bloomington, Ind.: Indiana University Press, 1986).
Leclaire, Serge, 'Sexuality: a Fact of Discourse', in Stambolian, 1979, pp. 42–55.
Leclerc, Annie, *Parole de femme* (Paris: Grasset, 1974).
Le Guin, Ursula, *The Left Hand of Darkness* (New York: Walker, 1969).
McCallum, Pamela, 'New Feminist Readings', in Kroker, 1985, pp. 127–32.
McCarty, Mari, 'Possessing Female Space', in Eisinger, 1981b, pp. 367–74.
Maccoby, Eleanor Emmons and Carol Nagy Jacklin, *The Psychology of Sex Differences* (Stanford, Calif.: Stanford University Press, 1974).
McConnell-Ginet, Sally, 'Difference and Language: a Linguist's Perspective', in Eisenstein and Jardine, 1980, pp. 157–65.
Makward, Christiane, 'Interview with Hélène Cixous', *Sub-stance*, 13 (1976) 19–37.
Makward, Christiane, 'Colette and Signs', in Eisinger and McCarty, 1981a, pp. 185–92.
Marini, Marcelle, 'Féminisme et critique littéraire', in *Stratégies des femmes* (livre collectif) (Paris: Tierce, 1984).
Marks, Elaine, *Colette* (New Brunswick, N.J.: Rutgers University Press, 1960).
Marks, Elaine, 'Lesbian Intertextuality', in Stambolian, 1979, pp. 353–77.
Marks, Elaine and Isabelle de Courtivron, 'Introduction', in *New French Feminisms* (Amherst, Mass.: University of Massachusetts Press, 1980).
Micciolo, Henri, *Moderato cantabile de Marguerite Duras* (Paris: Hachette, 1978–9).
Miller, Nancy K., 'Emphasis Added', in Showalter, 1985, pp. 339–60.
Miller, Nancy K., 'Changing the Subject', in Lauretis, 1986, pp. 102–20.
Minorgue, Valerie, *Nathalie Sarraute and the War of the Words* (Edinburgh: Edinburgh University Press, 1981).
Moi, Toril, 'The Missing Mother: the Oedipal Rivalries of René Girard', *Diacritics*, 12 (1982) 21–31.
Moi, Toril, *Sexual/Textual Politics* (London: Methuen, 1985).
Montefiore, Jan, *Feminism and Poetry* (London: Routledge and Kegan Paul, 1987).
Montrelay, Michèle, *L'Ombre et le nom* (Paris: Minuit, 1977).

Moskos, George, 'Women and Fictions in Marguerite Duras's *Moderato cantabile*', *Contemporary Literature*, 25 (1984) 28–52.

Mulford, Wendy, 'Notes on Writing', in Wandor, 1983, pp. 31–41.

Mulvey, Laura, 'Feminism, Film and the *Avant-Garde*', in Mary Jacobus (ed.), *Women Writing and Writing About Women* (London: Croom Helm, 1979) pp. 177–95.

Munich, Adrienne, 'Notorious Signs, Feminist Criticism and Literary Tradition', in Greene, 1985, pp. 238–59.

Munley, Ellen W., 'I'm Dying But It's Only Your Story', *Contemporary Literature*, 24 (1983) 233–58.

Murphy, Carol, *Alienation and Absence in the Novels of Marguerite Duras* (Lexington, Ky: French Forum, 1982).

Nixon, Rob, 'Approaching Post-Modernism: Issues of Culture and Technology', *Critical Arts*, 3 (1984) 25–34.

Owens, Craig, 'The Discourse of Others: Feminists and Postmodernism', in Hal Foster (ed.), *The Anti-Aesthetic: Essays on Postmodern Culture* (Port Townsend, Wash.: Bay Press, 1983).

Peyre, Henri, 'Contemporary Feminine Literature in France', *Yale French Studies*, 27 (1961) 47–65.

Pillet, Anna, 'Sorcières . . . nos traversées', *Sorcières*, 7 (1977) 6.

Polis, Milène, Comments in collective article, 'Choisir ou créer', *Les Cahiers du Grif*, 7 (1975) 10–21.

Pratt, Annis, *Archetypal Patterns in Women's Fiction* (Brighton: Harvester, 1981).

Rambures, Jean-Louis de, 'Comment travaillent les écrivains', *Le Monde* (14 January 1972) p. 16.

Relyea, Suzanne, 'Polymorphenic Perversity', in Eisinger and McCarty, 1981a, pp. 150–63.

Resch, Yannick, *Corps féminin, corps textuel* (Paris: Klincksieck, 1973).

Richards, Janet Radcliffe, 'Is There a Woman's Way of Thinking?', *The Times Higher Education Supplement* (17 July 1981) p. 15.

Richardson, Joanna, *Colette* (New York: Franklyn Watts, 1984).

Robbe-Grillet, Alain, 'What Interests Me Is Eroticism?', in Stambolian, 1979, pp. 87–100.

Robert, Marthe, *The Origins of the Novel* (Bloomington, Ind.: Indiana University Press, 1980).

Roberts, Michele, 'Questions and Answers', in Wandor, 1983, pp. 62–8.

Rochefort, Christiane, 'The Privilege of Consciousness', in Stambolian, 1979, pp. 101–13.

Romanowski, Sylvie, 'A Typology of Women in Colette's Novels', in Eisinger, 1981, pp. 66–74.

Rose, Jacqueline, 'Introduction – II', in Juliet Mitchell and Jacqueline Rose (eds), *Feminine Sexuality* (London: Macmillan, 1982).

Russo, Mary, 'Female Grotesques: Carnival and Theory', in Lauretis, 1986, pp. 213–29.

Rykiel, Sonia, Interview with Nathalie Sarraute, *Les Nouvelles* (9–15 February 1984) pp. 40–1.

Saporta, Marc, 'Portrait d'une inconnue' (interview with Nathalie Sarraute), *Arc*, 95 (1984) 5–23.

Sarraute, Nathalie, *Martereau* (Paris: Gallimard, 1953); trans. Maria Jolas (New York: Braziller, 1959).

Sarraute, Nathalie, *Portrait d'un inconnu* (Paris: Gallimard, 1956); *Portrait of a Man Unknown*, trans. Maria Jolas (New York: Braziller, 1958).

Sarraute, Nathalie, *Le Planétarium* (Paris: Gallimard, 1959); trans. Maria Jolas (New York: Braziller, 1960).

Sarraute, Nathalie, 'New Movements in French Literature', *The Listener*, 65 (1961) 428.

Sarraute, Nathalie, *Entre la vie et la mort* (Paris: Gallimard, 1968); *Between Life and Death*, trans. Maria Jolas (New York: Braziller, 1969).

Sarraute, Nathalie, 'Ce que je cherche à faire', in Jean Ricardou and Françoise van Rossum-Guyon (eds), *Nouveau roman: hier, aujourd'hui. 2: pratiques* (Paris: Union générale d'éditions, 1972) pp. 25–40 and discussion, pp. 41–57.

Sarraute, Nathalie, *L'Usage de la Parole* (Paris: Gallimard 1980); *The Use of Speech*, trans. Barbara Wright (New York: Braziller, 1983).

Sarraute, Nathalie, *Enfance* (Paris: Gallimard, 1983); *Childhood*, trans. Barbara Wright (New York: Braziller, 1984).

Sayers, Janet, *Biological Politics* (London: Tavistock, 1982).

Schweickart, Patrocinio, 'Comment', *Signs*, 8 (1982) 170–6.

Schweickart, Patrocinio, 'What Are We Doing Really?', in Kroker, 1985, pp. 148–64.

Segal, Naomi, 'Letter', *London Review of Books* (20 June 1985) p. 4.

Showalter, Elaine, 'Feminist Criticism in the Wilderness', in Abel, 1982, pp. 9–35.

Showalter, Elaine (ed.), *The New Feminist Criticism* (New York: Pantheon, 1985).

Spender, Dale, *Man Made Language* (London: Routledge and Kegan Paul, 1980).

Spivak, Gayatri, *In Other Worlds* (New York: Methuen, 1987).

Stambolian, George and Elaine Marks (eds), *Homosexualities and French Literature* (Ithaca, N.Y.: Cornell University Press, 1979).

Stewart, Joan Hinde, 'The School and the Home', in Eisinger, 1981b, pp. 259–72.

Stewart, Joan Hinde, *Colette* (Boston, Mass.: Twayne, 1983).

Stimpson, Catharine, 'Zero Degree Deviancy', in Abel, 1982, pp. 243–59.

Stockinger, Jacob, 'The Test of Love and Nature', in Eisinger and McCarty, 1981a, pp. 75–94.

Suleiman, Susan Rubin, '(Re)writing the Body', in Susan Rubin Suleiman (ed.), *The Female Body in Western Culture* (Cambridge, Mass.: Harvard University Press, 1986) pp. 7–29.

Sullerot, Evelyne (ed.), *Le Fait féminin* (Paris: Fayard, 1978).

Wandor, Michelene (ed.), *On Gender and Writing* (London: Routledge and Kegan Paul, 1983).

Weigel, Sigrid, 'Double Focus', in Ecker, 1985, pp. 59–80.

Wenzel, Hélène Vivienne, 'The Text as Body / Politics', *Feminist Studies*, 7 (1981) 264–87.

Willis, Sharon, *Marguerite Duras: Writing on the Body* (Champaign, Ill.: University of Illinois Press, 1987).

Wittig, Monique, *L'Opoponax* (Paris: Minuit, 1964); trans. Helen Weaver (New York: Simon and Schuster, 1966).

Wittig, Monique, *Les Guerillères* (Paris: Minuit, 1969); trans. David Le Vay (London: Peter Owen, 1971).

Wittig, Monique, *Le Corps lesbien* (Paris: Minuit, 1973a); *The Lesbian Body*, trans. David Le Vay (New York: Morrow, 1975).

Wittig, Monique, 'Je crois aux amazones', *Politique-Hebdo* (22 November 1973b) p. 29.

Wittig, Monique, Interview, *L'Art Vivant*, 45 (1974) 24–5.

Wittig, Monique, 'Paradigm', in Stambolian, 1979, pp. 114–21.

Wittig, Monique, 'One is Not Born a Woman', *Feminist Issues*, II (1981) 47–54.

Wittig, Monique, 'Le Cheval de Troie', *Vlasta*, 4 (1985a) 36–41.

Wittig, Monique, *Virgile, non* (Paris: Minuit, 1985b); *Across the Acheron*, trans. David Le Vay (London: Peter Owen, 1987).

Wittig, Monique, Article accompanying programme for *Le Voyage sans fin* (Paris, 1985c).

Woolf, Virginia, 'Women and Fiction', in *Collected Essays*, vol. 2 (New York: Harcourt Brace, 1967) pp. 141–8. (Essay originally published in 1929.)

Yaguello, Marina, *Les Mots et les femmes* (Paris: Petite Bibliothèque Payot, 1978).

Yourcenar, Marguerite, *'Alexis' and 'Le Coup de Grâce'* (Paris: Gallimard Folio, 1971); *Alexis*, trans. Walter Kaiser in collaboration with the author (New York: Farrar, Straus and Giroux, 1984); *The Coup de Grâce*, trans. Grace Frick in collaboration with the author (New York: Farrar, Straus and Giroux, 1957).

Yourcenar, Marguerite, *Mémoires d'Hadrien* (Paris: Gallimard, 1974); *Memoirs of Hadrian*, trans. Grace Frick in collaboration with the author (New York: Farrar and Straus, 1963).

Yourcenar, Marguerite, *Souvenirs pieux* (Paris: Gallimard, 1974b).

Yourcenar, Marguerite, *L'Œuvre au noir* (Paris: Gallimard, 1968; page numbers from Folio Edition, 1976); *The Abyss*, trans. Grace Frick in collaboration with the author (New York: Farrar, Straus and Giroux, 1976).

Yourcenar, Marguerite, Interview with Françoise Ducout, *Elle* (1979) 27.

Yourcenar, Marguerite, *Les Yeux ouverts*, with Matthieu Galey (Paris: Le Centurion, 1980).

Yourcenar, Marguerite, *The Dark Brain of Piranesi, and Other Essays*, trans. Richard Howard (New York: Farrar, Straus and Giroux, 1984).

Yourcenar, Marguerite, *Comme l'eau qui coule* (Paris: Gallimard, 1985); *Two Lives and a Dream*, trans. Walter Kaiser in collaboration with the author (New York: Farrar, Straus and Giroux, 1987).

Index

Micciolo, Henri, 137, 138
Michelet, Jules, 67
Miller, Nancy, K., 11, 44, 50
Millet, Kate, 2
Minorgue, Valerie, 87, 89, 94, 202
Moi, Toril, 7, 13, 17, 18, 42, 50, 159, 197
Molière (Jean-Baptiste Poquelin), 24, 67
Montefiore, Jan, ix, 177, 197
Montrelay, Michèle, 139
Mörhmann, Renate, 200
Moskos, George, 138, 143
Mulford, Wendy, 39
Mulvey, Laura, 54
Munich, Adrienne, 39
Munley, Ellen, 86–7, 103, 202
Murphy, Carol, 150

Nixon, Rob, 48
Noguez, Dominique, 162, 205

Owens, Craig, 48–9, 50

Pascal, Blaise, 174
Peyre, Henri, 2
Pezzuoli, Giovanna, 200
Phelps, Robert, 57
Phenarete, 171
Piatier, Jacqueline, 30
Pillet, Anna, ix–x
Plath, Sylvia, 39
Plato, 15, 101
Polis, Milène, 51
Pratt, Annis, 44–6, 50–1, 54
Pritam, Amrita, 204
Proust, Marcel, 52, 53, 63, 64, 82, 85, 88, 100, 122, 123, 159, 201

Rambures, Jean-Louis de, 88
Relyea, Suzanne, 61
Resch, Yannick, 68
Rich, Adrienne, 39, 188, 197, 200
Richards, Janet Radcliffe, 26
Richardson, Joanna, 58, 201
Richman, Michèle, 199
Robbe-Grillet, Alain, 29, 87, 202, 204
Robert, Marthe, 51–2
Roberts, Michèle, 39

Rochefort, Christiane, 27
Romanowski, Sylvie, 59
Rose, Jacqueline, 10
Rousseau, Jean-Jacques, 167, 197
Royer, Clémence, 25
Rushdie, Salman, 48
Russo, Mary, 13, 197
Rykiel, Sonia, 85

St Exupéry, Antoine de, 31
Saporta, Marc, 85, 87, 91, 92, 105
Sappho, 176
Sarraute, Nathalie, 40, 43, 85–107, 111, 134, 192, 193, 194, 195, 196, 202
  Enfance, 94, 104–6
  Entre la vie et la mort, 96, 99–100, 104
  L'Ère du soupçon, 86, 91
  Les Fruits d'or, 96
  Martereau, 88, 91–5, 96
  Le Planétarium, 95–9, 202
  Portrait, d'un inconnu, 87, 89–91, 92, 96, 194
  Tropismes, 100
  L'Usage de la parole, 100–4, 111, 192, 202
Sartre, Jean-Paul, 87, 89, 197
Saussure, Ferdinand de, 12
Sayers, Janet, 10
Scali, Marion, 202
Schweickart, Patrocinio, x, 189, 201
Segal, Naomi, 201
Sévin, Alexandra, 101
Shakespeare, William, 129, 201
Shelley, Mary, 54
Showalter, Elaine, 21, 50
Socrates, 171
Spender, Dale, 26, 198
Spivak, Gayatri Chakrovorty, 6, 197
Stella, Frank, 191, 206
Stendhal (Marie-Henri Beyle), 159
Stetson, Dorothy, 197
Stewart, Joan Hinde, 57, 65
Stimpson, Catharine, 46
Stockinger, Jacob, 61
Suleiman, Susan, 197
Sullerot, Evelyne, 9, 197